Chengchao Qu

Facial Texture Super-Resolution by Fitting 3D Face Models

Karlsruher Schriften zur Anthropomatik
Band 37
Herausgeber: Prof. Dr.-Ing. habil. Jürgen Beyerer

Eine Übersicht aller bisher in dieser Schriftenreihe erschienenen Bände finden Sie am Ende des Buchs.

Facial Texture Super-Resolution by Fitting 3D Face Models

by
Chengchao Qu

KIT Scientific Publishing

Dissertation, Karlsruher Institut für Technologie
KIT-Fakultät für Informatik

Tag der mündlichen Prüfung: 17. Mai 2018
Gutachter: Prof. Dr.-Ing. Jürgen Beyerer
Prof. Dr.-Ing. Rainer Stiefelhagen

Impressum

KIT Scientific Publishing

Karlsruher Institut für Technologie (KIT)
KIT Scientific Publishing
Straße am Forum 2
D-76131 Karlsruhe

KIT Scientific Publishing is a registered trademark
of Karlsruhe Institute of Technology.
Reprint using the book cover is not allowed.

www.ksp.kit.edu

Print on Demand 2018 – Gedruckt auf FSC-zertifiziertem Papier

ISSN 1863-6489
ISBN 978-3-7315-0828-1
DOI 10.5445/KSP/1000085134

Facial Texture Super-Resolution by Fitting 3D Face Models

zur Erlangung des akademischen Grades eines

Doktors der Ingenieurwissenschaften

der Fakultät für Informatik
des Karlsruher Instituts für Technologie (KIT)

genehmigte

Dissertation

von

Dipl.-Inform. Chengchao Qu

aus Shanghai

Tag der mündlichen Prüfung: 17. Mai 2018
Erster Gutachter: Prof. Dr.-Ing. Jürgen Beyerer
Zweiter Gutachter: Prof. Dr.-Ing. Rainer Stiefelhagen

Abstract

Facial image analysis has been an active research area in the past decades, resulting in a myriad of applications in security, entertainment, human–computer interaction, *etc.* Although human-level performance has been reached or even surpassed by some recent systems on several benchmark datasets, it can drop dramatically under non-cooperative conditions such as surveillance scenarios, where the subjects are acquired at a distance with arbitrary pose, expression and illumination, giving rise to diverse detrimental effects in the input images, in particular the low spatial resolution.

This thesis proposes to solve the low-resolution (LR) facial analysis problem with face super-resolution (FSR). In contrast to generic super-resolution (SR), FSR can leverage prior domain knowledge. The common face configuration can be used to hallucinate high-resolution (HR) output images with finer details. In order to provide FSR with such semantic guidance, a 3D representation of the face is adopted, which offers accurate and dense correspondence immune to shape and pose variation of the LR faces. However, incorporating 3D modeling for FSR is extremely challenging, especially in light of the ill-posed LR scenario.

To deal with this issue, a workflow coupling automatic localization of 2D facial feature points and 3D shape reconstruction is developed, leading to a novel LR fitting pipeline. First of all, the fundamental aspects of the cascaded shape regression method including the core regression engine, feature descriptors and fitting strategies are incrementally revisited and evolved to obtain state-of-the-art landmarking precision and robustness against image quality degradation. The following dense shape reconstruction module addresses the discrepancy of correspondences between detected 2D points and annotated 3D vertices on the face model with an adaptive fitting scheme. The nonlinear Levenberg–Marquardt Iterative Closest Point (LM–ICP) algorithm with Distance Transform (DT) is employed to relax the unfavorable fixed mapping assumption on the facial contour, which achieves superior and stable shape recovery across pose.

In order to exploit the obtained 3D shape and pose for FSR, a resolution-aware approach for registering the training 3D faces with the LR input is designed to avoid warping the LR face. To facilitate hallucination of the 3D facial texture, the widespread LR image formation process from HR images is first reformulated for the 3D face mesh using an intuitive and straightforward interpolation procedure. On the basis of this interpretation, the classic Lucas–Kanade algorithm is extended to the case of 3D deformable models to rectify the imperfect landmark-based face modeling on LR images in a posterior fashion. In this way, the final patch-wise SR stage is able to produce a HR facial texture robust to intrinsic and extrinsic sources of variation, and to faithfully synthesize the self-occluded half of the face for non-frontal poses.

Moreover, a novel Real-FSR dataset, which contains both LR and HR pairs acquired with a special dual-camera imaging system, is collected to study the genuine image characteristics related to SR. Further experiments on other publicly available datasets reveal the capabilities of the presented 3D FSR framework regarding high-quality SR for in-the-wild faces with an interocular distance (IOD) of as few as five pixels. Finally, the frontalized HR texture is also verified to help boost the performance of cross-pose face recognition (FR).

Zusammenfassung

Die Analyse von Gesichtsbildern ist in den vergangenen Jahrzehnten ein aktives Forschungsgebiet geworden, was zu einer Vielzahl von Anwendungen im Sicherheitsbereich, der Unterhaltung oder der Mensch–Computer–Interaktion führt. Obwohl auf manchen Datensätzen die menschliche Leistung von einigen neueren Systemen erreicht oder sogar übertroffen wird, kann diese unter nicht kooperativen Bedingungen wie in Überwachungsszenarien deutlich fallen. Die Ursache hierfür sind Gesichter mit beliebigen Kopfposen, Gesichtsausdrücken und Lichtbedingungen, welche zudem aus der Ferne aufgenommen sind. Die daraus resultierenden Störfaktoren in den Eingangsbildern, insbesondere die geringe Auflösung, wirken sich nachteilig für die vorhandenen Ansätze der Gesichtsanalyse aus.

Diese Arbeit versucht, diese Problematik mittels Gesichtssuperresolution (GSR) zu lösen. Im Gegensatz zur allgemeinen Superresolution (SR) kann die GSR Vorkenntnisse aufgrund der Einschränkung auf Gesichter nutzen, so dass hochaufgelöste Gesichter mit feineren Details erzeugt werden können. Um der GSR solche semantische Information zur Verfügung zu stellen, wird ein 3D-Modell des Gesichts verwendet, das eine dichte Korrespondenz und Beständigkeit gegen Gestalt- und Posenvariation der niedrigaufgelösten Gesichter bietet. Allerdings ist die Integration von 3D-Modellierung in die GSR extrem anspruchsvoll, vor allem angesichts der mangelnden Auflösung.

Um diese Schwierigkeit zu bewältigen, wird eine neuartige Verarbeitungskette bestehend aus einer automatischen Detektion von 2D-Merkmalspunkten und einer 3D-Modellrekonstruktion speziell für niedrigaufgelöste

Gesichter entwickelt. Zunächst werden die grundlegenden Aspekte des kaskadierten Regressionsverfahrens zur Landmarkenlokalisierung, d. h. der Kernalgorithmus für die Regression, die Merkmalsdeskriptoren und die Anpassungsstrategien verbessert, um eine sehr hohe Präzision und Robustheit gegenüber geringer Bildqualität zu erhalten. Das folgende Modul für die dichte 3D-Modellrekonstruktion adressiert die Abweichung der Korrespondenz zwischen detektierten 2D-Punkten und annotierten 3D-Eckknoten auf dem Gesichtsmodell mit einem adaptiven Anpassungsschema, das den nichtlinearen Levenberg–Marquardt Iterative Closest Point (LM–ICP) Algorithmus zusammen mit der Distanztransformation (DT) einsetzt, um die ungünstige Annahme der festen Zuordnung auf der Gesichtskontur zu lockern. Damit werden bessere und stabile Rekonstruktionsergebnisse über verschiedene Kopfposen von bis zu ±45° erzielt.

Anschließend wird ein auflösungsadaptiver Ansatz für die Registrierung der 3D-Trainingsgesichter mit dem Eingangsbild entworfen, um Detailverluste durch Verzerrungen des niedrigaufgelösten Gesichts zu vermeiden. Zur SR der 3D-Gesichtstextur wird das Bildentstehungsmodell niedrigaufgelöster Bilder auf das 3D-Gesichtsmodell mittels einfacher Interpolation ermöglicht. Der klassische Lucas–Kanade Algorithmus wird dann anhand dieser Formulierung auf den Fall der 3D-deformierbaren Modelle erweitert und die grobe landmarkenbasierte 3D-Anpassung lässt sich dadurch nachträglich verfeinern. Auf diese Weise kann eine realistische Gesichtstextur, auch in der abgewandten Gesichtshälfte für nicht frontale Posen, in der letzten 3D-GSR Phase synthetisiert werden.

Zur Untersuchung tatsächlicher SR-Bildeigenschaften entstand darüber hinaus im Rahmen dieser Arbeit ein neuer Datensatz, in dem niedrig- und hochaufgelöste Bildpaare mit einem Zwei-Kamera-System gleichzeitig aufgenommen werden. Durch weitere Evaluation auf mehreren öffentlichen Datensätzen ist es klar ersichtlich, dass das vorgestellte 3D-GSR Verfahren hochwertige SR-Ergebnisse für Gesichter mit einem Augenabstand ab fünf Pixeln erzeugt. Abschließend kann gezeigt werden, dass die synthetisierte Gesichtstextur durch eine Posennormalisierung die Leistung der posenübergreifenden Gesichtswiedererkennung steigert.

Acknowledgments

I would like to express my sincerest gratitude to my advisor Prof. Jürgen Beyerer for giving me the chance to work at the Vision and Fusion Laboratory (IES) of the Karlsruhe Institute of Technology (KIT) and encouraging me to grow as a research scientist. This doctoral thesis would not have been possible without his guidance and support. His passion, patience and immense knowledge always incented me to strive towards my goal. I am heartily grateful to my co-advisor Prof. Rainer Stiefelhagen for his mentorship, understanding and friendship, who also opened the door of computer vision for me and encouraged me to start my academic career when I was a graduate student in his lab.

This thesis is the result of close collaboration with tons of great people at the department Video Exploitation Systems (VID) of the Fraunhofer Institute of Optronics, System Technologies and Image Exploitation (Fraunhofer IOSB).

I am greatly indebted to Dr. Eduardo Monari, my former group leader, for offering me the opportunity to join his group, always showing his trust and support, and giving the right amount of freedom and supervision at the same time. I would also like to thank Dr. Tobias Schuchert, who dedicated his time to discussing my ideas and problems despite his busy schedule after undertaking the leader role of the neighboring group. They have been a source of inspiration to me, both professionally and personally.

I would like to thank all fellow doctoral students at VID and IES, in particular Ding Luo, Daniel Manger, Arne Schumann, Lars Wilko Sommer, and of course, my former office mate Christian Herrmann, for the fruitful discussions, for the days and nights we were working together before deadlines, for the beers we shared, and for all the fun we have had in the past few years. I would like to express my appreciation to the colleagues in my group at VID, Thomas Golda, Jürgen Metzler, Thomas Pollok, Sascha Voth and Heiko Widak, for the great atmosphere, friendship and support. Special thanks also go to the non-scientific staff Gaby Gross and Angelika Schreiber. I really feel honored to have the privilege of working with these wonderful people.

Moreover, I am very grateful to my friends Dr. Hazım Kemal Ekenel, Dr. Hua Gao and Dr. Yaokun Zhang for their encouragement and invaluable advices during my pursuit of the doctoral degree.

Last, but by no means least, I would like to acknowledge the unending love and unbridled support from my beloved wife Yizhou Yao, since we first met in 1999. I would not be the person I am today without her by my side. Her brightness, understanding and devotion have guided me all the way through this long journey. I dedicate this thesis to her with love and gratitude.

Karlsruhe, July 2018 Chengchao Qu

Contents

1 Introduction

1.1 Motivation

Face data compare favorably to other kinds of biometrics like fingerprint and iris due to its convenience and non-intrusive nature of collection. Less than two centuries after the oldest known portrait photograph of Robert Cornelius was taken by himself (a.k.a. selfie, see Figure 1.1), acquiring images of oneself or somebody else has never been as simple as it is today thanks to the rapid development of digital imaging technologies in the past few decades. As an example, for the case of photo or video selfies alone, a total of 24 billion of those were uploaded to Google Photos in the first 12 months since its launch in May 2015[1]. The ubiquitous access to the "Big Bang" of data has not only benefited our daily life in the "Informatization"[2] era, but also greatly pushed forward machine learning research, where sufficient training data is of paramount importance. To this end, a number of large-scale datasets [Hua08, Kem16, Ng14, Wol11] have been built upon a tremendous amount of uncontrolled face data on the Internet.

The analysis of such data has attracted broad interest from the computer vision society ever since the pioneering PhD thesis of Prof. Takeo Kanade [Kan73]. With the aid of mass data from unconstrained environments,

[1] `https://blog.google/products/photos/google-photos-one-year-200-million/`

[2] `https://en.wikipedia.org/wiki/Informatization`

several confounding factors such as pose, expression, occlusion and lighting are extensively studied, leading to recent advances in many facial analysis tasks to close the gap to human-level performance, *e.g.*, in face recognition (FR) [Tai14] and facial landmark detection [Fan16], as well as a dramatic boost of applications in multimedia [Bäu13], entertainment [Thi16], human–computer interaction [vAgr08], *etc.*

Figure 1.1: The oldest known (self-)portrait photo taken in 1839 by Robert Cornelius[1].

Nowadays, analysis of face images acquired by Closed-Circuit Televisions (CCTVs) has become ever more prevalent in the context of security and counter terrorism. Despite the high public concern regarding invasion of privacy, a vast increase of surveillance CCTVs has been estimated. For instance, around five million surveillance cameras had been installed in the United Kingdom by 2013, or equivalently one for every 11 people[2]. In the year 2016 alone, more than 800,000 new camera systems were expected to be put into operation in Germany, with a total of 5.2 million by the end of the year[3]. The deployed CCTVs so far have been shown to be an invaluable source of information for law enforcement agencies, as 95% of Scotland Yard murder cases used CCTV footage as evidence in 2009[2].

On the other hand, where the amount of video footage quickly exceeds the capacities of the prosecution authorities, automatic video analysis techniques, *e.g.*, FR[4], can play a critical role to assist the traditional surveillance systems with human operators in front of large video walls of monitors. However, one pitfall that prevents most existing facial analysis algorithms from successful incorporation into this practical setup is the low quality and resolution of the captured images. In spite of the deployment of new

1 https://publicdomainreview.org/collections/robert-cornelius-self-portrait-the-first-ever-selfie-1839/

2 http://www.telegraph.co.uk/technology/10172298/One-surveillance-camera-for-every-11-people-in-Britain-says-CCTV-survey.html

3 http://www.professionalsecurity.co.uk/products/cctv/german-surveillance-camera-market/

4 https://www.perpetuallineup.org/

hardware like Full HD or even 4K cameras, this problem still cannot be entirely circumvented, because wide-angle lenses are common choices for surveillance purposes in order for the coverage area to be as large as possible. As a consequence, the imaged faces often occupy a very small region, *e.g.*, with a resolution of under 10 pixels in width from a Full HD camera covering 20 m wide area [Whe11]. Moreover, limited hardware and acquisition conditions can also give rise to other deteriorations like interlacing, noise, sensor and motion blur, *etc.*

To address the negative impacts as a result of the surveillance scenario, especially the low-resolution (LR) problem, a sizable body of efforts has been made for individual facial analysis applications, *e.g.*, recognition [Hen08] and expression analysis [Kha13]. In contrast, this thesis focuses on restoring the high-resolution (HR) facial information that is lost during the LR imaging process, with the goal that the existing algorithms can be utilized without further adaptation. In particular, given a LR face image, the objective is to generate a HR version with enhanced details of the target person. Typically, such an image magnification task is realized with super-resolution (SR). In the special case of faces though, the domain-specific face super-resolution (FSR) approach is a natural choice compared to generic SR by virtue of the exploitation of common facial features. Even with as few as a single input image, learning-based FSR can take advantage of the external training data to synthesize the non-existing high-frequency information in the LR face, hence also called face hallucination (FH) in the literature [Bak02]. This property is sometimes essential in practice, *e.g.*, in a manhunt, as often no usable frames with well-illuminated, blurring-free and non-occluded face of the suspect can be extracted from the footage, due to the unconstrained nature of video surveillance. Thus, FSR gives a sound solution for both automatic face matching in the database and better human recognizability for the authority and the public.

In order to leverage learning-based FSR, one needs to couple a number of submodules, *e.g.*, alignment, subspace mapping and artifact suppression. While conventional 2D systems concentrate on improvements over variants of the subtasks, the presented framework attempts to explore a novel 3D workflow to solve the entire FSR problem, which can not only provide accurate fitting of the complex facial geometry for aligning training and test data, but also facilitate direct 3D texture SR. The latter allows for 3D frontalization of the SR faces to compensate for head rotation, which is proved crucial for

FR across pose [Bla03, Zhu16b]. Therefore, this appealing feature conveys the ultimate goal of this thesis: generating a 3D face with pose-normalized HR texture from a single non-frontal LR surveillance image.

1.2 Challenges

SR is an ill-posed inverse procedure to infer missing high-frequency information lost in the image degradation process. On the other hand, fitting 3D face models to 2D images is also a very sophisticated optimization problem [Rom05]. Hence, one can expect that incorporating these two tasks into a 3D FSR engine would pose an even bigger challenge. Furthermore, the subject being captured can unintentionally or sometimes intentionally behave in such a way that the performance of the system may be severely impaired. In this section, various sources of these factors for the FSR routine are discussed.

1. Image quality
   - **Resolution** originates from the discrete sampling of the continuous signal of the real-world objects acquired by the camera. It is a measure of how much spatial information there is available for digital image processing. Faces of low image resolution usually lack descriptive facial features, which are critical for the preprocessing modules of 3D FSR, namely face detection [Hu17], alignment [Her15] and 3D fitting [Hu12].
   - **Blurring** can have different causes, including low spatial resolution of the optics, out of focus, as well as object motion or camera shake with long integration time at low illumination levels. Blurring reduces contrast, sharpness and most importantly, the amount of details in images.
   - **Noise** is the undesired random deviation from the real pixel values produced during image acquisition. Noise is a common phenomenon in surveillance footage taken under low-light indoor condition with increased camera gain, which also becomes more prominent in the context of LR images than for HR data.
2. Face variation
   - **Pose** is one of the dominant extrinsic factors that can dramatically alter the appearance of a 3D object in 2D images. Variation

in the camera view angles relative to the subject leads to different projections on the 2D image plane, causing the apparent size and spatial distribution of facial components to vary. In addition, the visibility of certain parts of the face may change considerably w.r.t. the pose.

- **Expression** conveys the internal emotional state or intention in social interaction, which also has a major impact on the facial appearance. Depending on the type and intensity of the expression, facial components may alter shape, move location or even become invisible, further aggravating the complexity of dense face alignment for 3D FSR.
- **Illumination** has a direct bearing on the quality of the captured images. Blurring and imaging noise are mostly prevalent in low-light environment. On account of the complicated 3D geometry of faces, strong directional light can cast shadows or create specular highlights on the face, resulting in inaccurate registration and suboptimal texture SR.
- **Occlusion** occurs when objects are located on the line of projection in front of the face. Apart from self-occlusion of face parts at non-frontal poses, accessories, such as glasses or hats, and external sources may partially occlude the camera view, which can cause areas of abrupt changes to the faces in images that cannot be correctly modeled.
- **Style** is referred to as beard, mustache or makeup that substantially increases the variation of facial appearance. Unlike external objects in the case of occlusion, facial style can still be dealt with by statistical models for face registration [Bla99, Coo98], however, at the expense of robustness.

Besides the main challenging aspects summarized above, image or video artifacts such as interlacing and ringing or blocking effects in consequence of image compression [Gon07], aging effects like wrinkles and double chin owing to overweight [Cas09] may adversely affect the FSR routine as a whole or in part as well.

Typical samples related to low image quality and large face variation are illustrated in Figure 1.2, which originate from a collection of several popular in-the-wild face datasets [Sag13a]. Although each image is entitled with a single specific challenge, a combination of multiple detrimental effects can be observed in most examples. Figure 1.2a demonstrates a LR face with approximately 20 pixels in width, which is not yet an extremely LR scenario. Nevertheless, the eyes are composed of merely a few dark pixels so that, *e.g.*, the lash, eyelids, and pupils are barely recognizable, which renders the localization of fiducial facial landmarks and synthesis of plausible and natural HR texture a tough task, while a similar situation is drawn by the out-of-focus blur and shadow in the area around the eyes in Figure 1.2b. In other cases, like the non-frontal head pose, the occluding space helmet and the thick beard in Figures 1.2d, 1.2g and 1.2h, correspondence ambiguity on the 3D model remains an open question. In-plane rotation with the unseen half of the face due to out-of-plane rotation, and the unmodeled external object in addition to the intrinsic appearance variation give rise to severe degradation. Thus eventually, these combined factors can make the images in Figure 1.2 more challenging in contrast to the first portrait photo in Figure 1.1 taken more than one hundred years ago.

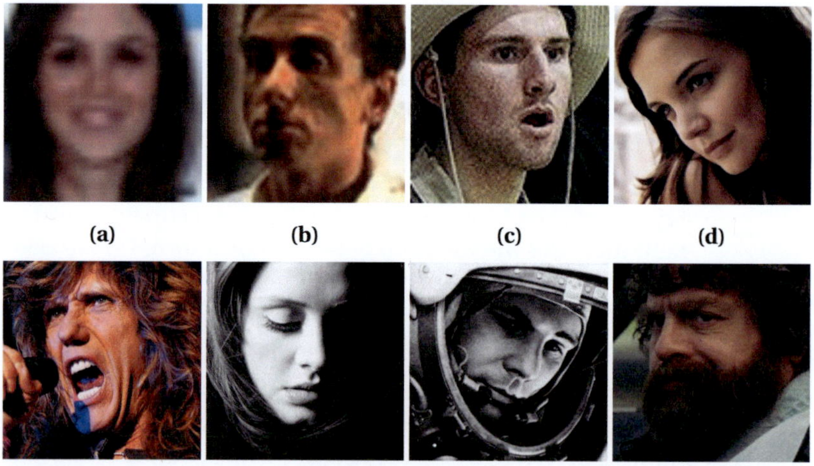

(a) (b) (c) (d)

(e) (f) (g) (h)

Figure 1.2: Example face images with different kinds of challenges: (a) resolution, (b) blurring, (c) noise, (d) pose, (e) expression, (f) illumination, (g) occlusion, (h) facial style [Sag13a].

Among the aforementioned challenges, some appear to do more damages than others, especially resolution and pose in the respective categories, which are also the primary focus of the presented 3D FSR framework, whereas the rest is not left unaddressed. For blurring, its mathematical model—the blurring kernel, is explicitly defined in the standard observation model of SR [Par03, Yan10a]. Although this means that a known kernel is a prerequisite for SR [Mic13], class-specific deblurring methods for face images, *e.g.*, [Anw15], can offer a reliable estimate of it. The remaining challenges of FSR have likewise a close connection to the uncontrolled settings as well. Therefore, robust landmark-based 3D fitting [Qu15d] in conjunction with HR 3D facial texture recovery based on local patches [Qu17] rather than the conventional holistic procedure [Bla99] as in [Mor09, Sch15] is exploited, since it tends to struggle with in-the-wild scenarios [Hu15, p. 86]. The proposed FSR work can instead leverage face data with richer variation [Gro10] within locally independent patch subspaces to cope with extreme illumination and facial styles. Even artifacts for non-neutral expressions can thereby be ameliorated to a certain extent. At the same time, noise is also implicitly mitigated thanks to the averaging effect of neighboring patches [Ma10]. Note that expression and occlusion are not explicitly handled in this thesis. Integrating extra expression variation into a bilinear face model [Cao14a] and employing an occlusion-aware sparse landmarking [Bur13] or dense fitting [Egg16] scheme usually suffice to bypass these problems.

1.3 Contributions

This thesis aims to design a performant 3D FSR system with a complete processing chain consisting of submodules for 2D facial landmark localization, 3D face shape fitting and 3D facial texture SR. The work presented in this thesis makes the following contributions to the field of LR facial analysis:

- A comprehensive review and critical analysis of the current approaches that straddle the boundary of general and LR face alignment, modeling and SR are conducted.
- As opposed to the synthetically generated LR data widely applied so far in the SR community, a novel FSR dataset with ground truth HR and LR image pairs is collected with a dual-camera hardware setup in combination with accurate HR–LR image registration, which is made publicly accessible to researchers [Qu16].

- The cascaded regression algorithm for sparse facial landmark detection is revisited and several core components w.r.t. the regression method, local image feature and fitting strategies are explored, which achieves top localization accuracy and low failure rate in the presence of various nuisances as a result of unconstrained LR images [Qu15c].
- While analyzing the fundamental issue of inconsistent correspondence of 2D and 3D landmarks caused by head pose for the landmark-based 3D face shape reconstruction approach, a new problem of localization ambiguity along the facial contour is identified for the first time, and subsequently addressed jointly by a novel dynamic online mapping algorithm [Qu14, Qu15d]. This leads to an automatic, efficient, robust and illumination-invariant alternative to the traditional fitting method.
- The proposed 3D FSR framework is the first ever attempt that integrates the standard LR image formation model into a 3D patch-based facial texture SR method. With a LR-friendly fitting strategy [Qu15b], a 3D extension of the Lucas–Kanade registration algorithm combined with a statistical morphable model is exploited to improve fitting and FSR on ill-posed LR images. Moreover, patch-based FSR carried out directly on the 3D face mesh is able to handle wide face variation and filling the self-occluded facial texture because of non-frontal head pose [Qu17].
- Extensive evaluation on several publicly available datasets demonstrates superior FSR performance in both effectiveness and efficiency over state-of-the-art approaches and remarkable improvement in FR as an application of FSR. Furthermore, this is also the first 3D FSR method capable of processing in-the-wild LR images.

1.4 Thesis Outline

This thesis is organized as follows:

Chapter 2: Related Work This study begins with an extensive survey of the existing literature within the scope of this thesis, *i.e.*, methods for landmark detection, 3D face reconstruction and SR. For the sake of clarity, the chapter is divided into separate sections related to the respective components. Current approaches covering one or multiple submodules are introduced and their advantages and the potential room for enhancement are reviewed.

Chapter 3: Concept This chapter depicts the design concept and choices behind the proposed 3D FSR processing chain. Crucial differences to other systems are discussed to briefly outline the theoretical merits of the presented workflow.

Chapter 4: Facial Landmark Detection Chapter 4 details the first module of this work, which localizes 2D fiducial facial feature points given a face image. Key improvements on the components of the cascaded regression algorithm are made incrementally to present the process of building a more robust landmark detector.

Chapter 5: 3D Face Reconstruction From Sparse Landmarks In this chapter, the theoretical knowledge of 3D face modeling, which is used throughout this thesis, and its practical adaptation for landmark-based 3D face shape reconstruction are described first. Next, after introducing the crux of the current problem in the facial contour landmarks, a novel adaptive correspondence algorithm is proposed to alleviate the drifting landmarks.

Chapter 6: 3D Patch-Based Facial Texture Super-Resolution Given the previously recovered 3D face shape, a resolution-aware 3D-assisted FSR method across pose is devised first. On the basis of this approach, a pure 3D algorithm for direct facial texture SR on the mesh is detailed, which is composed of a complete LR imaging model, an extra enhancement stage to circumvent the ill-posed 3D fitting problem and a local patch-based 3D texture SR approach.

Chapter 7: Experiments In the first part of Chapter 7, the newly collected FSR dataset containing ground truth HR and LR image pairs and its hardware and algorithmic implementation are described. Then, qualitative and quantitative performance is systematically evaluated in the context of the separate preprocessing submodules as well as the 3D FSR framework.

Different aspects for the robustness analysis are taken into account and an example application for LR FR is given.

Chapter 8: Concluding Remarks Finally, outcomes of this work are summarized with directions for future research.

2 Related Work

An overview of the existing work that covers the relevant modules of this thesis is given in this chapter. The goal is to exploit 3D information for learning-based FSR. Therefore, the preprocessing stages like alignment and reconstruction for faces in the presence of various challenging aspects play as crucial a role as the actual SR engine. In this sense, the chapter is broken down into three sections, *i.e.*, facial landmark detection in Section 2.1 and 3D face reconstruction in Section 2.2 prior to the main SR part in Section 2.3. Note that for lack of dedicated algorithms for the LR scenario, the majority of the preprocessing work introduced here is originally designed for standard face data, which may most probably suffer a decline in performance when applied to LR images. This will also be discussed at the end of the sections.

2.1 Facial Landmark Detection

The fiducial facial landmarks convey semantic information of faces. Facial landmark localization, a.k.a. face alignment, aims to detect these anchor points usually located at facial features that have descriptive meaning, *e.g.*, eyes, nose, mouth and chin. The sharp edges and corners near the feature points are leveraged to approach the true landmark location.

Reliable landmark detection algorithms are of vital importance for a number of facial analysis routines. As an example, face alignment is named after the traditional face recognition pipeline, *i.e.*, face detection, landmark localization, and eventually, image registration with linear or nonlinear transforms to obtain normalized faces for recognition [Gao09]. Similarly, robust landmark detection can benefit a wide spectrum of other researches and applications within the context of human faces, such as realistic face swapping for animation [Gar14], deformable face tracking [Chr17], head pose estimation [Mur09] or facial expression classification [Mar16], to name a few, all of which require accurate correspondence of the non-rigid facial structure across different images or video frames. Clearly, it is no exception for FSR as well [Wan14b].

After decades of active research, automatic facial landmark detection has developed into one of the spotlight topics in the facial analysis community and reached recently a high level of maturity. In spite of a plethora of diverse approaches to the problem so far, the most popular methods can be categorized into a few classes, *i.e.*, deformable appearance models, constrained shape models and shape regression. Other classification schemes, like the ones in [Jin16, Wan14a], are also found in the literature.

2.1.1 Deformable Appearance Models

Faces convey many pieces of intrinsic and extrinsic variations like shape, skin color, expression, pose, illumination, *etc.*, which are irreversibly blended into a single bitmap image during the capturing procedure. Deformable face models try to separate the face image into two simple parametric representations—shape and appearance. A shape model is typically in the form of a fixed sequence of the desired facial feature points, while appearance refers to the facial texture in correspondence with the face shape that helps to infer the appropriate shape w.r.t. the input image. As such, deformable appearance models can be regarded as a joint optimization problem in terms of shape and appearance to best fit the learned texture description to the query face.

According to the modeling principles in pattern recognition, deformable appearance models can be further grouped into *generative* and *discriminative* ones. Generative methods seek to minimize the distance between a rendered model instance and the face image. The Active Appearance Models (AAMs) proposed by Cootes *et al.* [Coo98] are undoubtedly the most famous generative appearance methods. In the data preparation phase of the AAM, the face images are manually annotated with a fixed set of N feature points $\mathbf{s} = [\mathbf{x}_1, \mathbf{x}_2, \dots, \mathbf{x}_N]^\top \in \mathbb{R}^{2N}$ representing the face shape, where $\mathbf{x}_i = [x_i, y_i]$ is the 2D location of the ith landmark. After aligning all shapes and applying Principal Component Analysis (PCA) to obtain a linear shape subspace with reduced dimensionality, the shape model, namely the Point Distribution Model (PDM), is constructed, which can be briefly interpreted as

$$\mathbf{s}(\mathbf{p}_s) = \bar{\mathbf{s}} + \mathbf{S}\mathbf{p}_s, \tag{2.1}$$

where $\mathbf{p}_s$ denotes the shape coefficients of the eigenface dictionary $\mathbf{S}$, and $\bar{\mathbf{s}}$ is the mean shape. The appearance model can be obtained in a similar fashion. Concretely, the face images need to be transformed onto the frame of the mean shape $\bar{\mathbf{s}}$ before PCA is conducted, which yields

$$\mathbf{a}(\mathbf{p}_a) = \bar{\mathbf{a}} + \mathbf{A}\mathbf{p}_a, \tag{2.2}$$

where $\bar{\mathbf{a}}$ and $\mathbf{A}$ denote the mean and eigenvectors of the appearance respectively, and $\mathbf{p}_a$ is the parameter. Based on the models built offline, the online fitting process is as described in a generative manner

$$\min_{\mathbf{p}_s, \mathbf{p}_a} \left\| \bar{\mathbf{a}} + \mathbf{A}\mathbf{p}_a - \mathbf{I}(\mathbf{W}(\mathbf{p}_s)) \right\|_2^2, \tag{2.3}$$

where the image $\mathbf{I}$ is warped via the warping operator $\mathbf{W}$ parametrized by the shape vector $\mathbf{p}_s$. This optimization problem has been extensively studied since the original linear regression approach coupling shape and appearance parameters by Cootes *et al.* [Coo98], leading to a gradient descent version [Coo01] and several inverse compositional variants [Gro05, Mat04, Tzi13] that can precompute Jacobian and Hessian matrices to increase efficiency [Bak03].

Most conventional generative AAMs optimize on the whole facial texture. However, this holistic approach is criticized for its lack of generalization power for unseen subjects and image conditions. To overcome the high dimensionality of the optimization problem, some recent generative AAM methods [Ant15, Tzi14] choose to operate on the local neighborhoods surrounding the facial landmarks only. Since part-based models are less sensitive to occlusion and lighting, they are shown to outperform holistic AAMs by a large margin and achieve state-of-the-art performance when trained on in-the-wild face datasets.

In contrast to the generative AAM family, discriminative AAM fitting leverages the learned correlation between the appearance feature and landmark displacement from the training data. A nonlinear boosted regression with an ensemble of weak learners using rectangular Haar-like features is presented by Saragih and Goecke [Sar07]. Only the shape parameters are updated with the nonlinear mapping. Liu [Liu09] treats deformable fitting as a classification problem. Similar to [Sar07], integral features are employed by weak classifiers to build a strong function to distinguish the correct PDM parameters from the wrong ones. Following this discriminative approach, Gao *et al.* propose a series of improvements exploring alternative features, like pseudo consensus transform [Gao11] and random pixel intensity differences [Gao13], as well as learning strategies like ranking and regression trees [Gao12], greatly increasing fitting accuracy and robustness given noisy initialization and data compared to generative AAMs.

2.1.2 Constrained Shape Models

Constrained shape models typically incorporate discriminatively learned local detectors or regressors with a certain type of shape constraint. This kind of methods has a long history in face alignment, dating back to the pioneering Active Shape Model (ASM) by Cootes *et al.* in 1992 [Coo92]. The ASM, along with a large body of succeeding work, belongs to the popular Constrained Local Model (CLM) framework. CLMs fit the face shape to the input image through a cost function jointly optimizing the shape prior and local response maps. Standard CLMs share the same PDM with AAMs, which serves as the prior knowledge of landmark configuration $p(\mathbf{p}_s)$ to constrain the fitting process. By assuming conditional independence between each landmark detector, the CLM objective is to maximize the posterior of the shape parameter [Sar11], which takes the form

$$\max_{\mathbf{p}_s} p\left(\mathbf{p}_s \mid \{l_i = 1\}_{i=1}^{N}, \mathbf{I}\right) \tag{2.4}$$

$$= \max_{\mathbf{p}_s} p\left(\mathbf{p}_s\right) \prod_{i=1}^{N} p\left(l_i = 1 \mid \mathbf{x}_i, \mathbf{I}\right), \tag{2.5}$$

where $l_i \in \{1, -1\}$ indicates whether the ith facial point is aligned or not. Figure 2.1 illustrates the CLM optimization w.r.t. its two components, *i.e.*, the PDM and the response maps of independent local experts, which can have different implementations for computing the response of each detector when convolved with an image patch during the exhaustive search. The

ASM [Coo92] defines the 1D distance between the profile normal to the edges. Linear Support Vector Machine (SVM) is utilized in [Sar11, Wan08] to classify positive detections and those with large distance to the true location as negative ones. Subsequently, logistic regression is employed to obtain a probabilistic output. Within this framework, a range of methods have been developed to approximate the true response maps to make the gradient descent tractable, including isotropic Gaussian in the probabilistic formulation of the original ASM [Coo92], anisotropic Gaussian [Wan08], Gaussian Mixture Models (GMMs) [Gu08] and the nonparametric kernel density estimation [Sar11].

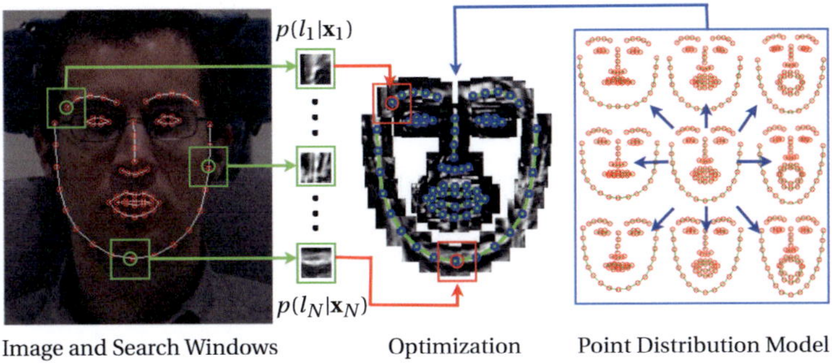

Figure 2.1: Illustration of the components of the CLM optimization: the response maps and the PDM [Sar11].

Apart from the mainstream CLMs, new attempts explore the possibilities to ditch the classic routine with PDM plus classifiers. Cootes *et al.* [Coo12] replace the SVM experts with regression using random forest [Bre01] to directly predict the shape update for each evaluated patch. Accumulated votes then generate the response maps, boosting both runtime and accuracy. Asthana *et al.* [Ast13] also regress the PDM parameter update from the low-dimensional projection of the response maps, and further adopt the Histogram of Oriented Gradients (HOG) feature [Dal05] to outperform raw pixel intensity on unconstrained face images. Finally, Belhumeur *et al.* present a novel nonparametric exemplar-based approach in [Bel11] to remedy the limitation of the PDM. On the basis of the rich patch representation using Scale-Invariant Feature Transform (SIFT) [Low04], the global shape is regularized by one of the closest transformed training exemplars sampled with a Random Sample Consensus (RANSAC)-like strategy [Fis81]. Thanks to this flexible shape model, fitting performance is comparable to that of human labeling on one of the first in-the-wild face alignment datasets [Bel11], however, at the expense of a high computational burden.

2.1.3 Shape Regression

Despite the massive attention received in the past decades and considerable progress achieved for deformable appearance and shape models, explicitly optimizing the face shape is proved to be ineffective when dealing with unconstrained face images. In particular, statistical shape models like the PDM may struggle with novel faces. Furthermore, it is usually tricky to balance the local and global constraints as well. To this end, a new group of regression-based algorithms have emerged recently, which directly map the image appearance features to the target shape

$$\mathcal{R} : \mathbf{\Phi}(\mathbf{I}) \mapsto \mathbf{s}, \tag{2.6}$$

where $\mathcal{R}$ denotes the mapping of shape regressors based on the features extracted from the image $\mathbf{I}$ by $\mathbf{\Phi}$. Unlike independent part detectors [Din08, Vuk05], shape regression can implicitly learn to regularize the whole shape to eliminate invalid point constellations through the training images.

The algorithm of Valstar *et al.* [Val10] is among the first attempts in this case. By training the local regressors with Support Vector Regression (SVR), direction and distance to the landmarks provide an initial prediction. The pairwise relation of the nodes are then encoded to ensure invariance to in-plane rotation, isotropic scaling and translation. The Markov Random Field (MRF) optimization, although not an absolutely optimal solution, refines the landmarking accuracy iteratively. But the ambiguity of local appearance models as in CLMs remains unsolved.

In [Dan12], Dantone *et al.* extend the regression forest to condition on the head pose to overcome the tendency of fitting the mean face due to the averaging effect of the random forest [Bre01]. The fitting stage first estimates the pose and then determines the tree distribution to be selected in the separate forests trained on different poses. Subsequently, Yang and Patras [Yan13d] propose to sieve regression voting with two levels of criteria, *i.e.*, the distance to the center of the whole face and each accumulated map, forcing the votes to be more reliable than in [Dan12].

Unarguably, the latest surge and explosive progress made in facial point localization can boil down to the success of cascaded regression-based approaches. Inspired by the novel cascaded pose regression by Dollár *et al.* [Dol10], a series of regressors can be successively stacked to fit the landmarks progressively, which circumvents the difficulty of regressing the face shape in a single attempt. The core methodology of cascaded shape regression is illustrated in Algorithm 1. In each stage t, the *shape-indexed feature*[1] $\boldsymbol{\phi}^{(t-1)}$ that depends on the previous shape estimate is extracted. Applying the learned regressor $\mathbf{R}^{(t)}$ straightforwardly produces an update $\Delta\mathbf{s}$, which is added to the current shape. After T iterations, the face shape is fitted in a coarse-to-fine manner.

Algorithm 1: Face alignment with cascaded shape regression

Input: Image $\mathbf{I}$ and initial shape $\mathbf{s}^{(0)}$
Output: Fitted shape $\mathbf{s}^{(T)}$

for $t = 1$ **to** T **do**
 $\boldsymbol{\phi}^{(t-1)} = \boldsymbol{\Phi}\left(\mathbf{I}, \mathbf{s}^{(t-1)}\right)$ ▷ Extract shape-indexed feature $\boldsymbol{\phi}^{(t-1)}$
 $\Delta\mathbf{s} = \mathbf{R}^{(t)}\left(\boldsymbol{\phi}^{(t-1)}\right)$ ▷ Apply regressor $\mathbf{R}^{(t)}$
 $\mathbf{s}^{(t)} = \mathbf{s}^{(t-1)} + \Delta\mathbf{s}$ ▷ Update shape $\mathbf{s}^{(t)}$
end

The breakthrough two-level boosted regression algorithm is devised by Cao *et al.* in [Cao12]. Each of the first-level regressors $\mathbf{R}^{(t)}$ is composed of a second-level cascade of random ferns [Özu10] with pixel-difference features extracted from the whole image. A correlation-based random feature selection strategy is further adopted for real-time capability. Motivated by the state-of-the-art performance of the two-level cascaded regression, Burgos-Artizzu *et al.* [Bur13] make several extensions of [Cao12]. The

[1] Note that the shape-indexed feature in this thesis has a general meaning, which is not restricted to the pixel-difference feature first proposed in [Cao12].

pixel-difference features are computed using linear interpolation of two landmarks rather than a fixed offset w.r.t. one landmark in [Cao12]. Their regressors also involve an extra occlusion property in addition to the landmark update for robust reasoning of invisible facial parts. In [Kaz14], Kazemi and Sullivan replace the random fern regressor [Özu10] with an ensemble of regression trees [Has09], achieving top and stable results with perturbed initialization [Yan15b] in the millisecond range.

In comparison with the two-level cascades, Xiong and De la Torre [Xio13] give a concise and elegant formulation to the cascaded shape regression, which regards the problem as a sequence of supervised gradient descent steps. The handcrafted SIFT features [Low04] extracted around the facial landmarks are fed into linear least squares and the descent direction is learned to guide the current shape estimate towards the desired location. Starting from the derivation of the nonlinear Newton optimization for the AAM [Coo98], they show the advantages of such supervised Newton update. Like other shape regression methods, though nonparametric in both shape and appearance, the implicit shape constraint still holds since each shape increment lies on the manifold of the training data, providing better generalization to novel faces. Inspired by the project-out AAM [Mat04], Tzimiropoulos [Tzi15] learns the descent directions of PDM parameters in a subspace orthogonal to the facial appearance variation coined Project-Out Cascaded Regression (PO–CR), which greatly propels robustness under extreme conditions. Ren *et al.* [Ren14] argue the drawbacks of both handcrafted features in [Xio13] and globally extracted features in [Cao12], and design the local binary features. It bears some similarity to [Kaz14] by using random forest [Bre01] to train local features as input to the linear regressor cascade, resulting in even faster fitting than [Kaz14]. Zhu *et al.* [Zhu15a] propose a cascaded shape search framework in a coarse-to-fine fashion with various feature descriptors [Cal10, Low04] to compromise over precision and speed, which accounts for large pose and local optima due to poor initialization. In other work, solutions for incremental and parallel training of different cascade stages [Ast14] and ranking of multiple shape hypotheses [Yan13a] are studied as well.

Finally, amid the hot trend of unconstrained face alignment, two challenges for static images [Sag16, Sag13a] and one challenge for video tracking [She15] have been organized within a short time span, leading to valuable datasets, algorithms and discussions, which will surely spur more research interest in the future.

2.1.4 Discussion

The facial landmark detection research has traveled a long journey from the person-specific AAMs [Coo98] to the state-of-the-art cascaded shape regression and Deep Neural Networks (DNNs) [Sun13, Tri16, Zha15, Zha14a, Zha14b, Zha16, Zho13] in uncontrolled environment. This justifies the design choice of first localizing 2D facial points in this thesis for 3D face SR, since some of the challenges discussed in Section 1.2 have already been addressed, whereas it is obviously not the case for the common statistical 3D face modeling algorithms [Hu15, Mor09]. Nevertheless, despite the broad interest, face alignment for LR faces remains a largely unattended apart from very few exceptions. Liu *et al.* [Liu06] build a pyramid of AAMs to adapt to a variety of image resolutions. Dedeoğlu *et al.* [Ded06] point out that the traditional AAM procedure causes information loss when warping the LR image onto the model coordinate frame. Instead, they devise an inverse fitting algorithm that takes the LR image formation process into consideration. With both approaches employing the aged generative AAM engine [Coo98], the eligibility of newer methods for the LR condition must be verified in the first place.

2.2 3D Face Reconstruction

The merit of a pose, expression and illumination invariant description of 3D faces has attracted considerable attention and research effort over the past decades. Hindered by the high cost and practical difficulties, 3D cameras [Dri13] and structured light techniques [Zha10] are still limited from being deployed outside of the lab. Hence, in this section, a compact review of image-based 3D face reconstruction is given.

2.2.1 Statistical Morphable Model

The seminal work of the 3D Morphable Model (3DMM) by Blanz and Vetter [Bla99] establishes the fundamental idea of describing human faces as linear shape and texture subspaces obtained with aligned 3D scans. Particularly, a collection of 3D face scans is first captured with a 3D scanner, where each scan consists of both geometry and albedo of the enrolled subject. To enforce the same ordering and dense correspondence of each vertex across all scans, an iterative registration process, *e.g.*, [Amb07] in [Pay09], is applied on the triangulated mesh, which in addition also fills the missing data (see Figure 2.2a). An example of the cleaned result after registration is depicted in Figure 2.2b. As such, the 3D shape and texture of human faces as shown in Figure 2.2c can be written as

$$\mathbf{s} = \left[x_1, y_1, z_1, \ldots, x_P, y_P, z_P\right]^\top \tag{2.7}$$

$$\mathbf{t} = \left[r_1, g_1, b_1, \ldots, r_P, g_P, b_P\right]^\top \tag{2.8}$$

respectively, where P is the number of vertices of the registered faces. Applying PCA to the shape and texture data individually yields

$$\mathbf{s} = \bar{\mathbf{s}} + \mathbf{S}\boldsymbol{\alpha} \tag{2.9}$$

$$\mathbf{t} = \bar{\mathbf{t}} + \mathbf{T}\boldsymbol{\beta}, \tag{2.10}$$

where $\bar{\mathbf{s}}$ and $\bar{\mathbf{t}}$ are the mean vectors. $\mathbf{S} \in \mathbb{R}^{3P \times Q_s}$ and $\mathbf{T} \in \mathbb{R}^{3P \times Q_t}$ denote the respective principal modes of variation rescaled by their standard deviation. In this way, the 3DMM is representable as $\{\bar{\mathbf{s}}, \mathbf{S}, \bar{\mathbf{t}}, \mathbf{T}\}$ and the normally distributed coefficients $\boldsymbol{\alpha} \in \mathbb{R}^{Q_s}$ and $\boldsymbol{\beta} \in \mathbb{R}^{Q_t}$ with unit variance suffice to describe any valid face within the PCA subspaces [Pay09]. It is worth noting that other shape models like local wavelet PCA is beyond the scope of this thesis. The reader is referred to [Bru14] for a comparative study.

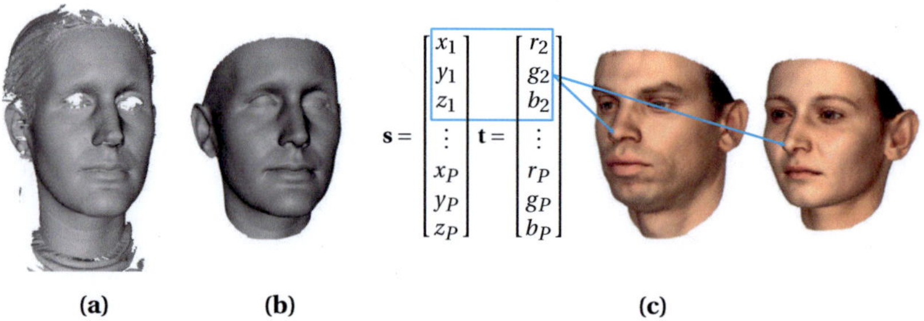

Figure 2.2: 3D registration for building a 3DMM: (a) a raw 3D scan, (b) the registered scan with filled holes, (c) vectorized face representation in shape and texture [Pay09].

Fitting a 3DMM to a 2D image is treated as an *analysis-by-synthesis* problem by Blanz and Vetter in [Bla99] akin to the AAM [Coo98], in which the model is used to render an image and the error between the synthesized and the input image is minimized to optimize the sought parameters. By explicitly modeling the Phong reflection $\boldsymbol{\gamma}$ [Hug13], the analysis-by-synthesis objective is then

$$\min_{\boldsymbol{\alpha},\boldsymbol{\beta},\boldsymbol{\gamma},\boldsymbol{\tau}} \left\| \mathbf{I}_{\text{input}} - \mathbf{I}_{\text{model}}\left(\boldsymbol{\alpha},\boldsymbol{\beta},\boldsymbol{\gamma},\boldsymbol{\tau}\right) \right\|_2^2, \tag{2.11}$$

where $\boldsymbol{\tau}$ denotes the camera parameters.

In their original work [Bla99], Blanz and Vetter simultaneously update all parameters using stochastic optimization based on a random selection of pixels, which is extended in [Bla03] with an additional term of several manually annotated anchor points. Romdhani *et al.* [Rom03] introduce the inverse compositional algorithm of 2D AAMs [Mat04] (see Section 2.1.1) into the 3DMM for acceleration. Later, they propose the Multi-Features Fitting (MFF) strategy to leverage auxiliary features like edge and specular highlights to diminish the risk of falling into local minima [Rom05]. Alternatively, the joint fitting process can be decomposed into geometric and photometric parts [Ald13, Rom02, Zha06a]. However, compromises on the camera and lighting models must be made to simplify the separate optimization tasks.

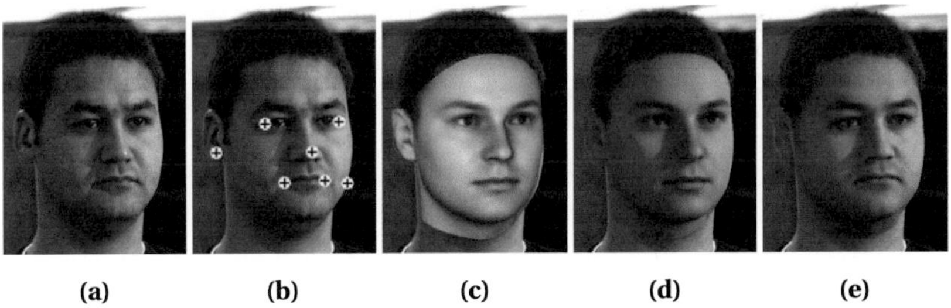

Figure 2.3: Face reconstruction from a single image using the 3DMM: (a) an input image, (b) the annotated feature points, (c) fitted initial shape using the features, (d) estimated illumination, (e) final optimization result w.r.t. shape, texture, transformation and illumination [Bla03].

A sample workflow of fitting a 3DMM to a single image is demonstrated in Figure 2.3. From the manually labeled features and shape initialization to the recovered illumination and the final textured face model, the analysis-by-synthesis framework can generate highly detailed and photo-realistic shape and texture. Nevertheless, drawbacks such as the low fitting speed and the demand for high-quality images as input impede these 3D statistical deformable models from broader application.

2.2.2 Shape from X

Instead of adopting the model-driven approaches, 3D shape of the face can be recovered by traditional computer vision techniques as well.

Structure from Motion (SFM) can reconstruct a 3D scene with a sequence of monocular images taken from different viewpoints, which resembles the ability of human beings that perceive 3D information by moving around objects. Many SFM algorithms begin with a track of sparse feature landmarks and then infer their depth. Lee *et al.* [Lee11] construct a shape conversion matrix to mitigate displacement of the self-occluded points in the cheek area caused by head rotation while converting 2D landmarks to 3D, and employ Thin-Plate Spline (TPS) [Boo89] for the dense mean model adaptation. Roy-Chowdhury and Chellappa [Roy03] make use of optical flow for SFM [Sri00] and regularize the output mesh with a generic head template. In general, SFM-based approaches still require a reference face model to densify the tracked sparse features. Yet the fidelity is limited and single-frame reconstruction is not possible. Therefore, landmark-based methods (see Section 2.2.3) that rely on statistical deformable shape models have gained popularity over SFM.

Shape from Shading (SFS) can recover the surface normals using shading information from a single image [Hor70], which is a special case of Photometric Stereo (PS), where multiple images under different lighting conditions are used [Woo80]. Generally speaking, SFS has an ill-posed setup with a large number of unknowns. Some authors integrate the symmetry of faces [Dov04, Zha01] as prior to reduce the ambiguity. In other cases, it is more common to exploit a 3D reference model. In the work of [Kem11a], Kemelmacher-Shlizerman and Basri "mold" the generic model to the single input face image and solve for the unknown lighting, boundary conditions and albedo. For personal or Internet image collections, PS is applied to the near-frontal faces with normalized expression to obtain more consistent normals locally [Kem11b] than the single-view reconstruction

[Kem11a]. Motivated by the promising result, Roth *et al.* extend [Kem11b] with a generic [Rot15] or personalized template [Rot16] to facilitate profile poses to enhance the depth of 3D faces. In light of these applications, SFS and PS are regarded as a complementary instrument to alleviate model dominance of the statistical 3DMM, which can produce outstanding facial details [Pat12].

2.2.3 Landmark-Based Shape Reconstruction

2D landmarks have long served as a plausible way to initialize the 3DMM fitting [Bla03]. Despite the impressive achievements, the analysis-by-synthesis framework is often criticized for its extremely time-consuming and challenging non-convex optimization w.r.t. the enormous parameter space for shape, texture, camera calibration, lighting, *etc.* Fortunately, thanks to the latest breakthrough of face alignment in the wild, by leveraging the fiducial feature points, it is viable to dramatically reduce the dimensionality by leaving out the entire motion, albedo and illumination parameters, as only the 3DMM shape coefficients need to be reconstructed. Moreover, the shrinkage from tens of thousands of dense vertices to merely dozens of sparse ones can also contribute to a huge speedup.

Besides the well-known analysis-by-synthesis 3DMM fitting [Bla99], Blanz *et al.* [Bla04] first show that landmarks alone are sufficient for obtaining useful shape estimates in their own rights. With the aid of less than 20 manually labeled anchor points, the complete 3D shape can be approximated via the shape coefficients within the span of the underlying 3DMM

$$\min_{\boldsymbol{\alpha}} \left\| \left(s\mathbf{R}_{[1:2,:]} \left(\bar{\mathbf{s}}_l + \mathbf{S}_l \boldsymbol{\alpha} \right) + \mathbf{o} \right) - \mathbf{l} \right\|_2^2, \tag{2.12}$$

where the subscript l denotes the corresponding vertices of the $F \ll P$ facial landmarks $\mathbf{l} \in \mathbb{R}^{2F}$ on the 3DMM. In order to have a closed-form formulation, the weak perspective camera parameters including scale s, 2D projection of the rotation matrix $\mathbf{R}_{[1:2,:]}$ and translation $\mathbf{o}$ are linearized and solved along with $\boldsymbol{\alpha}$ using least squares. As such, 3D reconstruction is significantly simplified and the prior knowledge from the 3DMM helps to overcome the otherwise ill-posed problem using incomplete sparse features.

As an extension of [Bla04], Faggian *et al.* [Fag06] first involve facial landmark detection with the help of a person-specific AAM [Mat04] towards fully automatic shape reconstruction. By considering multiple images, an extension of [Fag06] is devised to enhance robustness across frames [Fag08]. Jiang *et al.* [Jia05] also use a similar least squares approach to build an initial personalized 3D face model from a single frontal image, which is interpolated [Oli90] to better adapt to the 2D landmarks. Later, Zhao *et al.* [Zha06b] propose to add a second profile shape model to improve the depth estimate.

Aldrian and Smith [Ald10a, Ald10b] loose the assumption in [Bla04] that observations of all landmarks are subject to uncorrelated Gaussian noise with a uniform variance, as they learn the individual generalization errors by projecting out-of-sample data onto the 3DMM subspace. Without the need for a 3DMM, Rara *et al.* [Rar11] exploit 3D faces directly with Principal Component Regression (PCR) to model the 3D shape as a linear combination of the samples instead of 3DMM eigenfaces as in previous work. A nearly identical evaluation result is reported. Following this idea, Dou *et al.* [Dou14] learn a regression subspace for 2D and 3D sparse landmarks, and a second dictionary for 3D sparse and dense shapes. By forcing them to share the same weights in a coupled representation, their underlying relationship is encoded. In this way, the 3D shape is reconstructed with the transfered coefficients, whereas the pose is also implicitly recovered.

Self-Occlusion

In the previous efforts that try to connect automatic facial point localization and 3D shape inference, a crucial difference between 2D face alignment algorithms and 3D face models has been ignored while empirically assuming a fixed mapping between 2D and 3D features. Since the contour landmarks of 2D AAMs are originally defined as the jawline that becomes easily occluded even with small head poses, the points on the face boundary in the image plane are detected instead, which have a considerable distance to their true locations. This phenomenon is depicted in Figure 2.4. If the fixed annotations in blue rather than the actual correct contour vertices in red are utilized for shape reconstruction, bad distortion is likely to happen.

To mitigate the negative impact of the erroneous observation, Lee *et al.* [Lee12] propose to discard these self-occluded landmarks while reconstructing non-frontal faces. Experimental results show that this straightforward idea appears to be helpful. Asthana *et al.* [Ast11] are also aware of this issue when normalizing poses for face recognition. They manually label the 2D–3D correspondence for 199 poses with yaw angles from $-45°$ to

+45° and pitch angles from −30° to +30° to build a lookup table, leading to good recognition scores with frontalized faces. Wang *et al.* [Wan04a] employ an Expectation–Maximization (EM) algorithm to infer the shape and pose parameters iteratively and set the directional constraints individually for contour points. In [Cao14a], Cao *et al.* are faced with an inverse problem, which aims to locate the 2D landmarks from 3D faces. For this purpose, dense samplings of vertices arranged in many horizontal lines are annotated. Only one vertex perpendicular to the view direction per line is connected as the contour curve, from which the corresponding vertices to the 2D landmarks are selected equidistantly. Zhu *et al.* [Zhu15b] follow [Cao14a] and present a landmark marching scheme, which integrates this dynamic correspondence into the shape optimization step. Lately, Bas *et al.* [Bas16] completely drop the contour landmarks and use edges of the face as a substitute to constrain the facial geometry.

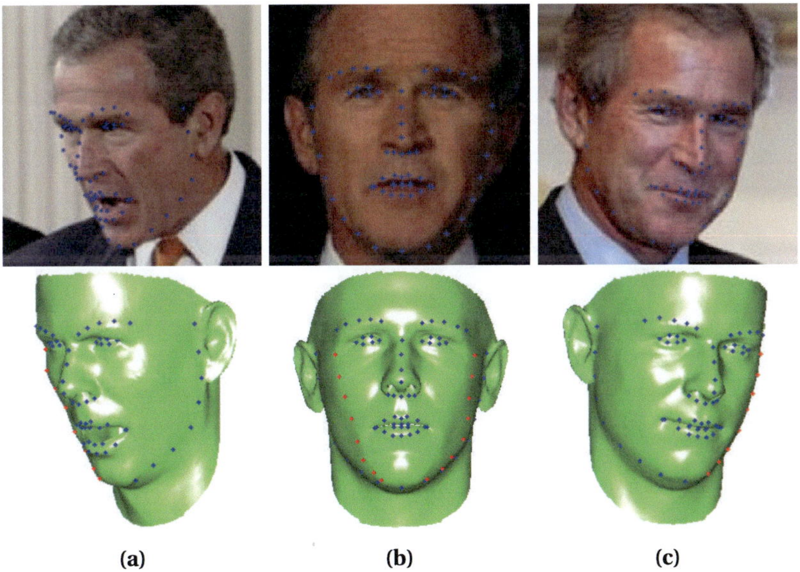

Figure 2.4: The phenomenon of vertex mismatch for contour landmarks. The blue points on the 3D face are standard landmark annotations. The red ones are the actual vertices corresponding to the self-occluded contour landmarks [Zhu15b].

Chapter 5 again analyzes the phenomenon of vertex mismatch thoroughly and details a novel soft correspondence approach that allows for a fast and effective solution to the existing and newly identified challenges.

2.2.4 3D Shape Regression

3D approaches are widely accepted to have advantages over 2D w.r.t. representational power and robustness to large pose. Recent advances in 2D shape regression have raised the question whether a 3D interpretation is possible, and to what extent the benefit will be.

Cao *et al.* [Cao13] employ the two-level cascades [Cao12] for facial landmarks to track a person-specific blend-shape model in videos, which is generalized to a person-independent system in [Cao14a]. A correction step is needed to resolve inconsistency at the facial contour as stated in Section 2.2.3. In comparison, without this step, Zhu *et al.* [Zhu15c] adopt HOG feature around landmarks akin to [Xio13], which is only capable of regressing frontal faces. Like [Cao13], Jeni *et al.* [Jen15] track 3D faces, which are tessellated into a dense grid of 3D feature points, so vertex displacement for 2D silhouette landmarks does not occur. [Tul15] uses the same strategy to tackle the problem. [Xio13] and [Kaz14] act as the regression backbones for [Jen15] and [Tul15] respectively.

Similar to 2D shape regression (*c.f.* Section 2.1.3), DNNs are beginning to prevail for discriminative 3D shape fitting. Jourabloo and Liu [Jou16] extract local features using piecewise affine warping, which are collated into a single image to feed the network that outputs the 3DMM shape coefficients. Zhu *et al.* [Zhu16b] use the whole face image and the depth map of 3D coordinates encoded in the RGB representation as the input, which is extended with an extra normal map by Richardson *et al.* in [Ric17]. A novel unsupervised loss emulating the SFS principle can generate additional fine details.

One advantage of 3D regression-based methods is that large pose can be circumvented naturally and efficiently via the cascaded regression [Jou15] or DNNs with end-to-end training [Jou16, Zhu16b]. Unfortunately, a major downside emerges, which potentially renders the large body of in-the-wild 2D face datasets of little avail. The sought 3DMM shape parameter for training is either fitted by means of 2D landmark-based approaches (see Section 2.2.3) [Jou16], or generated by synthesizing random 3D faces [Jen16, Ric16], which may hamper robustness and generalization for unconstrained data. Only in [Zhu16b], in-the-wild face profiling is conducted with their full-head rotation technique including background warping [Zhu15b].

2.2.5 Discussion

The development of statistical 3D face models has significantly lowered the barriers of entry for researchers, engineers and end-application developers interested in recovering facial geometry for diverse purposes. Nevertheless, the LR scenario puts a higher risk of failure for 3D frameworks by virtue of its more complex parameterization and optimization. Few algorithms targeting the LR problem are fully dedicated to the analysis-by-synthesis case for faces in controlled quality, including a pyramid of 3DMMs for different resolutions by Hu *et al.* [Hu12], and incorporation of the LR blurring into [Bla03] by Schumacher *et al.* [Sch15] and MFF [Rom05] by Mortazavian *et al.* [Mor12]. On the other hand, the prerequisite for DNN-based systems is in most situations a high spatial resolution [Kri12] to allow for a deep structure of convolution and pooling layers. Upscaled LR images turn out to be inadequate for good performance [Her16]. Therefore, LR 3D face reconstruction for surveillance data is not a trivial task.

2.3 Super-Resolution

SR offers an affordable way to boost quality and details of LR images *after* acquisition. The basic idea behind SR is to exploit non-redundant cues from internal or external sources to produce high-frequency details that are permanently lost during the LR image formation

$$\mathbf{Y}_k = \mathbf{D}_k\mathbf{B}_k\mathbf{W}_k\mathbf{X} + \mathbf{n}_k, \quad k \in \{1,2,\ldots,K\}, \tag{2.13}$$

where $\mathbf{Y}_k$ is the kth LR observation from the camera for the HR scene $\mathbf{X}$. $\mathbf{W}_k$, $\mathbf{B}_k$ and $\mathbf{D}_k$ denote operations for motion compensation, blurring due to out of focus, moving subject or camera, or the imaging device, *i.e.*, the Point Spread Function (PSF), as well as downsampling respectively, while $\mathbf{n}_k$ denotes the additive noise term.

Except for early frequency-domain techniques like the pioneering work by Tsai and Huang [Tsa84], prevalent generic SR algorithms address this ill-conditioned problem in the spatial domain, which can be roughly categorized into reconstruction-based and learning-based methods. Furthermore,

FSR that is designed for class-specific images, is gradually recognized as a separate branch, which is of particular interest to this thesis.

2.3.1 Reconstruction-Based Super-Resolution

To combat the intractable SR problem, many approaches turn to multiple LR frames to find out the missing HR details. Ur and Gross [Ur92] explore several spatially shifted LR images with known displacement to register and interpolate them on a HR lattice before applying restoration for blur removal. Elad and Hel-Or [Ela01] present a fast algorithm for pure translational motion and space-invariant blur, where a similar idea is found in current high-end cameras for generating a HR output using images taken with high-speed sensor shift by a half and a whole pixel[1]. For interpolating irregularly sampled data, Delaunay triangulation can be employed [Ler02].

In order to better regularize the HR result and account for registration error, noise and blurring effects, statistical approaches have a Maximum a Posteriori (MAP) interpretation minimizing the Lagrangian

$$\hat{\mathbf{X}} = \arg\min_{\mathbf{X}} \{\Pr(\mathbf{X} \mid \mathbf{Y})\} \tag{2.14}$$

$$= \arg\min_{\mathbf{X}} \{\Pr(\mathbf{Y} \mid \mathbf{X},\mathbf{H}) \Pr(\mathbf{X})\} \tag{2.15}$$

$$= \arg\min_{\mathbf{X}} \left\{\|\mathbf{Y} - \mathbf{H}\mathbf{X}\|_2^2 + \lambda \mathbf{A}(\mathbf{X})\right\}, \tag{2.16}$$

where $\mathbf{H}$ is the composition of image degradation operators $\mathbf{W}$, $\mathbf{B}$ and $\mathbf{D}$. λ denotes the Lagrange multiplier balancing the fidelity to the data w.r.t. the reconstruction constraint in the first term $\|\mathbf{Y} - \mathbf{H}\mathbf{X}\|_2^2$, and the second regularization term $\mathbf{A}(\mathbf{X})$ w.r.t. the HR image prior to control smoothness.

When the prior is not taken into consideration, the equivalent Maximum Likelihood Estimation (MLE) is then purely dependent on the data term. As an example, the popular Iterative Back-Projection (IBP) method by Irani and Peleg [Ira91] back-projects the reconstruction error in Equation (2.16) between the LR input and the simulated LR image onto the HR estimate to iteratively minimize the energy of error.

[1] `https://www.dpreview.com/reviews/olympus-om-d-e-m5-ii/4`

The choice of the image prior $\mathbf{A}(\mathbf{X})$ is one of the main focuses of MAP algorithms. Some heuristic priors can place spatial constraints on the local image neighborhoods in a MRF fashion, *e.g.*, the smoothness-preserving Gaussian MRF prior in [Ngu01] and the edge-preserving Huber MRF in [Sch96]. In [Far04], Farsiu *et al.* study the Total Variation (TV) [Rud92] prior with ℓ_1 norm for its sparse gradient-preserving nature and noise resistance, and devise a Bilateral Total Variation (BTV) generalization following the bilateral filtering [Tom98] for fast and robust SR.

Most aforementioned methods assume a known motion model and PSF. Tipping and Bishop [Tip02] address SR with a novel Bayesian formulation to marginalize over the unknown HR image, which is later extended by Pickup *et al.* in [Pic06] to integrate over the motion and blurring parameters for speed concerns.

As another well-known stream in SR, Projection onto Convex Sets (POCS) [Sta89, You78] treats multiple pieces of prior knowledge as convex sets with non-empty intersections. POCS performs recursive projection of an initial guess to these convex sets to find the HR image within the intersection set fulfilling the desired constraints. To remedy the slow convergence, Elad and Feuer [Ela97] propose a hybrid approach to embrace the merits of MLE, MAP and POCS.

2.3.2 Learning-Based Super-Resolution

In spite of the popularity of reconstruction-based SR with multiple images, Baker and Kanade [Bak02] prove that the SR reconstruction constraint provides less and less useful information as the magnification factor increases and produces overly smooth outputs with very little high-frequency information regardless of how many LR observations are used. Lin and Shum [Lin04] go a step further and derive theoretical upper bounds for images with local translation under realistic and synthetic conditions. As suggested by [Bak02], internal or external cues can be exploited for SR with high upsampling ratio. In the literature, this learning-based SR family is commonly referred to as single-image SR. Indeed, apart from some exceptions using natural image statistics [Kim10] and edge or gradient profiles [Fat07, Sun08], the predominant and most successful single-image SR algorithms are the learning-based ones [Yan14].

Generic learning-based SR is also known as patch-based or example-based methods, because the LR input image is partitioned into overlapping regions, for which the closest LR patches in the training data are searched, so that the HR reconstruction can be realized as a mapping from the LR patches. Freeman *et al.* [Fre02, Fre00] propose a MRF to model the relationship between the LR observation and the respective underlying HR patches, as well as the compatibility between the adjacent HR patches. Specifically, from the k-Nearest Neighbors (kNN) w.r.t. the LR patch, a loopy Belief Propagation (BP) algorithm [Fre00] or a one-pass approximation [Fre02] is utilized to select the best patch in favor of the Markov network. When merging the HR patches, the pixels in the overlapping area are averaged for smooth transition free of artifacts.

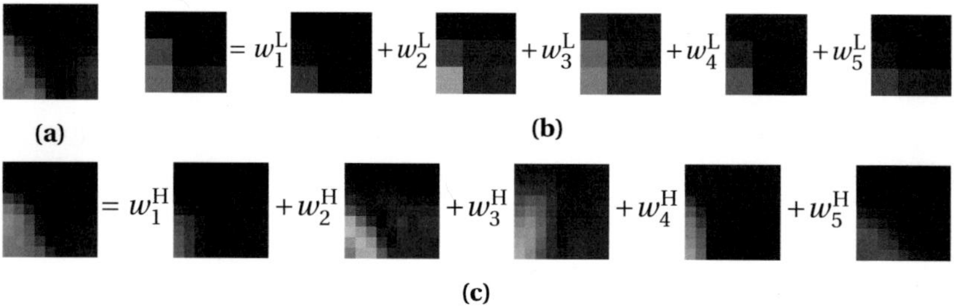

Figure 2.5: Learning local LR and HR embeddings for SR: (a) the ground truth HR patch, (b) five nearest neighbors in the training set are selected to linearly represent the LR patch, (c) SR result using the same or mapped weights from the LR reconstruction [Cha04].

The crux of the example-based SR lies in the ambiguity of finding HR correspondences solely based on the LR observation with a fraction of the number of pixels compared to those in HR patches. Apparently, it is a one-to-many problem, demonstrated exemplarily in Figure 2.5. The LR patch and the closest patches in the training set determined by kNN with $k = 5$ are shown in Figure 2.5b. Although the third exemplar is visually akin to the original LR patch, their HR counterparts have totally different image gradient directions (*c.f.* Figures 2.5a and 2.5c). To this end, Chang *et al.* [Cha04] explore local manifolds of LR and HR training data with Locally Linear Embedding (LLE) [Sau03]. Rather than inferring the absolutely best match out of the kNN with BP [Fre02], linear weights $\mathbf{w}^{\mathrm{L}}$ are computed to reconstruct the LR patch $\mathbf{y}$

$$\min_{\mathbf{w}^{\mathrm{L}}} \left\| \mathbf{y} - \sum_{\mathbf{y}_i \in \mathcal{N}(\mathbf{y})} w_i^{\mathrm{L}} \mathbf{y}_i \right\|_2^2, \text{ s.t. } \left\| \mathbf{w}^{\mathrm{L}} \right\|_1 = 1, \tag{2.17}$$

where $\mathcal{N}(\mathbf{y})$ includes the neighbors of $\mathbf{y}$ among all training patches. Subsequently, the SR patch can be recovered using the corresponding weights $\mathbf{w}^{\mathrm{H}}$ and neighbors in the HR manifold

$$\hat{\mathbf{x}} = \sum_{\mathbf{x}_i \in \mathcal{N}(\mathbf{x})} w_i^{\mathrm{H}} \mathbf{x}_i, \tag{2.18}$$

where $\mathcal{N}(\mathbf{x})$ is the HR version of $\mathcal{N}(\mathbf{y})$. Following the heuristics that HR and LR manifolds have similar local geometries, it can be assumed that $\mathbf{w}^{\mathrm{H}} = \mathbf{w}^{\mathrm{L}}$. Otherwise, locality constraints can be imposed to validate the LLE assumption [Li09].

By virtue of the efficacy of the LLE [Cha04], size of the patch database can be made remarkably smaller than for the case of example-based SR [Fre02]. However, the choice of k for the kNN is nontrivial. Yang *et al.* [Yan08] offer a solution driven by the compressive sensing theory [Don06], which indicates that with an over-complete dictionary, a test image patch can be reconstructed with a sparse linear combination on the support of the dictionary. By replacing the NP-hard ℓ_0 norm with the ℓ_1 norm, the optimization problem is hereby tractable. In the follow-up version [Yan10b], the authors train an optimal coupled dictionary of atoms instead of sampled raw patches, achieving comparable results with far less patches. In [Wan12], a semi-coupled dictionary with a mapping between LR and HR sparse codes is used to relax the tightly coupled one in [Yan10b], which is claimed to ensure fidelity of the hidden spaces.

Treating SR from the global perspective [Cha04] is believed to be neither efficient nor effective on account of the low affinity between remote image atoms in the embeddings. In this sense, methods exploiting locally linear regression emerge. [Yan13c] groups the entire patch database into local clusters and learns a regression function from LR to HR patches within each cluster in advance. During the SR inference, a simple multiplication with the mapping function of the right cluster suffices. Timofte *et al.* [Tim13] follow this local strategy, but employ ridge regression [Hoe70] with precomputed inverse matrices for each neighborhood. Improvements incorporating atom sharing among clusters and advanced training techniques are proposed in [Tim15] and [Tim16] respectively.

Alongside the conventional external database driven SR, Glasner *et al.* [Gla09] explore the possibility of solely exploiting the intrinsic LR and HR feature recurrence of natural scenes across scales in the test image itself. To accelerate the time-consuming seek for self-similarity exemplars, Yang *et al.* [Yan13e] restrict the search area to limited externally localized neighborhoods. Huang *et al.* [Hua15] accommodate perspective transformation for local patches to take advantage of the redundant textural appearance variations in natural and urban images.

By intuition, DNNs are not originally intended to produce a HR output from a LR input. In light of this, Dong *et al.* [Don14] upscale the LR patch before feeding it into a Convolutional Neural Network (CNN) with three layers that conceptually perform patch extraction and representation, nonlinear mapping and reconstruction, in various configurations [Don16a]. A deconvolution layer [Zei11] is appended in the last stage to allow for fast processing with a compact network operating on the LR grid [Don16b]. Shi *et al.* [Shi16] also work on the LR input directly for real-time capability, but simply reorder the second last channels as subpixels for the HR output. In contrast to the shallow structures in the previous approaches, Kim *et al.* present two very deep networks with residual learning [He16] and recursion in [Kim16a] and [Kim16b] respectively, with impressive performance.

2.3.3 Face Super-Resolution

FSR is an emerging topic in computer vision. Unlike generic SR, which produces HR images with finer details from a wide variety of LR images, *e.g.*, landscape and text, FSR is able to generate faces with higher magnification from input images of lower resolution owing to the constrained domain [Yan10b]. On the other hand, contrary to single-image patch-based SR applicable to universal image categories with no extra need of registration, the HR–LR training data and the LR query image in FSR are preferably well aligned, so that the prior knowledge of shared structural information, *e.g.*, eyes, noses and mouths, can be leveraged. Hence, FSR is nowadays acknowledged as an independent branch within the SR family.

Traditional Face Super-Resolution

The reconstruction-based SR in Section 2.3.1 is in general also suitable for face images. In such methods, image registration is an indispensable step [Par03], which aligns multiple LR frames to the HR grid w.r.t. an appropriate motion model to estimate the HR image. Although simple assumptions can be made for static scenes to compensate for frame-to-frame motion, the complex geometry, non-rigid deformation and self-occlusion in human faces may sometimes render global motion models useless. Therefore, Wheeler *et al.* [Whe07] hinge on the LR AAM [Liu06] to warp triangulated 2D meshes from the facial landmarks to the reference frame. The ℓ_1 norm for the reconstruction constraint and the BTV as regularization [Far04] are utilized for SR. In [Yu08], Yu and Bhanu deform the virtual lattice overlay using Free-Form Deformation (FFD) with B-splines [Hua06] to alleviate slight expression changes in the video frames. Optical flow is another option to obtain dense correspondence between images [Sch12], whereas special attention must be paid to flow consistency [Zha02]. These non-rigid registration schemes can cope with very limited pose and expression variations. Furthermore, reconstruction-based SR degrades dramatically and the overly smooth HR outputs lack high-frequency details when the magnification factor increases [Bak02].

The groundbreaking concept of FH [Bak00a] paves the way for learning-based FSR. In this work and the subsequent theoretical analysis [Bak00b, Bak02], Baker and Kanade establish pixel-by-pixel statistical gradient priors from the training faces using feature pyramids and solve the FSR problem in a MAP manner. Besides the likelihood term ensuring the faithfulness of LR and the predicted HR image, the gradient priors model the relationship between the training data and the test image for each specific location. Inspired by the seminal studies of Baker and Kanade, Su *et al.* [Su05] argue that a single pixel does not convey meaningful information and adopt steerable pyramids with a bank of oriented filter kernels in their gradient priors to facilitate patch-based interference rather than that of independent pixels, encouraging coherence of the output faces.

Like some early FR systems that function in a holistic fashion, the PCA prior, or the eigenface algorithm [Tur91], is one of the most widely used methods in FSR. Capel and Zisserman [Cap01] model the HR subspace with PCA, where $\boldsymbol{\mu}$, $\mathbf{V}$ and $\boldsymbol{\Sigma}$ denote the mean, the eigenfaces, and their variance, respectively. By assuming Gaussian noise, two MAP priors, namely the Face

Space–Maximum a Posteriori (FS–MAP) and the Image Space–Maximum a Posteriori (IS–MAP), are introduced. For FS–MAP, the PCA coefficient vector **c** is obtained via

$$\min_{\mathbf{c}} \left\{ \left\| \mathbf{H} \left(\boldsymbol{\mu} + \mathbf{V}\mathbf{c} \right) - \mathbf{Y} \right\|_{\boldsymbol{\Sigma}}^{2} + \lambda \left\| \mathbf{c} \right\|_{2}^{2} \right\}. \tag{2.19}$$

In contrast, the IS–MAP directly solves for the HR face in the form of

$$\min_{\mathbf{X}} \left\{ \left\| \mathbf{H}\mathbf{X} - \mathbf{Y} \right\|_{2}^{2} + \lambda \left\| \left(\mathbf{I}_{\mathrm{id}} - \mathbf{V}\mathbf{V}^{\top} \right) \left(\mathbf{X} - \boldsymbol{\mu} \right) \right\|_{2}^{2} \right\}, \tag{2.20}$$

where $\mathbf{I}_{\mathrm{id}}$ stands for the identity matrix. As such, the appearance variation is projected out to make the estimated image lie near the PCA subspace. An alternative to [Cap01] is the eigentransformation by Wang and Tang [Wan05], *i.e.*, projecting the LR input image onto the LR training PCA subspace and reusing the same weights for HR face reconstruction on the HR subspace.

Since holistic approaches are susceptible to many kinds of nuisance factors, Liu *et al.* [Liu01] devise a novel two-step FSR method, compensating for the residual of the global PCA face with a MRF defined on the homogeneous image lattice [Fre02] to enhance local texture details. In [Liu07], they elaborate more on the soft and hard constraint for the global PCA model, add bilateral filtering [Tom98] as post-processing to remove artifacts, and accurately align LR faces with the Lucas–Kanade algorithm [Luc81]. By virtue of the theoretical and practical benefits, this two-step procedure eventually becomes a long-time rule of practice for FSR. Jia and Gong [Jia08] replace PCA with a generalized hierarchical tensor analysis to simultaneously deal with multiple face modalities, *e.g.*, identities, expressions, poses and resolutions, and generate HR faces with different expressions regarding the LR input. Zhuang *et al.* [Zhu07] employ Locality Preserving Projection (LPP) [He04] for feature embedding extraction and Radial Basis Function (RBF) regression for the global image SR, and the LLE SR technique [Cha04] for local residual compensation. In [Par08] by Park and Lee, given a LR frontal morphable model [Vet97], the shape displacement and texture are super-resolved by example-based holistic HR face recovery similar to eigentransformation [Wan05]. Finally, as the second contribution of [Yan10b] (*c.f.* Section 2.3.2), a two-step FSR system is proposed. Yang *et al.* argue that PCA bases are suboptimal, which allow negative coefficients and tend to generate smooth faces close to the mean, and turn to Nonnegative Matrix

Factorization (NMF) for an additive part-based subspace, followed by sparse coding SR [Yan08] for local detail refinement.

Ma *et al.* [Ma10] discuss the necessity of such two-step global–local framework, and bypass it with the Position-Patch (PP), which borrows the idea of the generic LLE SR and imposes explicit positional restriction for faces, *i.e.*, separate embeddings for each patch of a specific location on the face. This strategy successfully incorporates the common facial structure as prior information into SR within a single stage. Additionally, the time-consuming global search in LLE [Cha04] is alleviated at the same time. Due to the simplicity and performance edge, numerous extensions exist on top of [Ma10]. Jung *et al.* [Jun11] prefer sparsity [Yan10b] to the collaborative least squares representation over the whole training samples in [Ma10]. Jiang *et al.* publish a series of studies [Jia12, Jia13] with a locality constraint to encourage close matching between the query and training patches.

Modern Face Super-Resolution

Prevailing 2D FSR algorithms adopt simple alignment of faces as preprocessing. Transformation by similarity using the eyes [Liu01, Wan05, Yan10b] or affinity with an extra point at the tip of the nose [Bak02] or center of the mouth [Ma10] is a widespread technique. On the other hand, pixel-wise registration [Luc81] is arguably a better option for LR faces, which estimates the transformation by energy minimization w.r.t. the entire image window instead of a few feature points that may be localized imprecisely on LR images [Jia08, Liu07]. In this thesis, this global parametric alignment is deemed as the traditional routine to conduct FSR.

The latest success of 2D FSR is partly attributed to the advanced registration techniques that remedy misalignment caused by out-of-plane rotation and complicated facial geometry to a certain extent. Hu *et al.* [Hu11] make use of optical flow [Bro04] to warp similar candidate training faces w.r.t. the query image. Surrounding local pixel structure is explored to reconstruct the HR patch. In [Li14], Li *et al.* favor sparse representation as the SR engine. Tappen and Liu [Tap12] mitigate non-frontal poses by matching and warping training exemplars close to the LR face with PatchMatch [Bar09] and SIFT flow [Liu11] respectively. A convex optimization scheme for the Bayesian SR method in [Tap12] is proposed in [Inn13]. However, this system struggles when the training set is small or it fails to find faces that can match the input well. Yang *et al.* [Yan13b] handle different image components separately.

On the basis of 2D AAM landmarks, main facial features are extracted and similar exemplars are aligned. In addition, statistical edge prior and PatchMatch [Bar09] are used to hallucinate contours and smooth regions. In [Jin13], Jin and Bouganis devise a unified MAP formulation exploiting holistic PCA prior to model blurring and motion, and prove that previous MAP FSR algorithms like the FS–MAP and the IS–MAP in [Cap01] and the soft and hard constraints in [Liu07] are just special cases of their framework, which is extended with a probabilistic patch-wise approach in [Jin15] for in-the-wild FSR. Nonetheless, homography in their parametric motion can only cope with near-frontal poses. Kolouri and Rohde [Kol15] consider FSR as a transport problem [Amb02], which constructs a nonlinear model for both pixel intensity and displacement for face images. A linear subspace that best describes the optimal transport is learned to constrain the space of HR images to those that can be morphed by the reference. This method is demonstrated to be pragmatic for frontal faces of very low resolution.

Opposite to DNNs for generic SR, which take image patches as input for training the networks, dedicated DNNs for FSR are usually exercised on the whole face crop to bring in domain knowledge. Zhou *et al.* [Zho15] present a bi-channel CNN to learn the missing HR detail and a coefficient for fusion with the LR image. Tuzel *et al.* [Tuz16] design a face upsampling network comprised of sequential global detail generation on top of the interpolated LR face with fully-connected layers and local refinement with convolution layers. Yu and Porikli [Yu16] employ exclusively deconvolution layers [Zei11] for generative FSR. Akin to [Tuz16], the Generative Adversarial Networks (GANs) [Goo14] are exploited to synthesize realistic HR images subject to the discriminative network. Either alternating fine-tuning [Tuz16] or integrated ℓ_2 regularization with the adversarial loss [Yu16] are shown to be effective. In [Zhu16a], Zhu *et al.* unite cascaded face alignment and FSR with a Cascaded Bi-Network (CBN). With a face correspondence field expressed in the form of 2D PDM, dense pixel displacement instead of sparse landmarks can be inferred with PO–CR [Tzi15]. Its output then guides to warp the high-frequency prior for facial components in a separate branch parallel to the common one for holistic upscaling, which are joined with a pixel-wise gate network. Thanks to the explicit modeling of spatial cues, CBN works extremely well for non-frontal LR faces.

3D Face Super-Resolution

In the previous part of this chapter, incorporating 3D information has proven to be instrumental in the context of facial analysis. However, limited application has been witnessed in FSR, probably because of the severe difficulty of fitting 3D models onto LR images. Note that some 3D approaches [Ber12, Pan06] focus on SR of the depth map rather than the facial texture, which is not reviewed here.

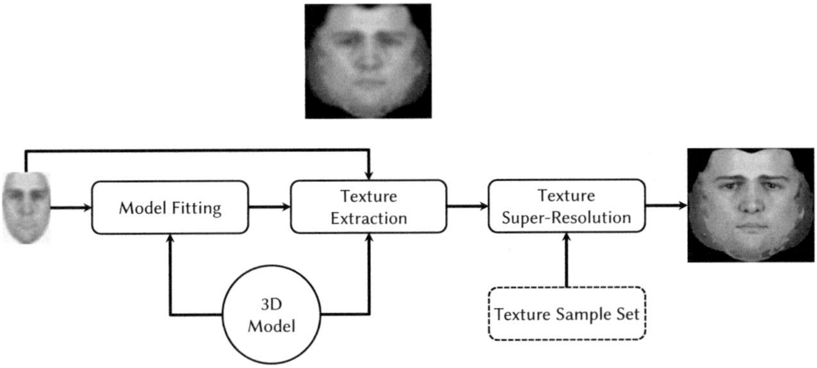

Figure 2.6: Workflow of the 3D FSR method in [Mor09].

In [Mor09], 3D-assisted FSR shows its strong potential for the first time. The processing chain suggested by Mortazavian *et al.* is composed of three independent modules, *i.e.*, model fitting, LR texture extraction and SR, as illustrated in Figure 2.6. After reconstructing the 3D shape using the standard analysis-by-synthesis algorithm [Bla03], the LR facial texture is extracted and mapped onto a predefined canonical grid [Ten07], so that facial geometry and pose are normalized, which is theoretically ideal for FSR. In case of self-occlusion, the missing data is filled with estimated 3DMM texture. Subsequently, the external texture set, stored in the same format, serves as the training data for the MAP FSR method by Baker and Kanade [Bak02]. It is worth mentioning that 3D models are merely leveraged to build dense correspondence between the LR image and the training faces. The 3D facial texture is treated as an ordinary 2D image during FSR, neglecting the actual observation process of the LR texture on the 3D mesh. Hence, it is strictly speaking a 3D-aided 2D approach, or 2.5D FSR.

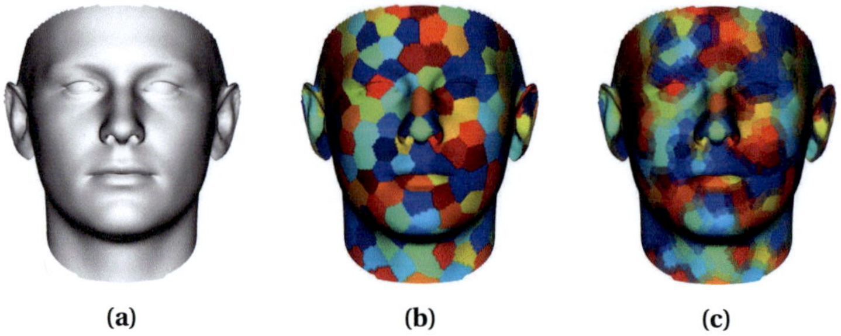

Figure 2.7: Face mesh segmentation in [Des15]: The mean face in (a) is uniformly segmented into patches in (b) at first, which are then enlarged to produce overlapping boundaries in (c).

The full capability of 3D FSR has been unleashed only until recently. Schumacher *et al.* [Sch15] modify the 3DMM fitting [Bla99] by adding the blurring effect into image synthesis within the iterative procedure. Unlike [Mor09], where an extra texture map SR is needed, the recovered 3D model here already includes HR texture inherently after the fitting process. The authors further fill details such as facial hair and blemish into the HR face from a best match exemplar in the dataset. Although both shape reconstruction and visual appeal are improved against the LR input, this holistic framework is restrained to well-controlled images. To combat this drawback, the novel example-based 3D FSR by Dessein *et al.* [Des15] is applicable. In this first and only existing patch-wise 3D method, the mesh of the mean face is segmented uniformly in the offline phase. In order to account for compatibility between neighboring patches, they are then expanded to share the boundary with adjacent cells, so that vertex color averaging in these areas is possible (see Figure 2.7). However, as in [Mor09], the image formation model is ignored and the LR pixels are directly back-projected onto the corresponding LR vertices to apply BP on the HR patches in a 3D MRF fashion [Fre02]. Despite the positive results on simulated LR faces, the inverse image formation model from LR pixels to LR vertices assuming Nearest Neighbor (NN) interpolation and forward BP with HR vertices within patches of fixed size rules out the flexibility to incorporate viable blurring kernels, since the convolution operation always involves a larger vicinity.

2.3.4 Discussion

Image SR, in spite of its ill-posed nature, has evolved to a certain level of maturity for both generic and face images (see the reviews for SR [Nas14, Par03, Yan10a] and FSR [Wan14b], as well as the benchmark study [Yan14]). A combined framework with successive modules, *e.g.*, recognition [Hen08, Wan16, Wan14c, Zou12], is also demonstrated to bring mutual benefits. Yet there exist several critical questions that remain unanswered. *All* SR algorithms are evaluated on synthetically downsized HR images for lack of real LR data. Is such setup objective and justified in this vein? Is it possible to obtain ground truth HR and LR image pairs? Moreover, except for very little work [Jin15, Whe07, Zhu16a], most FSR, especially the 3D variants [Des15, Mor09, Sch15], are all targeted for constrained face data acquired in studio environment. Is LR 3D model fitting and FSR viable on in-the-wild images? And if so, where is the limit for 3D FSR? The remaining part of this thesis will shed some light upon those issues.

3 Concept

The overall concept of the proposed framework is illustrated in Figure 3.1. Given a LR face image as input, the three modules performing facial landmark detection, 3D shape reconstruction and facial texture SR are highlighted in successive order, of which the individual concepts and algorithms will be detailed in the following chapters. Note that the 3D subsystem of this thesis is a model-based approach, which is realized by involving a 3D face dataset with preprocessed shape and texture data as prior knowledge, visualized in the left part of Figure 3.1.

Considering that input images of the deployed system are usually captured using surveillance cameras, 3D face reconstruction directly conducted on the input images can be extremely difficult given the challenges discussed in Section 1.2. Therefore, a more robust approach is to use sparse facial feature landmarks as an intermediate instrument to assist 3D shape modeling, which can be reliably detected by virtue of the recent advances in this field, immune to various negative impacts resulting from the unconstrained image acquisition condition "in the wild" [Qu15c]. The output of this stage as a list of 2D feature point locations w.r.t. the image coordinates can then be used as the anchor points to guide the morphable shape model during the process of 3D face reconstruction.

In order to recover the depth information from the 2D points, the intrinsic shape variation of the scanned faces within the 3D face dataset is utilized. With known correspondences and proper manipulation of the 2D and 3D landmarks, the dense 3D face shape can be computed without taking into account multiple aspects responsible for appearance changes, keeping the computational complexity at a very low level [Qu14, Qu15d].

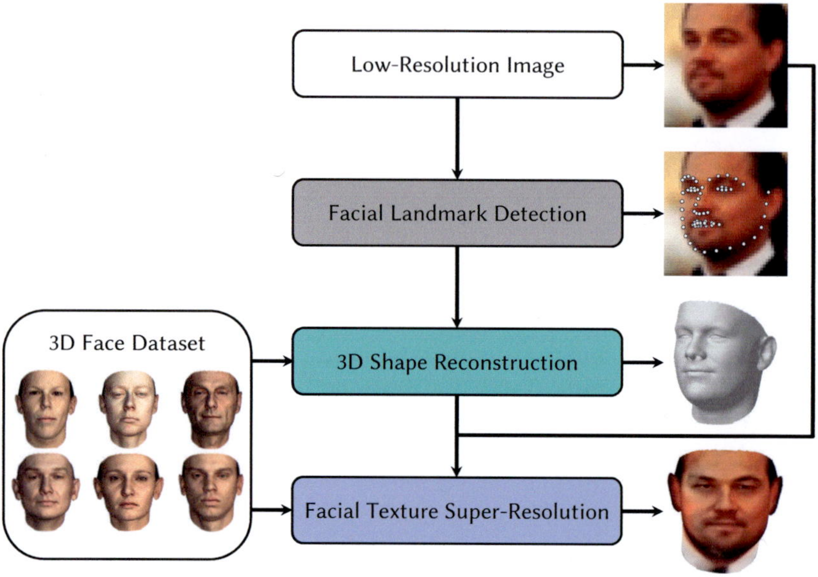

Figure 3.1: The overall concept of the proposed 3D FSR framework.

The final facial texture SR module is the essential part of the presented workflow, which takes the LR face image, shape and texture information from the 3D face dataset, as well as the previously obtained shape model as input. Dense correspondence between the textures in the dataset as training data and the LR face is established with the help of the fitted 3D model [Qu15b]. This allows not only for the synthesis of the SR texture, but also for a second-pass fine-tuning of the fitting result to improve the accuracy, which is of particular interest for the processing chain, since the initial shape reconstruction solely hinges on a few sparse landmarks located on the LR image. As a result, a person-specific 3D face model with photo-realistic facial texture and fine details is created [Qu17]. An example output of the algorithm is shown in the lower-right corner of Figure 3.1. This 3D face model, irrespective of the original head rotation of the input image, allows for normalization to the frontal pose or rendering a novel image in an arbitrary perspective, which is advantageous for many facial analysis applications, *e.g.*, FR.

3D face modeling and FSR are both well-studied topics in computer vision. A good deal of algorithms has been presented, which share similar ideas with some part of this work. However, there are several significant differences between the proposed concept and all of the existing ones in the literature:

3D vs. 2D

One of the dilemmas when designing computer vision systems is whether to make the extra effort to model the problem in 3D or to simply stick with the well-developed 2D methods. In the context of FSR, the related studies reviewed in Section 2.3.3 demonstrate a wide spectrum of approaches, of which the overwhelming majority is based on pure 2D information. More specifically, both image registration and SR face synthesis are directly carried out on 2D images.

Considering the challenges discussed in Section 1.2, FSR could take advantage of 3D fitting to mitigate the negative factors of diverse head poses and lighting conditions to generate plausible SR images. On the other hand, limited image resolution and poor image quality render 3D face modeling on LR data a highly difficult problem. Therefore, since properly aligning training and input images is an indispensable prerequisite to maximize the usage of information within the constrained face domain, most existing methods choose to adopt available global or local 2D alignment techniques and concentrate on novel FSR algorithms. Contrarily, this thesis makes the observation from another perspective and shows that superior performance can be achieved by leveraging the more precise 3D fitting, even with standard FSR approaches [Qu15b].

An intuitive comparison between the widely applied 2D alignment techniques and the employed 3D method in this thesis is depicted in Figure 3.2, where the mean faces of the *frontal* HR Multi-PIE [Gro10] images are generated with the respective procedure. With the similarity transformation using the center of two eyes, the nose and mouth are blurred in Figure 3.2a due to the varied length of human faces which is not normalized. This can be improved by adding the center of the mouth as a third point. By applying affine transformation, the mouth in Figure 3.2b becomes sharper.

Nevertheless, blurring in other facial components such as nose and eyebrows remains. In contrast, 3D fitting ensures correspondence of the dense vertices throughout all face samples, leading to rich details in Figure 3.2c. In this sense, one can expect FSR, which shares a similar principle while exploiting the training data, to benefit from a better alignment scheme.

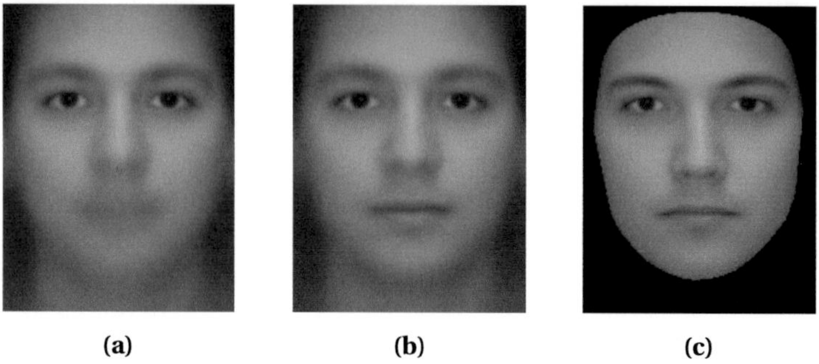

Figure 3.2: Mean faces of the Multi-PIE [Gro10] images aligned with (a) eyes, (b) eyes and mouth, and (c) the target 3D shape.

3D Fitting

Within the 3D FSR literature, some [Des15, Par08] assume pre-aligned input and training faces, whereas the general applicability for real-world LR scenarios is not verified. Only very few papers [Mor09, Sch15] address the LR fitting problem explicitly in a complete workflow, both of which follow the spirit of the 3DMM algorithm by Blanz and Vetter [Bla03]. This analysis-by-synthesis framework can generate accurate and photo-realistic 3D models given a wide range of pose and identity variations on HR data. However, due to its complicated optimization problem, direct application on "LR and small face yields unacceptable results" [Mor09]. At the same time, computational cost is also extremely high. In comparison, an alternative strategy is adopted in this thesis, which depends on a small set of facial feature points as shape constraints to fit the 3D deformable shape using the 3DMM. Thanks to the rapid progress from the facial landmark detection community in the past few years, the automatically detected landmarks are highly robust against a number of nuisance factors, such as pose, expression, occlusion and bad illumination. Unlike the comparative analysis-by-synthesis algorithms, which must compensate for appearance variation in their optimization task, the landmark-based approaches only need to take into account the fitting of these sparse landmarks to their correspondence on the 3DMM so that dense shape recovery can be accomplished highly efficiently [Qu14, Qu15d].

After reconstructing the shape of the LR face, the second design choice is how to align the training data with it to perform FSR. Mortazavian *et al.* [Mor09] extract the LR facial texture from the input image to a predefined coordinate frame with normalized pose and identity. Subsequently, FSR is conducted on this flattened texture frame. Alternatively, the training faces can be projected forwardly onto the LR image coordinates in the hope of preserving LR details, since this operation requires no interpolation of the LR image. Such a strategy, which was first introduced in the FSR module of the proposed processing chain [Qu15b], can also be found and is proved effective in other 3D FSR work, *e.g.*, [Des15, Sch15].

Facial Texture Super-Resolution

Dense model fitting can be straightforwardly regarded as a powerful tool to establish dense mapping for FSR [Par08]. The rendered facial texture is then treated as regular 2D image for conventional 2D methods. Despite the superior results owing to the better fitting, the advantage of involving 3D face models is not yet fully exploited [Qu15b]. For the following facial analysis tasks after the SR preprocessing stage, a textured HR 3D face is favorable. In this case, pure 3D FSR instead of 3D-assisted 2D FSR is preferred.

The newly published FSR work [Sch15] of the analysis-by-synthesis framework [Bla03] is able to generate 3D texture from the 3DMM within a unified optimization task. For other 3D fitting schemes, however, like the landmark-based one used in this thesis, a novel algorithm must be found. In addition, akin to the PCA model for 2D SR [Liu07], the holistic 3DMM texture variations may not have enough expressiveness for all kinds of real-world appearance and lighting conditions.

To overcome the aforementioned challenges, a novel patch-based 3D FSR algorithm is developed [Qu17], which fundamentally differs from the recent 3D MRF approach [Des15] in that the LR imaging model observed from the 3D face mesh is formulated, facilitating the incorporation of any realistic blurring kernels into the 3D FSR framework. Moreover, an extension of the Lucas–Kanade image registration method [Bak04a] for the applied LR 3D model-based scenario offers an extra post-refinement step to improve the error-prone initial 3D fitting on the LR data using landmarks. Hence, robustness of the proposed 3D FSR pipeline under degraded circumstances is thereby guaranteed.

Summary

The entire processing chain is comprised of components which may be interchangeable with other alternatives. For instance, in the first two modules which are responsible for 3D shape recovery, combined approaches using 3DMMs [Hu12, Mor12] or 3D dense face alignment [Jou15, Zhu16b] can be deployed. It is worth noting that in some failure cases which are caused by bad shape initialization in the early stage, minimal human assistance with manual landmark annotation can be introduced. This is however cumbersome for these methods to cope with. All in all, the whole concept proposed in this thesis is carefully designed with a focus on efficiency, robustness, automation and flexibility for the challenging problem of LR FSR.

4 Facial Landmark Detection

The first and foremost component in the processing chain of the proposed 3D FSR system is the detection of 2D fiducial facial feature points. Like many state-of-the-art solutions, the work presented in this chapter builds on the recent success of the cascaded shape regression algorithm [Cao12, Dol10, Xio13], which progressively predicts the shape update based on the previous shape estimate and its feature representation. Several core aspects of this framework are revisited, accompanied by incremental improvement analyses compared to the baseline [Xio13] on the benchmark Labeled Face Parts in the Wild (LFPW) dataset [Bel11] to provide a preliminary performance overview before extensive evaluation in Section 7.3.1.

The remainder of this chapter is mainly based on the author's publication [Qu15c], and is organized as follows. A brief introduction is given in Section 4.1. Section 4.2 recalls the baseline framework. The individual proposed improvements are discussed and analyzed in detail in Sections 4.3 to 4.5, respectively. Finally, the work is summarized in Section 4.6. Notation that commonly appears in this chapter is listed in Table 4.1.

Table 4.1: Notation used in Chapter 4.

Symbol	Description
D	Feature dimensionality
K	IRLS scaling factor for $\mathbf{W}$
N	Number of training samples
P	Number of facial landmarks
s	IRLS iteration number
S	Number of iterations for IRLS
t	Cascade level starting from initialization
T	Number of cascades
γ	Regularization weight for ridge regression
$\mathbf{b}$	Bias term for Regression
$\mathbf{I}$	Face image
$\mathbf{I}_{\text{id}}$	Identity matrix
$\mathbf{r}(\mathbf{I},\mathbf{x})$	A cascade for shape update
$\mathbf{R}$	Descent direction for Regression
$\widetilde{\mathbf{R}}$	Combined regressor composed of $\mathbf{R}$ and $\mathbf{b}$
$\mathbf{W}$	Diagonal weighting matrix of IRLS
$\mathbf{x}$	Shape vector
$\mathbf{x}^{\star}$	Ground truth shape
$\Delta\mathbf{x}$	Shape displacement to the ground truth
$\Delta\mathbf{X}$	Stacked shape increment for all training samples
$\mathbf{\Phi}(\mathbf{I},\mathbf{x})$	Operator for extracting shape-indexed feature
$\widetilde{\mathbf{\Phi}}$	Stacked shape-indexed features for all training samples

4.1 Introduction

As described in Section 2.1, localization of facial feature landmarks, a.k.a. face alignment, is an early but crucial step in the facial image analysis literature for the latter processing stages, which is of course also applicable to FSR [Wan14b]. Despite the broad interest and research effort since the seminal work ASM [Coo92] and AAM [Coo98], there still remain challenges under unconstrained conditions, *e.g.*, occlusion, extreme lighting, pose and shape variations.

Classic ASM and AAM approaches jointly optimize the shape parameters with local or global texture. In the last few years, a new family of face alignment algorithm has emerged, which directly learns regressors from image feature descriptors to the target shape update. These regression-based methods are gaining increasing popularity due to their leading performance and high efficiency in the face alignment task. Although recent studies [Cao12, Ren14] suggest that performance may have saturated on simple uncontrolled indoor (*e.g.*, BioID [Jes01]) or outdoor (*e.g.*, LFPW [Bel11]) datasets, reliable detection of facial feature points is still a distant promise on new challenging in-the-wild datasets (*e.g.*, 300 Faces in-the-Wild Challenge (300-W) [Sag13a] and Caltech Occluded Faces in the Wild (COFW) [Bur13]). Unlike previous approaches that try to mitigate the impact of occlusion [Bur13], feature selection [Ren14] and initialization [Yan13a] with specific solutions, this work instead revisits some of the low-level aspects of cascaded shape regression. By reconsidering the essential assumptions and design choices, it is possible to achieve a significant improvement and state-of-the-art performance without bells and whistles.

In the spirit of the baseline cascaded shape regression [Xio13], the approach in this thesis investigates the fundamentals and seeks for enhancement in quest of successful in-the-wild landmark localization based on a series of intermediate experiments. Highlights of this work include:

- **Robust regression**: As a core component of the underlying framework, the quality of regression has a huge influence on the trained model. Iteratively Reweighted Least Squares (IRLS) alleviates the impact of outliers and noises which are inevitable in real-world data, especially in the presence of extreme pose, occlusion and illumination condition in unconstrained face datasets.
- **RootSIFT**: The Hellinger distance proves to be preferable in many histogram-based matching problems [Ara12]. By taking the square root during the feature map space conversion, small histogram bin values get more emphasized. In this way, face alignment accuracy is boosted dramatically.
- **Fitting strategies**: Pose, novel expression and occlusion can all cause the initialized landmarks to drift far away from the true location. Thus, a larger local image patch size and compensation for in-plane face rotation account for fast convergence in early cascade stages, whereas a smaller patch size ensures high precision in the final stages.

4.2 Cascaded Shape Regression

Within the framework introduced in [Cao12, Dol10, Xio13], face alignment is naturally interpreted as a regression problem for the target output shape $\mathbf{x}$ given an input image $\mathbf{I}$ and an initial shape $\mathbf{x}^{(0)}$, which is typically chosen as the mean shape of the training data scaled and translated w.r.t. the region of interest (ROI) of the detected face. Here the vectorized shape

$$\mathbf{x} = [x_1, \ldots, x_P, y_1, \ldots, y_P] \in \mathbb{R}^{1\times 2P} \tag{4.1}$$

is parametrized by the image coordinates of the P facial landmarks, which is $P = 29$ for the LFPW annotation in Figure 4.1. The scattered points of all samples are a result of the unconstrained collection of Internet face data. A statistical shape model, like the PDM in conventional face alignment, is most of the time unnecessary (with the exception of the PO–CR [Tzi15]).

The objective is then to learn a regression function $\mathbf{r}(\cdot,\cdot)$ that returns an updated shape by minimizing the Euclidean distance to the ground truth $\mathbf{x}^\star$

$$\sum_{i=1}^{N} \left\| \mathbf{r}(\mathbf{I}_i, \mathbf{x}_i^{(0)}) - \mathbf{x}_i^\star \right\|_2^2, \tag{4.2}$$

where i denotes the index of the totally N training samples. While a one-pass regression is incapable of understanding the high complexity of the problem [Xio13], composition of multiple regressors

$$\mathbf{r} = \mathbf{r}^{(T)} \circ \mathbf{r}^{(T-1)} \circ \ldots \circ \mathbf{r}^{(1)}, \tag{4.3}$$

a.k.a. a cascade of regressions, proves to be effective, where the output shape of the previous regressor $\mathbf{r}^{(t-1)}$ is fed to the following one $\mathbf{r}^{(t)}$ as the input shape and T denotes the total number of stages.

Thanks to the additive nature of the linear shape updates, as long as the initial shape $\mathbf{x}^{(0)}$ is valid, the subsequent shapes $\{\mathbf{x}^{(t)}\}$ are guaranteed to lie in the linear subspace of the training shapes by regression. This implicit shape constraint not only makes the algorithm exempt from an explicit shape model, but also encourages to fit to novel shapes that share little similarity with the mean shape, which is favorable for in-the-wild settings.

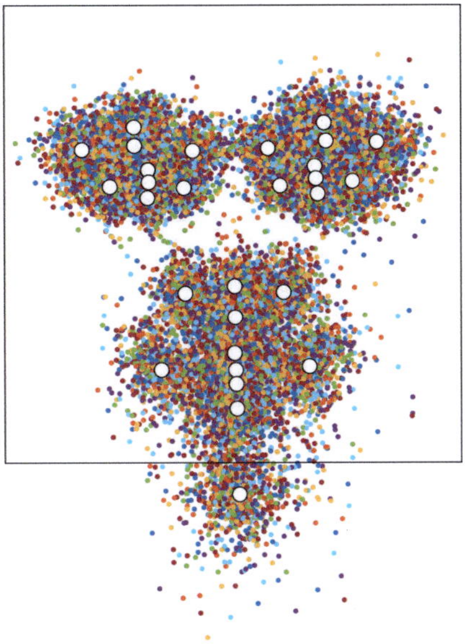

Figure 4.1: Aligned shapes of the training data on LFPW [Bel11] w.r.t. face detection and the resulting mean shape.

Next, the regression function $\mathbf{r}^{(t)}$ is specified as

$$\mathbf{r}^{(t)}\left(\mathbf{I}_i,\mathbf{x}_i^{(t-1)}\right) = \mathbf{x}_i^{(t)} = \mathbf{x}_i^{(t-1)} + \mathbf{\Phi}\left(\mathbf{I}_i,\mathbf{x}_i^{(t-1)}\right)\mathbf{R}^{(t)} + \mathbf{b}^{(t)}, \tag{4.4}$$

where $\mathbf{\Phi}(\mathbf{I},\mathbf{x}) \in \mathbb{R}^{1\times PD}$ extracts the local shape-indexed feature as in CLMs, such as raw intensity, binary difference features [Bur13, Cao12, Ren14] or SIFT [Xio13], in the proximity of $\mathbf{x}$ on the image $\mathbf{I}$, where D is the dimensionality of the feature. The descent direction $\mathbf{R}^{(t)} \in \mathbb{R}^{PD\times 2P}$ and bias term $\mathbf{b}^{(t)} \in \mathbb{R}^{1\times 2P}$ characterize the stage regressor $\mathbf{r}^{(t)}$ and are learned by incorporating Equation (4.4) into Equation (4.2)

$$\min_{\mathbf{R}^{(t)},\mathbf{b}^{(t)}} \sum_{i=1}^{N} \left\| \Delta\mathbf{x}_i^{(t-1)} - \mathbf{\Phi}\left(\mathbf{I}_i,\mathbf{x}_i^{(t-1)}\right)\mathbf{R}^{(t)} - \mathbf{b}^{(t)} \right\|_2^2, \tag{4.5}$$

where $\Delta\mathbf{x}_i^{(t-1)} = \mathbf{x}_i^{\star} - \mathbf{x}_i^{(t-1)}$ is the desired optimal increment regarding the current shape $\mathbf{x}_i^{(t-1)}$.

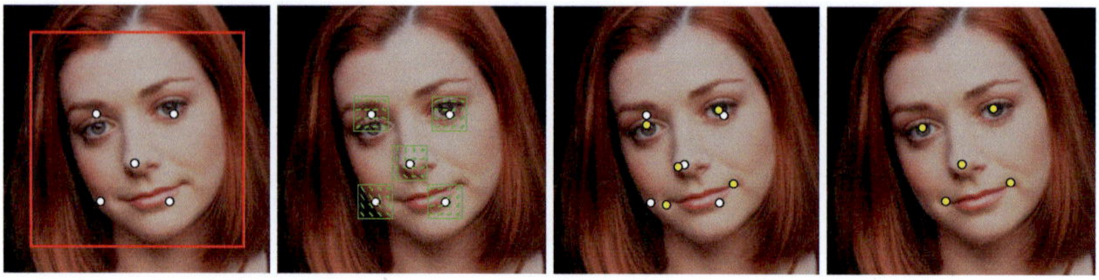

(a) (b) (c) (d)

Figure 4.2: Example fitting procedure of cascaded shape regression: (a) shape initialized from the detected face, (b) extracted shape-indexed feature, (c) first update iteration from the initial shape, (d) final fitting result.

The quadratic optimization problem in Equation (4.5) is usually solved with Newton's method. However, on the one hand, the shape displacement $\Delta\mathbf{x}$ is unknown at test time. On the other hand, the shape-indexed feature $\mathbf{\Phi}$ often appears to be non-differentiable. Hence, cascaded shape regression substitutes gradient descent with supervised learning on the training images. In particular, starting from the (perturbed) initial landmarks $\left\{\mathbf{x}_i^{(0)}\right\}$, after extracting the appearance feature $\left\{\mathbf{\Phi}\left(\mathbf{I}_i, \mathbf{x}_i^{(0)}\right)\right\}$ and computing $\mathbf{R}^{(0)}$ and $\mathbf{b}^{(0)}$ using least squares to minimize Equation (4.5), a new set of training shapes $\left\{\mathbf{x}_i^{(1)}\right\}$ is generated by applying Equation (4.4) to the regression output. A small number of iterations then suffice to successively converge $\left\{\mathbf{x}_i^{(t)}\right\}$ to $\{\mathbf{x}_i^{\star}\}$. Apparently, the fitting procedure is done with exactly the same routine, which is depicted in Figure 4.2. After the first cascade in Figure 4.2c, though a rough alignment is already fulfilled, further iterations are still needed for accurate localization.

4.3 Regression Algorithm

Minimizing Equation (4.5) is widely known as the linear least squares problem. In order to simplify the solution and obtain the regression parameters $\{\mathbf{R}^{(t)}, \mathbf{b}^{(t)}\}$ in closed form, a common practice is to concatenate the descent direction and bias term as a single unknown, and stack all N training samples, which yields

$$\Delta\mathbf{X}^{(t)} = \begin{bmatrix} \Delta\mathbf{x}_1^{(t)} \\ \vdots \\ \Delta\mathbf{x}_N^{(t)} \end{bmatrix} \in \mathbb{R}^{N\times 2P} \tag{4.6}$$

$$\widetilde{\boldsymbol{\Phi}}^{(t)} = \begin{bmatrix} \left[\boldsymbol{\Phi}(\mathbf{I}_1, \mathbf{x}_1^{(t)}), 1\right] \\ \vdots \\ \left[\boldsymbol{\Phi}(\mathbf{I}_N, \mathbf{x}_N^{(t)}), 1\right] \end{bmatrix} \in \mathbb{R}^{N\times(PD+1)} \tag{4.7}$$

$$\widetilde{\mathbf{R}}^{(t)} = \begin{bmatrix} \mathbf{R}^{(t)} \\ \mathbf{b}^{(t)} \end{bmatrix} \in \mathbb{R}^{(PD+1)\times 2P}. \tag{4.8}$$

To avoid the singularity problem, one can append a regularization term to Equation (4.5) as ridge regression [Hoe70]

$$\min_{\widetilde{\mathbf{R}}^{(t)}} \left\| \Delta\mathbf{X}^{(t-1)} - \widetilde{\boldsymbol{\Phi}}^{(t-1)} \widetilde{\mathbf{R}}^{(t)} \right\|_F^2 + \gamma \left\| \widetilde{\mathbf{R}}^{(t)} \right\|_F^2, \tag{4.9}$$

which can be solved straightforwardly

$$\widetilde{\mathbf{R}}^{(t)} = \left(\widetilde{\boldsymbol{\Phi}}^{(t-1)^\top} \widetilde{\boldsymbol{\Phi}}^{(t-1)} + \gamma \mathbf{I}_{\mathrm{id}} \right)^{-1} \widetilde{\boldsymbol{\Phi}}^{(t-1)^\top} \Delta\mathbf{X}^{(t-1)}. \tag{4.10}$$

Note that $\|\cdot\|_F$ in Equation (4.9) stands for the Frobenius norm for matrices.

Due to the inevitable existence of noise in the training data, including annotation errors and severe degradation, upright linear regression assuming the error to be normally distributed is suboptimal. In fact, it is well acknowledged that even a small number of gross outliers can hugely exacerbate the regressed model[1].

4.3.1 Iteratively Reweighted Least Squares

IRLS offers an iterative solution to diminish the negative influence of noisy data samples [Gre84]. At each iteration stage s, the original formulation of the cascaded shape regression in Equation (4.5) is extended with a weighted least squares version

[1] http://www.mathworks.com/help/stats/robustdemo.html

$$\min_{\mathbf{R}^{(s)},\mathbf{b}^{(s)}} \sum_{i=1}^{N} w_i^{(s)} \left\| \Delta\mathbf{x}_i - \mathbf{\Phi}(\mathbf{I}_i,\mathbf{x}_i)\mathbf{R}^{(s)} - \mathbf{b}^{(s)} \right\|_2^2, \tag{4.11}$$

where $w_i^{(s)}$ are the entries of the diagonal weighting matrix

$$\mathbf{W}^{(s)} = \operatorname{diag}\left(w_1^{(s)}, \ldots, w_N^{(s)} \right) \tag{4.12}$$

with the initial values set to $w_i^{(0)} = 1$, which means at the beginning, each training face image contributes equally to the regressor. For the purpose of clarity, the superscript (t) denoting regression stage is omitted here. Akin to Equation (4.10),

$$\widetilde{\mathbf{R}}^{(s+1)} = \left(\widetilde{\mathbf{\Phi}}^\top \mathbf{W}^{(s)} \widetilde{\mathbf{\Phi}} \right)^{-1} \widetilde{\mathbf{\Phi}}^\top \mathbf{W}^{(s)} \Delta\mathbf{X}. \tag{4.13}$$

Intuitively, the weighting matrix $\mathbf{W}^{(s)}$ should be updated inversely proportional to the residual after applying regressor $\widetilde{\mathbf{R}}^{(s)}$. Specifically, in case of the ℓ_1 norm,

$$w_i^{(s)} = \frac{K}{\left\| \Delta\mathbf{x}_i - \mathbf{\Phi}(\mathbf{I}_i,\mathbf{x}_i)\mathbf{R}^{(s)} - \mathbf{b}^{(s)} \right\|_1}, \tag{4.14}$$

where the scaling factor K as well as the regularization parameter γ from Equation (4.10) are experimentally determined.

The algorithm stops when $\mathbf{W}^{(s)}$ converges, which usually takes merely a few iterations in experiments. The mathematical representation of IRLS reduces the significance of outliers to the lowest level, which keeps the learned regression model as little affected as possible and robust against unconstrained conditions in the training data.

4.3.2 Experiments and Discussion

Intermediate experiments are conducted to briefly validate the necessity of each proposed improvement for building the final landmark detector and the progress incrementally. To keep the compactness of the experiments in this chapter, more details are discussed in Section 7.3.1. The widely used LFPW dataset [Bel11] is chosen as the benchmark. As some volatile URLs in LFPW are no longer valid, only 810 and 220 of the original 1,132 and 300 images could be collected for training and evaluation respectively. The baseline cascaded regression implementation resembles [Xio13] with ordinary least squares and SIFT feature. It is worth a mention that by reason of different size of data (*c.f.* [Bel11]), multiple initializations (*c.f.* [Cao12]) and manual correction of erroneous annotations in [Xio13][1], the exact numbers as reported in the respective papers on LFPW cannot be reproduced.

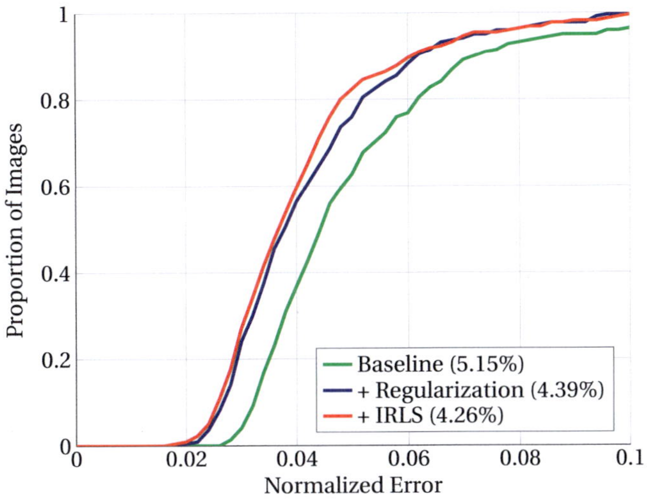

Figure 4.3: Performance on LFPW [Bel11] by combining better regression methods. NMEs are reported in parentheses.

As illustrated in Figure 4.3, simple ridge regression performs surprisingly well with considerable improvement in both *precision* and *convergence*. Here, a high precision is characterized with the curve located close to the left side of the plot, signalizing more results having a smaller error. Convergence, in contrast, suggests the curve approaching the top of the graphic, converging to 100% of all images, especially for difficult ones. With the adoption of IRLS, localization accuracy further increases by a small margin, indicating a more robust model against outliers during the learning. However, convergence remains almost unchanged, possibly because nearly all

[1] By direct correspondence with the author.

of the images have already a Mean Normalized Error (NME) less than 10% of the interocular distance (IOD). In Section 7.3.1, the benefit is more evident as expected.

4.4 Shape-Indexed Feature

Obviously, in the fundamental principle of training and using cascaded shape regression in Equations (4.4) and (4.5), the choice of feature extractor $\boldsymbol{\Phi}$ is a key design factor. Thus, it is reasonable to experiment with other features and mappings than SIFT alone in the baseline method [Xio13]. In this section, three popular image feature descriptors in computer vision, namely SIFT [Low04], HOG [Dal05] and Local Binary Patterns (LBP) [Oja02], are investigated.

A typical use case of SIFT is for matching local regions. Nevertheless, the key-point descriptor computing gradient histograms of patches around interest points can be leveraged separately for the facial landmarks. HOG is designed for object detection in the entire image frame. It resembles SIFT but introduces additional normalization within neighboring spatial bins. On the contrary, the LBP descriptor compares surrounding pixels with the value in the middle to make a binary number of zeros and ones, and builds a histogram of all possible patterns in the image window. Its illumination-invariant property [Oja02] could be helpful for uncontrolled face images.

Given the fact that SIFT, HOG and LBP are all histogram-based, the question naturally arises if the Euclidean distance employed in the regression objective in Equation (4.5) also yields inferior results in comparison with the square root (Hellinger) kernel, which is observed in many tasks like image retrieval [Ara12] and FR [Wol08].

Suppose $\mathbf{u}$ and $\mathbf{v}$ are SIFT histograms with unit Euclidean norm, *i.e.*, $\|\mathbf{u}\|_2 = \|\mathbf{v}\|_2 = 1$. The conventional dot product of these two vectors is

$$\langle \mathbf{u}, \mathbf{v} \rangle = \sum_i u_i v_i. \tag{4.15}$$

In contrast, the Hellinger kernel for ℓ_1 normalized vectors $\mathbf{u}'$ and $\mathbf{v}'$ with $\|\mathbf{u}'\|_1 = \|\mathbf{v}'\|_1 = 1$, is defined as

$$\mathbf{H}(\mathbf{u}', \mathbf{v}') = \sum_i \sqrt{u'_i v'_i}. \tag{4.16}$$

It is straightforward to prove that comparing transformed histograms in Euclidean space is equivalent to comparing the original descriptors in the Hellinger space [Ara12]. With the extra square root in Equation (4.16), the Hellinger distance augments counts belonging to small histogram bins, which are overwhelmingly suppressed by values of large bins in the Euclidean space. Therefore, to obtain higher localization precision, the benefit of ℓ_1 normalization and taking square root prior to utilizing the evaluated off-the-shelf feature descriptors is also studied.

4.4.1 Experiments and Discussion

With the IRLS algorithm fixed as the regression method according to the outcome of the previous section, SIFT, HOG and LBP with optional Hellinger distance mapping are tested as the shape-indexed feature, leading to six experimental analyses. Standard settings of HOG and LBP, namely 8×8 cell size, 2-by-2 blocks and 50% overlap for HOG, as well as $\text{LBP}_{8,2}^{u2}$ with eight sampling points of radius two and uniform patterns with at most two bitwise transitions, are deployed, which implies that SIFT, HOG and LBP have the dimensionality $\mathbb{R}^{128}$, $\mathbb{R}^{324}$ and $\mathbb{R}^{59}$, respectively. The Hellinger mapping is computed on the fly. Following Arandjelović and Zisserman [Ara12], the special case of SIFT in Hellinger space is denoted RootSIFT.

Figure 4.4 presents the contribution of the respective feature descriptors. At first sight, only HOG and SIFT+Hellinger (RootSIFT) successfully bring smaller NME than the baseline SIFT. Both LBP variants in Euclidean and Hellinger space cannot compete with the rest. Interestingly, HOG+Hellinger performs a bit worse than the original HOG, which is the only one of the three histogram-based features that fails to improve under Hellinger feature map. SIFT+Hellinger (RootSIFT) reveals the best result in spite of the degradation in convergence. This trend is visible in HOG and LBP as well, though less obvious. The reason might be self-explanatory by referring to the definition of the Hellinger space. Whilst emphasis on small bins improves fine fitting precision, suppression of larger bins leads to lower sensibility to severe shape variations. In the next section, this issue is addressed by looking for better fitting strategies to boost the convergence property on LFPW.

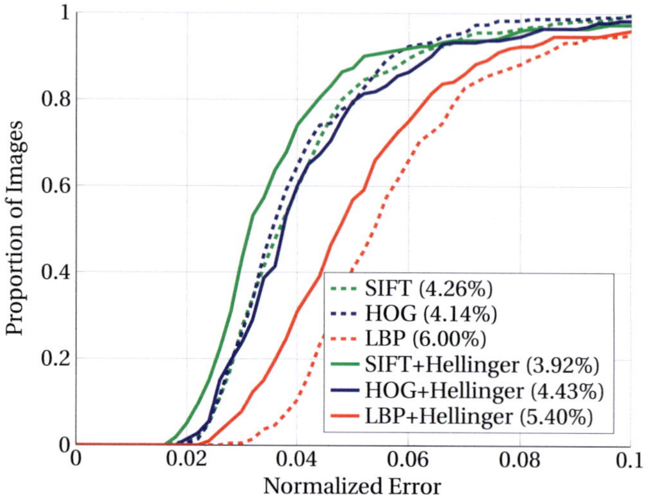

Figure 4.4: Performance on LFPW [Bel11] by comparing various feature descriptors and the Hellinger feature map. NMEs are reported in parentheses.

4.5 Fitting Strategy

In face alignment, the initial shape is usually determined as the mean shape of the training data scaled and translated w.r.t. the bounding box returned from a face detector. In addition, random perturbation is imposed to the initial shapes in the training stage to take into account more harsh conditions and accommodate imprecise initializations in the test phase. Asthana *et al.* [Ast14] show that in the course of training the cascaded regressors, the variance of the shape displacement reduces gradually, approaching the ground truth in the final stages. A similar tendency also exists in the fitting, which is demonstrated side by side in Figures 4.2c and 4.2d. After just one single iteration, the fitted landmarks are already very close to the ground truth. Subsequent cascades till the last one mainly refine the positions rather than correcting much discrepancy [Zhu15a]. Hence, a rational strategy is to use large local patches for feature extraction at early stages to allow for more uncertainty, whereas at later stages, fine-scale local patches facilitate accurate landmark localization.

Apart from that, modern face detectors, even trained for frontal upright faces, can tolerate a certain extent of in-plane rotation. On the other hand, most widely used feature descriptors for face alignment operated on ordinary image patches, *e.g.*, standard SIFT, HOG and LBP, are not rotationally invariant. The regressor must then model an extra degree of freedom, *i.e.*, the angle between the upright features in the image and the rotated face. This redundancy is mitigated by a two-pass strategy in fitting. In the first pass, an approximate shape is computed with the trained regressor. Afterwards, the similarity transform to the upright mean shape is calculated and this temporary shape is discarded. Finally, the regressor is applied in the second pass to the features extracted from the pose-normalized image scaled, rotated and translated subject to the similarity transform obtained in the previous step. For training, in order not to double the number of cascaded regressors through the second pass but still conform to the fitting scenario, similarity transform is carried out at the beginning of each iteration, which turns out to be effective in the test.

Figure 4.5 reveals a schematic comparison between the baseline and the proposed fitting strategy.

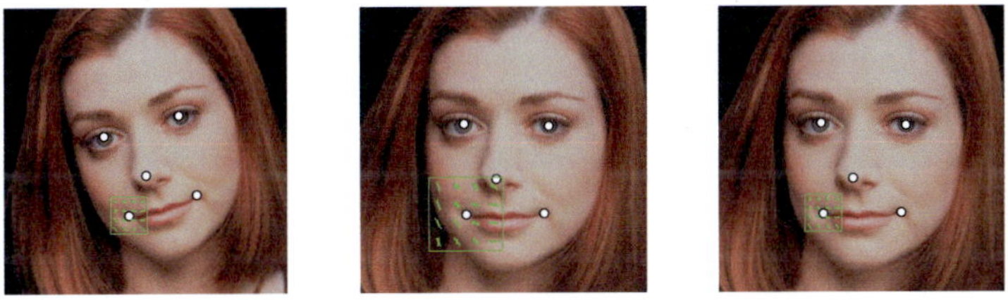

(a) (b) (c)

Figure 4.5: Local image feature extracted from (a) the original image and the pose-normalized image in (b) initial and (c) final cascade stages.

4.5.1 Experiments and Discussion

In the last section, the RootSIFT feature loses a few percent in convergence on the cumulative error curve while propelling the precision. Fortunately, this loss is immediately reclaimed and improved with the adaptive local patch size for different stages, which is demonstrated in Figure 4.6. The capability of covering a larger vicinity of the initial landmarks seems to be instrumental for challenging faces. The NME further decreases to the state-of-the-art level with the compensation of in-plane rotation in both learning and fitting. In Section 7.3.1, this fine-tuned landmark detector will be extensively benchmarked.

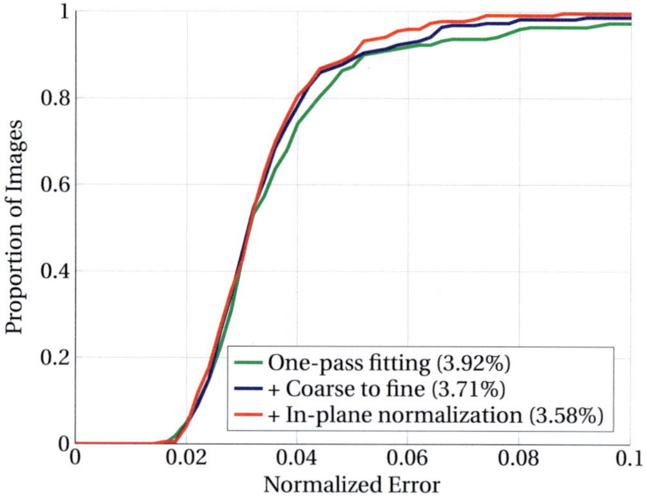

Figure 4.6: Performance on LFPW [Bel11] by combining better fitting strategies. NMEs are reported in parentheses.

4.6 Summary

Following the design flow of the cascaded regression framework, the essential components are revisited and a superior regression algorithm, a local feature descriptor and fitting strategies pursuing robust in-the-wild facial landmark localization are presented, which is summarized in Algorithm 2. As is seen in Figure 4.7, progressive experiments stage by stage help to identify the positive factors that get the best out of the baseline method [Xio13]. Ultimately, the final product is a composition of straightforward and essential improvements, yet strong enough to achieve top results over more sophisticated systems. Nevertheless, this approach is non-excludable. It is believed that incorporating these ideas in other state-of-the-art engines may provide further boost for the face alignment performance. All in all, a reliable module for 3D modeling within the 3D FSR processing chain of this thesis is found in the proposed landmark detector.

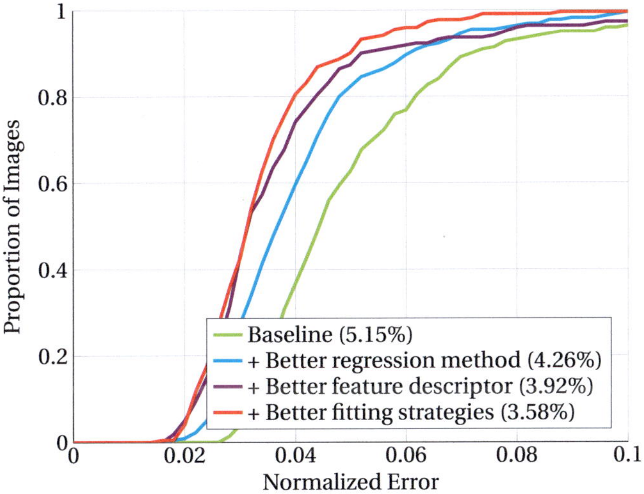

Figure 4.7: Overview of the performance gain through each proposed improvement on top of the baseline evaluated on LFPW [Bel11]. NMEs are reported in parentheses.

Algorithm 2: Training of the proposed cascade shape regression method.

Input: Face images $\{\mathbf{I}_i\}$ and labeled landmarks $\{\mathbf{x}_i^\star\}$
Output: Learned regressors $\{\mathbf{R}^{(t)},\mathbf{b}^{(t)}\}$

Detect face ROIs
Compute mean shape $\bar{\mathbf{x}}$
Perturb $\bar{\mathbf{x}}$ as initialization $\left\{\mathbf{x}_i^{(0)}\right\}$
for $t = 1 \rightarrow T$ **do**
    Normalize $\left\{\mathbf{x}_i^{(t-1)}\right\}$ w.r.t. $\bar{\mathbf{x}}$ using similarity transform
    Extract $\left\{\mathbf{\Phi}_{\text{SIFT}}\left(\mathbf{I}_i,\mathbf{x}_i^{(t-1)}\right)\right\}$ w.r.t. the ROI size subject to t
    Compute the Hellinger mapping $\left\{\mathbf{\Phi}_{\text{RootSIFT}}\left(\mathbf{I}_i,\mathbf{x}_i^{(t-1)}\right)\right\}$
    Conduct PCA on $\left\{\mathbf{\Phi}_{\text{RootSIFT}}\left(\mathbf{I}_i,\mathbf{x}_i^{(t-1)}\right)\right\}$ for dimensionality reduction
    Compute $\left\{\Delta\mathbf{x}_i^{(t-1)}\right\}$
    Initialize $\mathbf{W}^{(0)}$ with $\mathbf{I}_{\text{id}}$
    for $s = 1 \rightarrow S$ **do**
        Compute $\widetilde{\mathbf{R}}^{(s)}$ via Equation (4.13)
        Update $\mathbf{W}^{(s)}$ via Equation (4.14)
    end
    Update $\left\{\mathbf{x}_i^{(t)}\right\}$ via Equation (4.4)
end

5 3D Face Reconstruction From Sparse Landmarks

This chapter elucidates the reconstruction of the dense 3D face model with the aid of a set of sparse 2D facial landmarks detected with the method from the previous chapter. This approach offers an automatic, efficient and illumination-invariant alternative to the standard analysis-by-synthesis 3DMM fitting routine [Bla99], but at the same time suffers from inconsistent correspondence of 2D and 3D landmarks at the facial contour due to head rotation and localization ambiguity along the chin edge. After thoroughly analyzing the cause of this issue, a novel algorithm with fast convergence in mind is proposed to address the problem, facilitating adaptive landmark correspondence and dynamic fitting for robust estimation of the 3D face shape against pose variation.

The work presented in this chapter is mainly based on two of the author's publications [Qu14, Qu15d], and is organized as follows. An introduction to the general shape and pose estimation is given in Section 5.1. Section 5.3 first elaborates on the encountered problem as the motivation before going into details about the adaptive fitting framework. Finally, the work is concluded in Section 5.4. General notation used in this chapter can be found in Table 5.1.

Table 5.1: Notation used in Chapter 5.

Symbol	Description
D, D^x, D^y	Scalar pixel value of the DT image as well as its gradient images in x-direction and y-direction, given a pixel position
$\mathbf{D}, \mathbf{D}^x, \mathbf{D}^y$	Vector of pixel values of the DT image as well as its gradient gradient images in x-direction and y-direction, given a vector of pixel positions
F	Number of facial landmarks
M	Number of principal vectors for shape variation
n_z	z-component of the normal vector
P	Number of vertices in the 3DMM
η	Regularization weight for ridge regression
$\mathbf{I}_{\text{id}}$	Identity matrix
$\mathbf{Q}$	Simplified notation for shape variation w.r.t. the landmarks
$\mathbf{r}$	2D image coordinates of the facial landmarks
$\mathbf{s}$	3D dense shape of the face
$\bar{\mathbf{s}}$	Mean 3D shape of the 3DMM
$\mathbf{S}$	Principal modes of shape variation of the 3DMM
$\mathbf{y}$	2D landmark coordinates with the projection of the mean 3D shape subtracted
$\boldsymbol{\alpha}$	3DMM shape coefficients
$\mathbf{\Pi}$	Projection matrix
$\mathbf{\Phi}$	Matrix for mapping all dense vertices to those corresponding to the sparse landmarks

5.1 Introduction

Since the emergence of the 3DMM by Blanz and Vetter [Bla99], 3D face modeling with statistical face models has attracted broad interest and seen numerous applications in various facial analysis tasks, as is already introduced in Section 2.2. So one may ask why new approaches for 3D face reconstruction are required or why the existing methods are not or less applicable here. The motivation for that is the low quality and unconstrained conditions of the images. For instance, 3DMMs are originally intended for HR faces to allow for high-quality modeling in computer graphics [Bla99]. Fitting them to in-the-wild images still remains an open challenge according to the recently published PhD thesis of Hu [Hu15, p. 86]. Also, the small input size of LR images limits the allowed depth of DNN architectures, which could support the reconstruction. Upsampled LR faces lead to a significant performance drop as well [Her16].

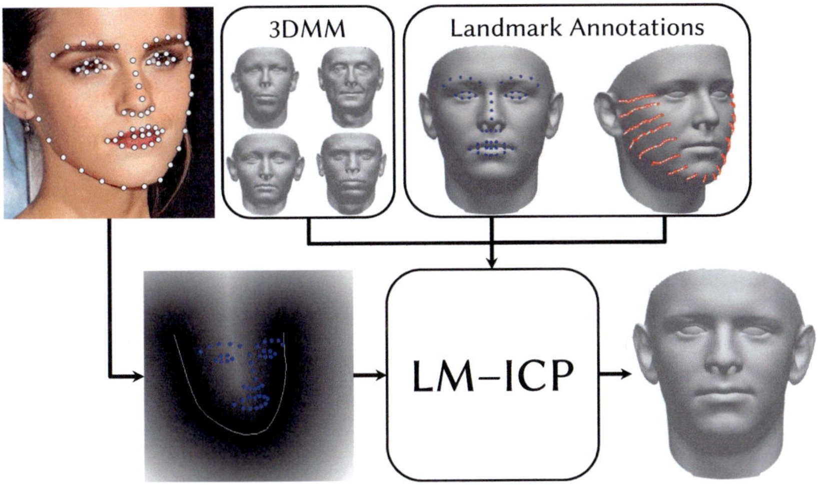

Figure 5.1: Overview of the proposed 3D face shape reconstruction algorithm using sparse landmarks. Blue and red points denote inner and candidate contour landmarks respectively.

Consider that for 3D FSR, 3D models primarily serve as a tool for finding accurate shape correspondence of the HR training and LR input data in terms of the *real* facial texture. The process of the analysis-by-synthesis 3DMM fitting [Bla99, Rom05], which models shape, texture and lighting parameters and solves for them simultaneously with gradient descent, results in prohibitively slow convergence and local minima for the actually unnecessary estimation of the albedo. To this end, the optimal strategy is to recover merely the 3D shape of the face. Unlike the analysis-by-synthesis framework, for lack of causal relation between the dense shape and the appearance in the whole face region, the fiducial facial landmarks are commonly leveraged as auxiliary points to guide the face shape reconstruction. Using these 2D landmarks manually labeled, or automatically localized as in Chapter 4, rigid motion and 3DMM shape parameters can be estimated with the help of the correspondence of these points on the 3D model. In some existing work [Ald10a, Bla04, Fag06, Jia05, Rar11], a fixed mapping from 2D to 3D is employed. However, this assumption is shown to be valid only for faces close to frontal view, since in the less visible half of the face, the 2D contour landmarks deviate greatly from the true 3D location because of self-occlusion in non-frontal poses. This phenomenon is illustrated in Figure 2.4 and partially discussed in Section 2.2.3.

This work goes a step further to account for ambiguous landmark positions along the facial contour for both halves of the face. In the course of shape reconstruction, fixed (inner) and flexible (contour) landmarks are distinguished and separately treated. Instead of directly minimizing the distance of the corresponding landmarks, Distance Transform (DT) is first applied to the line segments bounded by the 2D contour landmarks. At the same time, the proper 3D vertices can be chosen from a small candidate set. Subsequently, together with the fixed points, the projected distance is minimized by the Levenberg–Marquardt Iterative Closest Point (LM–ICP) algorithm and the 3DMM shape coefficients as the optimization parameters are obtained within a few iterations. The overall workflow of the proposed framework is depicted in Figure 5.1 and the main contributions of this chapter are summarized as follows:

- It is argued that not only the self-occluded landmarks on the facial contour, but also the visible ones are susceptible to 2D–3D correspondence discrepancy.
- By formulating the 3D face shape reconstruction as a general-purpose LM–ICP optimization problem incorporated with DT, a robust and unified solution for fixed and flexible landmark mapping is given without the loss of efficiency.
- A fast and effective method is presented to estimate the 3D silhouette vertices online in LM–ICP iterations.

5.2 Landmark-Based Shape Reconstruction

3DMMs [Bla99], built from 3D laser scans of several hundred subjects, usually consist of tens of thousands of vertices to densely represent human faces, resulting in a morphable model of 3D geometry and albedo. Contrary to conventional 3DMM fitting algorithms that reveal photo-realistic rendering at the cost of computational time, landmark-based methods are only interested in the recovery of the 3D geometry $\mathbf{s} = \left[x_1, y_1, z_1, \ldots, x_P, y_P, z_P\right]^\top \in \mathbb{R}^{3P}$ using incomplete sparse points, where the number F of the facial landmarks is much smaller than that of the 3D vertices, *i.e.*, $F \ll P$.

5.2.1 Landmark Mapping for 3D Models

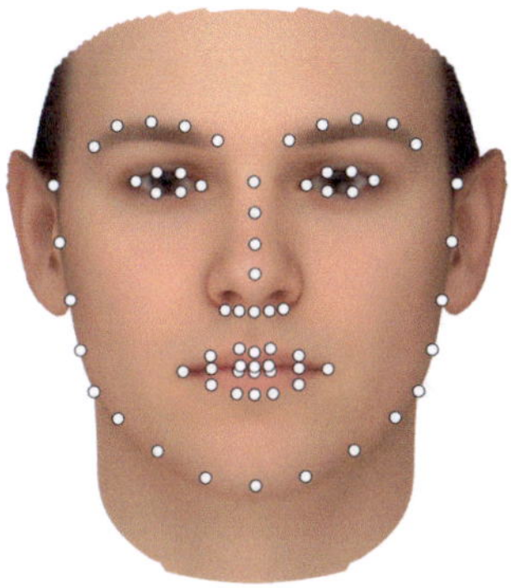

Figure 5.2: Annotation of the 68 facial landmarks on the BFM [Pay09].

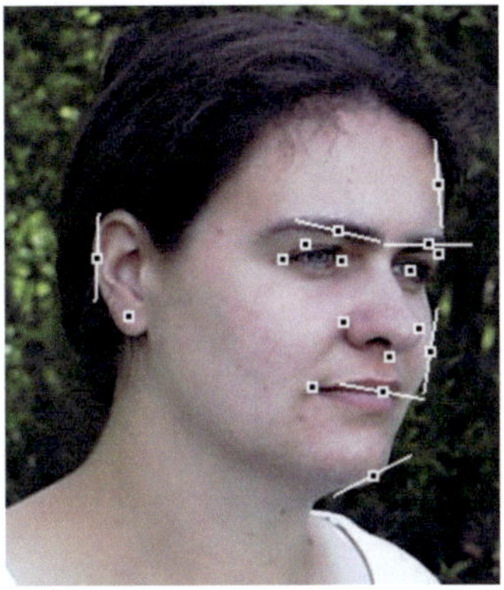

Figure 5.3: Manual feature point and directional annotation in [Bla04].

In order for this simplified 3D reconstruction pipeline to work, the mapping of the fiducial facial feature points from 2D images to the 3DMM should be known. In reality, though, the first and foremost step is to select a decent landmark annotation scheme. The reason is shown in an exemplary way in Figure 5.4. It is obvious to see in the example face images from six widely used public datasets, *i.e.*, Annotated Faces in the Wild (AFW) [Zhu12], Labeled Faces in the Wild (LFW) [Dan12, Hua08], LFPW [Bel11], Multi-PIE [Gro10], FaceWarehouse [Cao14b] and Helen [Le12], the creators follow completely different strategies when labeling the face data for their own purposes. For instance, Zhu and Ramanan [Zhu12] need merely few reliable feature points to estimate the head pose, while to make possible the high-quality editing of portraits, tight and dense landmarks as in ASM [Coo92] is essential for Le *et al.* [Le12]. This leads to diverse markups of non-interchangeable semantic meaning of the features[1], with the number ranging from six to a total of 194. Regarding 3D face modeling in this thesis, the contour of the face is highly important for constraining the general shape of the face. Also, Helen's markup is not optimal due to the computational burden for its large number of landmarks and lack of annotation on the tip of the nose, which might help to infer the depth for non-frontal faces. Therefore, the 68-point scheme in Multi-PIE is chosen. Compared to that of FaceWarehouse acquired under controlled conditions, it is one of the standard formats for in-the-wild images in the face alignment literature, as Sagonas *et al.* [Sag13a] re-annotate the AFW, LFPW and Helen datasets with this markup.

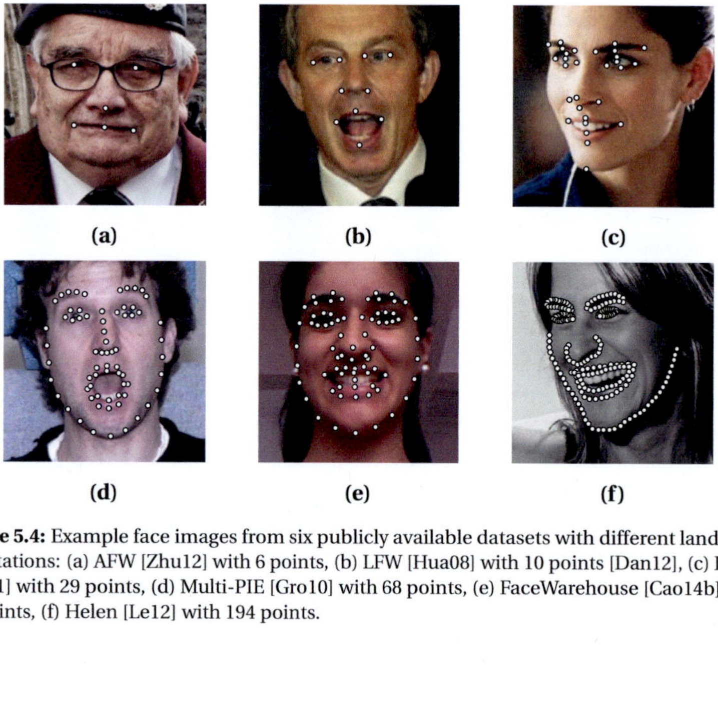

Figure 5.4: Example face images from six publicly available datasets with different landmark annotations: (a) AFW [Zhu12] with 6 points, (b) LFW [Hua08] with 10 points [Dan12], (c) LFPW [Bel11] with 29 points, (d) Multi-PIE [Gro10] with 68 points, (e) FaceWarehouse [Cao14b] with 74 points, (f) Helen [Le12] with 194 points.

[1] Their inherent relationship can still be exploited [Zha15].

These 68 landmarks are then manually labeled on the 3DMM, specifically, the Basel Face Model (BFM) [Pay09] in this work. To ensure precise annotation, the labeling procedure is done on all of the ten example 3D faces in BFM, and subsequently averaged in position to get the index of the nearest vertex. Symmetry is also taken into account for the landmarks on left and right face halves as well as for the ten points in the middle of the face. The final result is superimposed on the rendered mean face in Figure 5.2. Note that this offline annotation process is required just once for each landmarking scheme and 3DMM dataset. Online labeling for the directional constraints depicted in Figure 5.3 as for [Bla04] is not necessary.

5.2.2 Shape and Pose Estimation

With the fixed landmark mapping to hand, denoted $\mathbf{\Phi} \in \mathbb{R}^{P \times F}$, an efficient method for shape parameter estimation under unknown pose is developed. Obviously, in an ideal situation, the 2D facial landmarks $\mathbf{r} \in \mathbb{R}^{2 \times F}$ are the 2D projection of the corresponding vertices on the 3DMM, which can be expressed as

$$\mathbf{r} = \mathbf{\Pi} \Psi_{3 \times P} (\bar{\mathbf{s}} + \mathbf{S}\boldsymbol{\alpha}) \mathbf{\Phi}, \tag{5.1}$$

where $\bar{\mathbf{s}} \in \mathbb{R}^{3P}$ and $\mathbf{S} \in \mathbb{R}^{3P \times M}$ are the mean vector and principal variation matrix of the shape in the 3DMM respectively. The $\Psi_{3 \times P}(\cdot)$ operator reorders the 3D point entries and outputs a $3 \times P$ matrix. Since real-world faces are in general not aligned with the 3D model, it is essential to compute the non-trivial affine camera projection matrix $\mathbf{\Pi} \in \mathbb{R}^{2 \times 3}$ representing scaling, rotation and translation.

The problem of Equation (5.1) with two unknowns $\mathbf{\Pi}$ and $\boldsymbol{\alpha}$ is decomposed into two interleaved procedures, *i.e.*, estimation of the head pose, or the camera projection matrix $\mathbf{\Pi}$, with the 3D–2D landmark correspondence, and 3D shape recovery using the obtained pose information.

Pose Estimation

The task of finding the camera projection $\mathbf{\Pi}$ given the point correspondence of 2D and 3D landmarks resembles the traditional computer vision problem of computing the unknown linear point mapping from world to image. Thus, the Gold Standard Algorithm presented by Hartley and Zisserman [Har04] can be adopted here, too. With $\mathbf{x} \in \mathbb{R}^{2F}$ and $\mathbf{X} \in \mathbb{R}^{3F}$ as the vectorized 2D and ground truth 3D coordinates of the facial landmarks, the desired camera matrix $\mathbf{\Pi}$ should fulfill

$$\mathbf{x}_i = \mathbf{\Pi}\mathbf{X}_i \tag{5.2}$$

for each landmark i. If $\tilde{\mathbf{x}} \in \mathbb{R}^{3\times F}$ and $\tilde{\mathbf{X}} \in \mathbb{R}^{4\times F}$ are the homogeneous coordinates of the respective points, and given more than four such correspondences, there exists an over-determined solution of the normalized matrix $\tilde{\mathbf{\Pi}} \in \mathbb{R}^{3\times 4}$ with MLE minimizing the reprojection error

$$\sum_i \|\tilde{\mathbf{x}}_i - \tilde{\mathbf{\Pi}}\tilde{\mathbf{X}}_i\|_2^2 \tag{5.3}$$

subject to the affine constraint under the assumption of Gaussian measurement error. Stacking the individual correspondences in Equation (5.3) into a matrix representation of linear equations yields

$$\begin{bmatrix} \tilde{\mathbf{X}}^\top & \mathbf{0} \\ \mathbf{0} & \tilde{\mathbf{X}}^\top \end{bmatrix} \begin{bmatrix} \tilde{\mathbf{\Pi}}_{[1,:]}^\top \\ \tilde{\mathbf{\Pi}}_{[2,:]}^\top \end{bmatrix} = \begin{bmatrix} \tilde{\mathbf{x}}_{[1,:]}^\top \\ \tilde{\mathbf{x}}_{[2,:]}^\top \end{bmatrix}, \tag{5.4}$$

where the subscript $[j,:]$ denotes the jth row of the matrix. This equation system can be solved straightforwardly using least squares. Afterwards, Singular Value Decomposition (SVD) is applied to find the best-fit rotation matrix. Note that the 2D and 3D data are normalized to approximately the same range to guarantee numerical stability [Har04].

Alternatively, Blanz *et al.* [Bla04] linearize the scaling, rotation and translation as vectors and treat them as ordinary principal components of the shape variation $\mathbf{S}$ to allow for a closed-form solution.

Shape Estimation

Based on the 3D to 2D landmark projection in Equation (5.1) and assuming global zero-mean Gaussian white noise in the presence of 3DMM generalization error, the MAP formulation of the objective function is

$$E(\boldsymbol{\alpha}) = \min_{\boldsymbol{\alpha}} \left\{ \|\mathbf{\Pi}\,\Psi_{3\times P}(\mathbf{S}\boldsymbol{\alpha})\,\mathbf{\Phi} - (\mathbf{r} - \mathbf{\Pi}\,\Psi_{3\times P}(\bar{\mathbf{s}})\,\mathbf{\Phi})\|_2^2 + \eta\,\|\boldsymbol{\alpha}\|_2^2 \right\} \tag{5.5}$$

$$= \min_{\boldsymbol{\alpha}} \left\{ \|\mathbf{Q}\boldsymbol{\alpha} - \mathbf{y}\|_2^2 + \eta\,\|\boldsymbol{\alpha}\|_2^2 \right\}. \tag{5.6}$$

Here simplification is made by substituting the projected shape variation regarding $\mathbf{S}$ with $\mathbf{Q}$ and the mean-normalized 2D landmark coordinates $\mathbf{r}$ with $\mathbf{y}$. The reason for adding the regularization term $\eta \|\boldsymbol{\alpha}\|_2^2$ is that otherwise it tends to minimize the absolute projection error whenever possible, yielding overfitted and perceptually unrealistic shape coefficients $\boldsymbol{\alpha}$ [Hoe70]. Finally, by setting

$$\nabla_{\boldsymbol{\alpha}} E = \mathbf{0}, \tag{5.7}$$

the solution can be obtained in a regularized least squares fashion

$$\boldsymbol{\alpha} = \left(\mathbf{Q}^{\top}\mathbf{Q} + \eta\mathbf{I}\right)^{-1}\mathbf{Q}^{\top}\mathbf{y}. \tag{5.8}$$

In practice, as none of the shape and pose parameters is known at the beginning of the iterating process, the mean shape of the 3DMM with $\boldsymbol{\alpha} = \mathbf{0}$ is used for the Gold Standard Algorithm. Despite the rough initialization, typically the entire procedure is able to converge very fast.

5.3 Pose-Invariant Shape Reconstruction

Following the key idea introduced in the previous section for dense 3D face shape recovery using feature points localized by off-the-shelf landmark detectors, this section details fully automatic approaches to achieve pose-invariant reconstruction. To start with, the necessity of facilitating a flexible 2D–3D mapping of landmarks is argued and a novel algorithm that can effectively deal with self-occlusion and inaccurate landmark localization at the facial contour is proposed.

5.3.1 The Crux of Contour Landmarks

Self-Occlusion

According to Section 2.2.3, in the previous efforts towards automated 3D shape reconstruction by means of facial feature point detection, either they are exclusively applicable to frontal faces, or special measures must be taken to mitigate this landmark deviation issue that is raised by the gap in representation power between 2D face alignment and 3DMMs. Interestingly, as one of the original and most influential 2D frameworks, the AAM is a sibling of the 3DMM, which is as well a joint statistical model of shape and texture to fit an input image in an analysis-by-synthesis manner. A major practical difference lies in the dimensionality of the feature points, as the number of 3DMM vertices is orders of magnitude larger than that of the hand-labeled salient landmarks in AAMs. Hence, the distinction in the shape model imposes a great impact on the appearance model. 3DMMs represent the texture per vertex. Thanks to the dense sampling, the whole facial texture can be realistically rendered and self-occluded vertices are handled by nature with the 3D texture. On the other side, AAMs employ the whole image inside the convex hull of the landmarks while CLMs exploit the image structure surrounding the landmarks. That means, AAMs and CLMs only take advantage of 2D statistical texture models by design. Therefore, as can be observed in Figure 5.5, the automatically detected 2D facial contour landmarks in red differ remarkably from the respective 3D ground truth vertices in green. Obviously, with increasing yaw angle, huge deviation is seen in the self-occluded half of the face, since the 2D texture features are not able to infer the hidden 3D structure and only the detection of the face silhouette is possible, whereas the real invisible jawline of non-frontal faces turns out to be intractable, even with a 2.5D extension of the AAM [Mat07]. On the contrary, 3DMMs offer a much denser representation. Both geometry and albedo information is tightly coupled into the 3D vertices, which always correspond to the same place on the face independently from the pose variation.

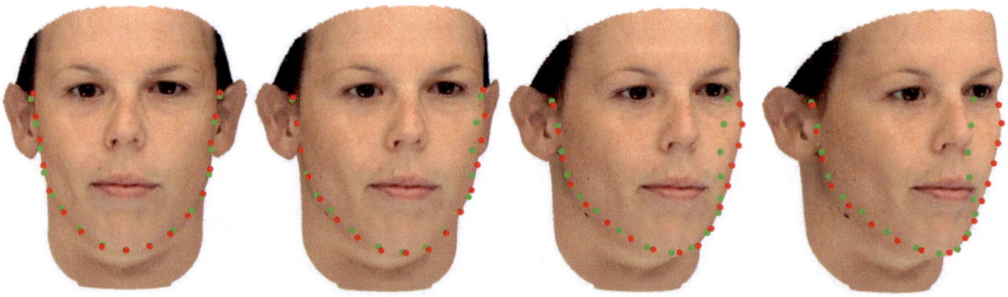

(a) **(b)** **(c)** **(d)**

Figure 5.5: Correspondence errors of 2D (red) and 3D (green) facial contour landmarks w.r.t. yaw angles of (a) 0°, (b) 10°, (c) 20° and (d) 30°.

To counteract the inappropriate fixed 2D–3D mapping scheme, an intuitive reconstruction method is first provided, which is illustrated in Figure 5.6. For non-frontal poses, the landmarks under potential occlusion situation are excluded from the pipeline introduced in Section 5.2.2. In this way, the 3D face shape is recovered on the basis of the remaining landmarks by optimizing the same objective function in Equation (5.6). Furthermore, this closed-form solution can be easily extended to multiple frames to compensate for the ignored feature points [Qu14].

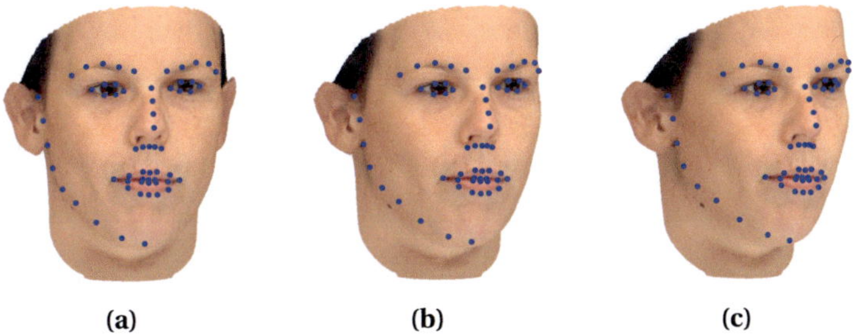

Figure 5.6: 3D reconstruction using visible landmarks for non-frontal faces with yaw angles of (a) 10°, (b) 20° and (c) 30°.

Correspondence Ambiguity

In spite of the continuous pursuit of pose-invariant landmark-based model fitting in the facial analysis society, *all* of the focus has been devoted to solving the occlusion problem. Nevertheless, after careful review of the original cause, the surprising outcome is that the issue related to the facial contour is more than just self-occlusion alone. A second view on Figure 5.5 reveals that the visible 2D and 3D contour landmarks are also affected by ambiguous correspondence, which again boils down to the 2D landmark localization routine.

It has long been demonstrated in the face alignment literature that the landmarking difficulty and precision of feature points in different parts of the face may vary considerably [Bel11], and the outer landmarks pose a larger challenge than the inner ones [Yan13a]. Most authors attribute it to pose, occlusion, vague boundary between foreground and background, *etc.* Irrespective of these extraneous causes, it is claimed in this thesis that intrinsic factors like the localization mechanism play a major role as well.

While detecting or regressing contour landmarks, change of the image gradient perpendicular to the jawline or the silhouette offers helpful information for determining the overall profile of the curve. However, unlike for the inner facial components such as the center of the pupil or the corner of the mouth, it lacks distinct image features to tell the absolute position on the contour, leading to the fact that those landmarks can freely move along the curve to a certain extent. Due to this ambiguity, an exact correspondence of the contour landmarks cannot be necessarily guaranteed. This implies that even in the frontal view, a fixed 2D–3D mapping scheme could well result in erroneous correspondence, which can be verified in Figure 5.5a. Unfortunately, authors in 2D and 3D areas are so far unaware of this crucial phenomenon that may influence both design and evaluation of 2D and 3D fitting approaches.

5.3.2 Fast Detection of Silhouette Vertices

After identifying the major cause that hinders landmark-based shape reconstruction, the question now arises as to how to alleviate these two issues effectively and efficiently. Discarding the occluded 2D landmarks during the fitting [Qu14] to combat self-occlusion in Section 5.3.1 is not considered here due to loss of valuable information in the first place. Furthermore, the visible landmarks cannot be ignored for the second situation, either. Otherwise the face shape would be totally unconstrained. Hence, a dynamic adaptation scheme for the annotated vertices of the contour landmarks must be conceived.

Recall that the 2D landmarks are always located at the boundary of the rotated faces, which varies w.r.t. shape and pose variations. A straightforward approach is to compute the boundary vertices using 3D geometric constraints. Mathematically, assuming a weak perspective camera model, the tangent plane of those vertices on the 3D face surface is perpendicular to the image plane

$$z = z_c, \tag{5.9}$$

where z_c is a constant, which is equivalent to the fact that the normal vector of silhouette vertices is parallel to this plane. In other words, the projection onto the z-axis of the world coordinate system is equal to zero. It is then an intuitive idea to treat those satisfying

$$|n_z| < t \tag{5.10}$$

as silhouette points [Rom05], where t stands for the upper bound for the absolute z-component of the normal vector $|n_z|$. By carefully choosing the threshold t and an appropriate face region, an example detection is shown in Figure 5.7d. At first sight, this method seems to give legitimate results. However, a universally valid threshold for all cases is hard to find, leaving the number of the selected vertices unstable. Secondly, the spatial distribution is uncontrollable, too. Both nuisance factors make it extremely challenging to derive a robust closed-form solution in connection with the facial landmarks. As a last point, the high computational effort of densely evaluating the normals rules out the possibility of online calculation within iterative methods, *e.g.*, LM–ICP in this thesis.

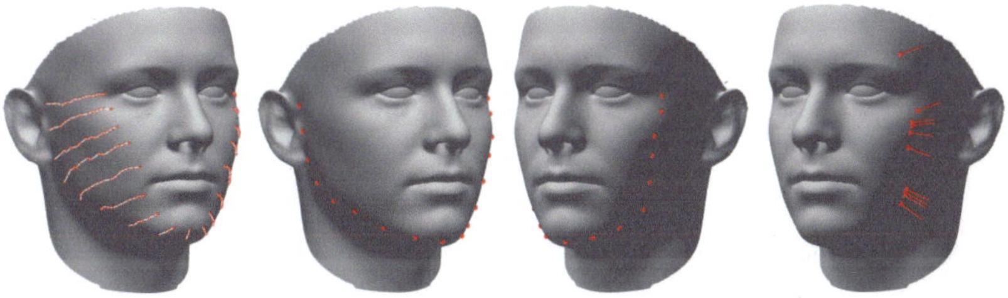

(a) **(b)** **(c)** **(d)**

Figure 5.7: Fast detection of silhouette vertices using (a) a few annotated candidates. (b) and (c) show the same result in different views compared to the direct approach in (d).

On the basis of this observation, though, a fast approach free of the aforementioned drawbacks for specifying the closest 3D silhouette vertices to the 2D landmarks can be presented. First, starting from each original contour landmark mapping on the 3D model, a maximum of 20 extended vertices towards the center of the face are labeled offline. During the fitting process, the ones with the smallest $|n_z|$ on each horizontal line are chosen. Despite following the principle of the direct approach [Rom05], the additional path constraints reduce the number of evaluated vertices while calculating the normals by two orders of magnitude to approximately 100. Moreover, the same number of 3D silhouette vertices as 2D landmarks with a uniform spatial distribution is guaranteed. An overview of the proposed silhouette detection method is illustrated in Figure 5.7. In contrast to Figure 5.7d, the vertices in Figures 5.7b and 5.7c preserve the smoothness and constant distance of the virtual contour landmarks.

Note that these vertices, now like those in the visible half of the face, are still subject to positional uncertainty along the path of 2D contour landmarks. The adaptive fitting in Section 5.3.3 addresses this point.

5.3.3 Adaptive Contour Fitting

In consequence of the apparently non-isotropic uncertainty w.r.t. the correspondence of contour vertices and landmarks (see Figure 5.5a), 3D shape recovery by separately modeling noise variances for each landmark [Ald10b] is not applicable. Since deviation of the 3D vertices detected in Section 5.3.2 should not be penalized, as long as they stay on the curve formed by the 2D landmarks, it makes sense to exploit the continuous curve instead of the discrete landmarks when reconstructing the shape. As a side effect, though, the coupled correspondence of 2D–3D contour feature points is lost, as all 2D coordinates on the curve are now eligible to give an optimal match. The new 2D features are exemplarily depicted in Figure 5.8a. Note that the contour landmarks are plotted solely as a reference. The actual features are just the connected edges in between.

In order to better understand the impact of the modified 2D features on the reconstruction algorithm in Section 5.2.2, it is helpful to start from scratch and revisit the basic formulation in Equation (5.6) to seek the solution. Assuming that the 2D–3D correspondence of the inner facial landmarks is detected plausibly by virtue of their informative image features, separating all landmarks in Equation (5.6) into two disjoint subsets of fixed and contour ones according to Figure 5.8 leads to

$$E(\boldsymbol{\alpha}) = \left\| \begin{bmatrix} \mathbf{Q}_{\text{contour}} \\ \mathbf{Q}_{\text{fixed}} \end{bmatrix} \boldsymbol{\alpha} - \begin{bmatrix} \mathbf{y}_{\text{contour}} \\ \mathbf{y}_{\text{fixed}} \end{bmatrix} \right\|_2^2 + \eta \, \|\boldsymbol{\alpha}\|_2^2 . \tag{5.11}$$

An unknown mapping denoted $\phi(i) = j$ which selects, for each 3D contour vertex i, the corresponding 2D pixel j with the shortest distance, is now also a part of the minimization process

$$E(\boldsymbol{\alpha},\phi) = \sum_i \left\| \mathbf{Q}_i \boldsymbol{\alpha} - \mathbf{y}_{\phi(i)} \right\|_2^2 + \left\| \mathbf{Q}_{\text{fixed}} \boldsymbol{\alpha} - \mathbf{y}_{\text{fixed}} \right\|_2^2 + \eta \left\| \boldsymbol{\alpha} \right\|_2^2 \tag{5.12}$$

$$E(\boldsymbol{\alpha}) = \sum_i \min_j \left\{ \left\| \mathbf{Q}_i \boldsymbol{\alpha} - \mathbf{y}_j \right\|_2^2 \right\} + \left\| \mathbf{Q}_{\text{fixed}} \boldsymbol{\alpha} - \mathbf{y}_{\text{fixed}} \right\|_2^2 + \eta \left\| \boldsymbol{\alpha} \right\|_2^2. \tag{5.13}$$

As a result, estimation of the shape parameter $\boldsymbol{\alpha}$ is formulated as a "minimization of minimization" problem

$$\min_{\boldsymbol{\alpha}} \left\{ \sum_i \min_j \left\{ \left\| \mathbf{Q}_i \boldsymbol{\alpha} - \mathbf{y}_j \right\|_2^2 \right\} + \left\| \mathbf{Q}_{\text{fixed}} \boldsymbol{\alpha} - \mathbf{y}_{\text{fixed}} \right\|_2^2 + \eta \left\| \boldsymbol{\alpha} \right\|_2^2 \right\}. \tag{5.14}$$

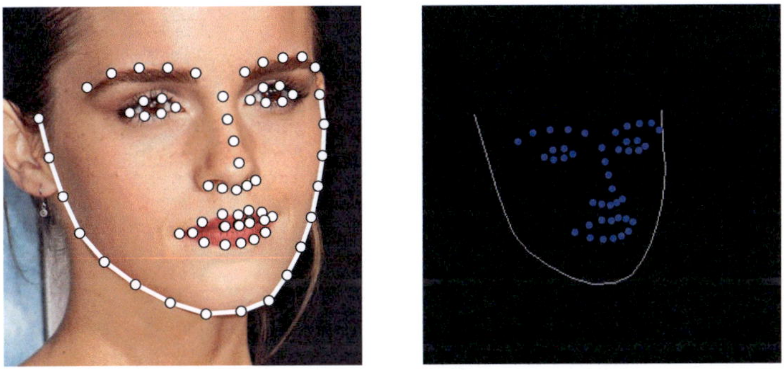

(a) **(b)**

Figure 5.8: (a) Improved 2D features with connected contour lines and (b) the realization using the Bresenham's algorithm [Bre65].

A common practice for solving such correspondence problem is the Iterative Closest Point (ICP) algorithm, which computes ϕ given fixed $\boldsymbol{\alpha}$ and updates $\boldsymbol{\alpha}$ on the basis of ϕ in a suboptimal alternating manner. Fitzgibbon [Fit01] addresses the deficiency with the LM–ICP algorithm, which tolerates a larger basin of convergence and allows for a closed-form solution and speedup. The Levenberg–Marquardt (LM) optimization procedure is in particular suited to the cost function $E(\boldsymbol{\alpha})$ in Equation (5.13) which is a sum of squared residuals. However, like conjugate gradient and Gauss–Newton, the requirement for first derivatives seems intractable for the discrete minimization over j within the summation in Equation (5.14). The trick to circumvent this difficulty is to apply DT to the 2D features, as shown in Figure 5.8b.

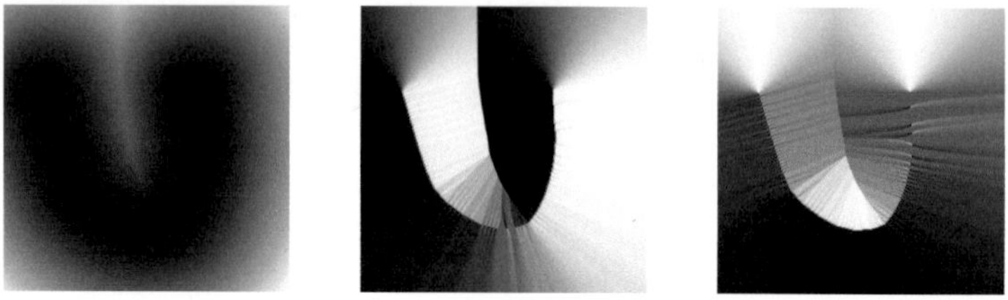

(a) D **(b) $\mathbf{D}^x$** **(c) $\mathbf{D}^y$**

Figure 5.9: (a) An example DT image of Figure 5.8b with its derivatives in (b) x-direction and (c) y-direction.

On the 2D image lattice $\mathbf{x}$, DT assigns each image pixel with the distance to its closest point on the contour lines

$$D(\mathbf{x}) = \min_j \|\mathbf{x} - \mathbf{y}_j\|_2. \tag{5.15}$$

Specifically, to retrieve all discrete contour pixels as binary code on a bitmap image, the Bresenham's algorithm [Bre65] is utilized, which counts as one of the earliest computer graphics algorithms to rasterize the line drawing using cheap operations. Once the DT image of the 2D contour is efficiently computed, it is reusable for the entire reconstruction procedure by virtue of its independence of the model parameter $\boldsymbol{\alpha}$. The Bresenham's and DT outputs of Figure 5.8a are illustrated in Figures 5.8b and 5.9a respectively. To make it possible for the matched vertices to be located above the top contour landmarks on each side, the first and last line segments are extended upwards (*c.f.* Figures 5.8a and 5.8b).

The merit of DT lies in that it precomputes the distance energy as a discrete "field" and the mapping function $\phi(i)$, or the minimization over j in the cost of Equation (5.12), then vanishes and is thereby simply replaced with

$$D(\mathbf{Q}_i\boldsymbol{\alpha}) = \min_j \left\|\mathbf{Q}_i\boldsymbol{\alpha} - \mathbf{y}_j\right\|_2. \tag{5.16}$$

Integrating Equation (5.16) into Equation (5.13) and vectorizing the DT over all contour vertices i yields

$$E(\boldsymbol{\alpha}) = \|\mathbf{D}(\mathbf{Q}_{\text{contour}}\boldsymbol{\alpha})\|_2^2 + \left\|\mathbf{Q}_{\text{fixed}}\boldsymbol{\alpha} - \mathbf{y}_{\text{fixed}}\right\|_2^2 + \eta\|\boldsymbol{\alpha}\|_2^2. \tag{5.17}$$

Rather than the sum of squares $E(\boldsymbol{\alpha})$ in Equation (5.17), LM–ICP demands the stacked vector of residuals

$$\mathbf{e}(\boldsymbol{\alpha}) = \begin{bmatrix} \mathbf{D}(\mathbf{Q}_{\text{contour}}\boldsymbol{\alpha}) \\ \mathbf{Q}_{\text{fixed}}\boldsymbol{\alpha} - \mathbf{y}_{\text{fixed}} \\ \sqrt{\eta}\boldsymbol{\alpha} \end{bmatrix}. \tag{5.18}$$

Differentiating the first entry in Equation (5.18) analytically subject to the shape parameter $\boldsymbol{\alpha}$ is possible with the chain rule [Rom05]

$$\frac{\partial D_i}{\partial \boldsymbol{\alpha}_j} = \frac{\partial D}{\partial x}\mathbf{f}_i \cdot \frac{\partial \mathbf{f}_i^x}{\partial \boldsymbol{\alpha}_j} + \frac{\partial D}{\partial y}\mathbf{f}_i \cdot \frac{\partial \mathbf{f}_i^y}{\partial \boldsymbol{\alpha}_j}, \tag{5.19}$$

where $\mathbf{f}_i = \mathbf{Q}_i\boldsymbol{\alpha}$, and thus $\frac{\partial D}{\partial x}\mathbf{f}_i = D^x(\mathbf{Q}_i\boldsymbol{\alpha})$ and $\frac{\partial D}{\partial y}\mathbf{f}_i = D^y(\mathbf{Q}_i\boldsymbol{\alpha})$, *i.e.*, the pixel values of the precomputed gradient images w.r.t. x-direction and y-direction in Figures 5.9b and 5.9c respectively, are applied to calculate the discrete derivatives of the contour cost $\boldsymbol{\nabla}_{\boldsymbol{\alpha}}\mathbf{D}(\mathbf{Q}_{\text{contour}}\boldsymbol{\alpha})$. The target Jacobian matrix $\mathbf{J}_{ij} = \frac{\partial \mathbf{e}_i}{\partial \boldsymbol{\alpha}_j}$ is then

$$\mathbf{J} = \begin{bmatrix} \mathbf{D}^x(\mathbf{Q}_{\text{contour}}\boldsymbol{\alpha}) \cdot \mathbf{Q}_{\text{contour}}^x + \mathbf{D}^y(\mathbf{Q}_{\text{contour}}\boldsymbol{\alpha}) \cdot \mathbf{Q}_{\text{contour}}^y \\ \mathbf{Q}_{\text{fixed}} \\ \sqrt{\eta}\mathbf{I}_{\text{id}} \end{bmatrix}, \tag{5.20}$$

where the superscript in $\mathbf{Q}_{\text{contour}}^x$ and $\mathbf{Q}_{\text{contour}}^y$ stands for the first two rows in the matrices. The closed-form Jacobian matrix dramatically reduces reconstruction time in comparison with finite difference approximation.

The final estimate of the 3DMM shape coefficients $\boldsymbol{\alpha}$ is solved for iteratively by means of the LM algorithm [Fit01], which is a damped version of Gauss–Newton [Mad04] combined with gradient descent for function minimization. In each iteration k, the first-order approximation of the objective function in Equation (5.17) w.r.t. the shape increment $\boldsymbol{\Delta\alpha}$ gives

$$E(\boldsymbol{\alpha}+\boldsymbol{\Delta\alpha}) \approx \mathbf{e}^\top\mathbf{e}+\boldsymbol{\Delta\alpha}^\top\mathbf{J}^\top\mathbf{e}+\boldsymbol{\Delta\alpha}^\top\mathbf{J}^\top\mathbf{J}\boldsymbol{\Delta\alpha}. \tag{5.21}$$

Differentiating this equation subject to $\boldsymbol{\Delta\alpha}$ and equating with zero reveals

$$\nabla_{\boldsymbol{\Delta\alpha}}E(\boldsymbol{\alpha}+\boldsymbol{\Delta\alpha}) = \mathbf{J}^\top\mathbf{e}+\mathbf{J}^\top\mathbf{J}\boldsymbol{\Delta\alpha} = \mathbf{0}, \tag{5.22}$$

so that the Gauss–Newton solution is

$$\boldsymbol{\Delta\alpha} = -\left(\mathbf{J}^\top\mathbf{J}\right)^{-1}\mathbf{J}^\top\mathbf{e} \tag{5.23}$$

providing the full-rank Jacobian matrix $\mathbf{J}$. Alternatively, gradient descent defines a factor λ to control the distance along the gradient direction in

$$\boldsymbol{\Delta\alpha} = -\lambda^{-1}\mathbf{J}^\top\mathbf{e} \tag{5.24}$$

to ensure the reduction of E with a sufficiently large λ, which is not necessarily the case with Gauss–Newton in general. By contrast, the convergence in the proximity of the stationary point may be slow compared to that of Gauss–Newton where the approximation holds. Therefore, a simple strategy that takes advantage of the strengths of both sides in the form of

$$\boldsymbol{\Delta\alpha} = -\left(\mathbf{J}^\top\mathbf{J}+\lambda\mathbf{I}_{\text{id}}\right)^{-1}\mathbf{J}^\top\mathbf{e} \tag{5.25}$$

is devised in the LM algorithm [Lev44, Mar63], which can interpolate flexibly using the damping parameter λ. Finally, the shape update is obtained by

$$\boldsymbol{\alpha}^{(k)} = \boldsymbol{\alpha}^{(k-1)}+\boldsymbol{\Delta\alpha}^{(k)} \tag{5.26}$$

$$= \boldsymbol{\alpha}^{(k-1)}-\left(\mathbf{J}^{(k)\top}\mathbf{J}^{(k)}+\lambda\mathbf{I}_{\text{id}}\right)^{-1}\mathbf{J}^{(k)\top}\mathbf{e}^{(k)}. \tag{5.27}$$

Discussion

Romdhani and Vetter [Rom05] also employ LM–ICP [Fit01] to simultaneously find the 2D–3D correspondence and minimize the error function in their MFF. Major differences that distinguish the contribution of this chapter from theirs are: (i) The contour is an indispensable 2D feature for the presented 3D shape reconstruction, while in MFF, it is merely one of the several supplementary features, *e.g.*, textured edges and specular highlights, to the analysis-by-synthesis framework [Rom03]; (ii) 2D contour landmarks in both face halves are exploited here, whereas MFF detects silhouette edges in the occluded face half; (iii) The proposed fast detection of silhouette vertices ideally facilitates online update within LM–ICP iterations. By comparison, direct global estimation in MFF can be done only once on the initial shape owing to performance reasons.

5.4 Summary

This chapter revisits the general framework of 3D face shape reconstruction from automatically localized 2D facial features and demonstrates the importance of properly modeling the entire contour landmarks. Instead of using the individual landmark positions, the connected curve feature leveraging DT and LM–ICP is studied, rendering the fitting algorithm flexible to tolerate discrepancy of 2D–3D correspondence, yet constrained enough to achieve robustness along the facial contour independent of pose variation. On the other hand, fast detection of silhouette vertices allows to keep the computational cost of the complex optimization process at a very low level. The workflow is summarized in Algorithm 3.

It is arguable whether the recovered 3D face solely based on less than a hundred feature points without any texture information is adequate for the following 3D FSR module. Nevertheless, in [Has15], Hassner *et al.* fit a single, non-deformable 3D model onto the face images and conduct pose normalization that effectively boosts the FR performance. Similarly, for the ill-conditioned LR data, the employed landmark-based method is an ideal compromise between efficiency, accuracy, and—finally but importantly—flexibility, since manually correcting a few 2D landmarks is always easier than manipulating the analysis-by-synthesis 3DMM fitting procedure.

Algorithm 3: Adaptive 3D face shape fitting from 2D facial landmarks robust to pose variation.

Input: Facial landmarks and a 3DMM with annotations for inner and candidate contour vertices
Output: 3DMM shape coefficients $\boldsymbol{\alpha}$

Compute the DT image and its gradient images w.r.t. the face ROI
Initialize $\boldsymbol{\alpha}^{(0)}$ with frontal mean 3D shape
for $k = 1 \to K$ **do**
    Estimate camera projection with the Gold Standard Algorithm
    Compute normals of the extended contour vertices
    Select silhouette vertices with the smallest $|n_z|$
    Compute the residual vector $\mathbf{e}^{(k)}$ via Equation (5.18)
    Compute the Jacobian matrix $\mathbf{J}^{(k)}$ via Equation (5.20)
    Perform LM to compute shape update $\boldsymbol{\Delta\alpha}^{(k)}$ via Equation (5.25)
    Update current shape $\boldsymbol{\alpha}^{(k)}$ via Equation (5.26)
end

6 3D Patch-Based Facial Texture Super-Resolution

As the last and most important component of the proposed framework, the FSR algorithm in this chapter should be capable of intelligently utilizing the 3D face structure recovered in the previous module and simultaneously avoid or better ameliorate the accompanying shortcomings in order to faithfully super-resolve the LR facial texture. In this sense, a resolution-aware approach for aligning the HR training faces with the input LR image is devised. By extending the 2D LR image formation process to the 3D domain, the classic Lucas–Kanade algorithm is exploited to improve the precision of the error-prone 3D model fitting on LR images. The established correspondence between the input image and 3D training textures then facilitates reconstruction of HR patches directly on the mesh, which can be employed to render realistic frontal faces for follow-up modules, *e.g.*, FR.

The content of this chapter is mainly based on two of the author's publications [Qu15b, Qu17], and is organized as follows. After the introduction in Section 6.1, the workflow for training data preparation is described in Section 6.2. Section 6.3 first presents a 3D-assisted 2D FSR method as a prologue and motivation of the novel 3D framework. Finally, a brief summary is given in Section 6.4. Common notation can be found in Table 6.1.

Table 6.1: Notation used in Chapter 6.

Symbol	Description
m	Upscaling factor for SR
P	Number of vertices in the 3DMM
Q_s	Number of principal vectors for shape variation
Q_t	Number of principal vectors for texture variation
s	Scaling factor for the 3D face shape
$\mathbf{H}$	LR image representation of 3D faces
$\mathbf{I}$	HR image representation of 3D faces
$\mathbf{I}_{\text{id}}$	Identity matrix
$\mathbf{k}$	Blurring kernel of dimension $K \times K$
$\mathbf{P}'$	Diagonal matrix of PCA eigenvalues of the training textures
$\mathbf{R}$	3D rotation matrix
$\mathbf{s}$	Dense 3D shape of the face
$\mathbf{s}^-$	Subsampled dense 3D shape of the face
$\bar{\mathbf{s}}$	Mean 3D shape of the 3DMM
$\mathbf{S}$	Principal modes of shape variation of the 3DMM
$\mathbf{S}_m$	Matrix representation for downsampling of factor m
$\mathbf{t}$	Dense 3D texture of the face
$\mathbf{t}^-$	Subsampled dense 3D texture of the face
$\bar{\mathbf{t}}$	Mean 3D texture of the 3DMM
$\mathbf{t}'$	Intermediate HR texture with FS–MAP
$\mathbf{t}_{2\text{D}}$	2D translation vector
$\mathbf{T}$	Principal modes of texture variation of the 3DMM
$\mathbf{T}'$	Principal modes of texture variation of the training textures
$\mathbf{T}_{\mathbf{k}}$	Toeplitz matrix representation of $\mathbf{k}$
$\mathbf{W}(\mathbf{s}^-;\boldsymbol{\theta})$	Warping of the sparse 3D shape $\mathbf{s}^-$ parametrized by $\boldsymbol{\theta}$
$\mathbf{x}$	HR image of dimension $mN_1 \times mN_2$
$\mathbf{z}$	Input LR image of dimension $N_1 \times N_2$
$\boldsymbol{\alpha}$	3DMM shape coefficients
$\boldsymbol{\beta}$	3DMM texture coefficients
$\boldsymbol{\beta}'$	Texture coefficients of the training textures
$\boldsymbol{\theta}$	Warping vector for global and local transformations
$\boldsymbol{\omega}$	3D rotation vector

6.1 Introduction

Contrary to generic learning-based SR normally with no extra need of registration, FSR can leverage shared information of similar facial features in a more restricted domain, achieving higher hallucination quality when properly aligned [Wan14a]. To this end, the question regarding the impact of various alignment techniques on the final FSR result may arise. To answer the question, the performance of the reviewed literature in Section 2.3.3 categorized into traditional and modern 2D approaches as well as the 3D ones is shown to more or less conform to the registration behind, and the general understanding of the capability of each method family listed in Table 6.2, too. Obviously, 3D fitting is ideal to compensate for the complex global motion, local deformation and pose variation of human faces.

Table 6.2: Summary of the capability of different alignment methods.

	2D basic	2D advanced	3D
Global motion	✓	✓	✓
Local deformation	✗	✓	✓
Out-of-plane rotation	✗	✗	✓

Then, given the dense 3D face model from the preceding pipeline, what is the best way to put the LR input face and the HR training data into correspondence? In this work, a fundamentally different scheme to the prior art [Mor09] is presented, which does not interpolate and map the LR image onto the canonical coordinates to prevent unnecessary degradation to the already poor LR texture. As such, 3D modeling can be straightforwardly utilized as a registration tool to render the 3D training textures as 2D images for conventional 2D FSR in the sequel.

In order to facilitate pure 3D FSR, a novel framework is proposed, of which the basis is a proper reinterpretation of the observation model from the mesh surface to the LR image plane. Moreover, fitting 3D models to 2D images is a challenging task, and the LR input could make things even worse for lack of high-frequency facial details. With this in mind, the classic Lucas–Kanade algorithm [Bak04a] can then be naturally extended to the

3DHR–2DLR scenario for robust fitting refinement in terms of both global motion (rotation, scaling and translation) and local deformation (3D shape) with the aforementioned imaging model. Patch-based FSR is then directly conducted on the mesh surface to give complete and dense HR texture (even for self-occluded regions), which can be deployed to render frontal face images to alleviate FR across pose. Highlights of this work are summarized as follows:

- A resolution-aware 3D alignment without interpolating the LR facial texture is devised.
- To the best of the author's knowledge, this is the first FSR algorithm that integrates the LR image formation model into a robust 3D patch-based facial texture SR method.
- The 3D extension of the Lucas–Kanade algorithm combined with a statistical texture model greatly improves fitting and FSR on the ill-posed LR images.
- Patch-based 3D FSR on the mesh naturally fills the hidden facial texture caused by large head poses.

6.2 Resolution-Aware HR–LR Alignment

Employing 3D modeling in learning-based FSR can remedy extra degrees of freedom in comparison with 2D registration, but the principal idea remains the same, *i.e.*, bring the HR training data as close as possible to the LR face so as to maximize similarity during SR inference. There are actually two possibilities to serve this purpose. After the 3D model of the LR test image is recovered, the intuitive idea would be to extract the LR texture from the image, and subsequently project it to a canonical frontal reference frame, which is the standard routine for many 2D or 3D face analysis methods, *e.g.*, AAMs [Coo98]. Mortazavian *et al.* [Mor09] (see Figure 2.6) follow the exact same concept and define a texture coordinate frame that is independent of the initial subject's shape and pose [Ten07]. Then, the pixel-based MAP algorithm of Baker and Kanade [Bak02] is performed on the 2D map to super-resolve the facial texture. The advantage of this approach lies in that merely the input image needs to be warped during the test time, while the set of training data can be transformed to the reference space offline.

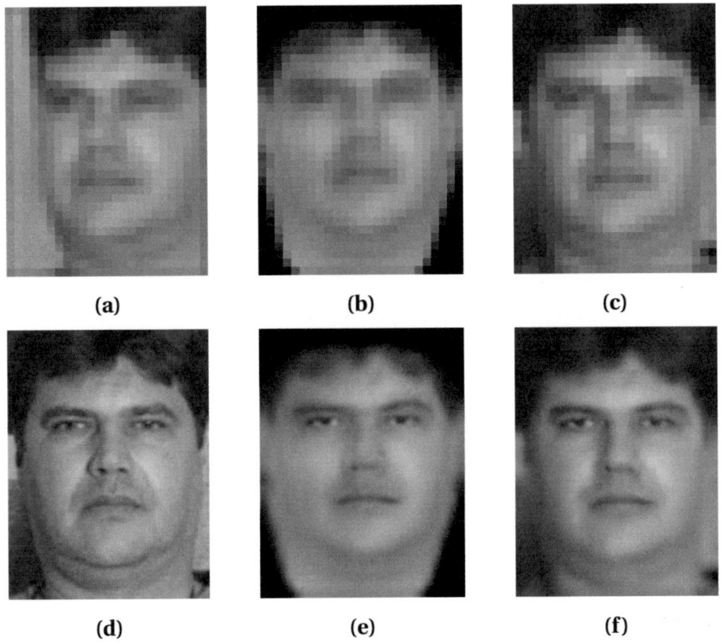

Figure 6.1: Example illustration for the impact of interpolating LR images: (a) a non-frontal LR input face, (b) the warped face of (a) after being projected onto the canonical frame, (c) the real LR image of the frontal face, (d) HR ground truth of (c), (e) FSR result of (b), (f) FSR result of (c).

However, it is argued in this thesis that the convenience comes at the cost of image quality loss. To explain the problem in detail, a closer look at the texture extraction in 3D modeling is taken. The polygon mesh of the fitted model is first projected to the image plane. Next, because the 3D texture is stored on the vertices in the 3DMM, which are scattered in the image with subpixel shifts, their values have to be interpolated non-uniformly from the image pixels. As a consequence, there is a certain degree of image deterioration resulting from the interpolation. It is known that in the context of SR, loss of LR details is critical, which is demonstrated in Figure 6.1 on the basis of the Multi-PIE images [Gro10] from multiple views. A non-frontal LR face in Figure 6.1a warped onto the canonical grid following a similar registration principle as in [Mor09] is illustrated in Figure 6.1b. Compared to the original frontal face in Figure 6.1c, the interpolated version lacks in contrast and loses some details, *e.g.*, of the eyes and nostrils. The subtle differences, though, are shown to have profound influence on the FSR results, where Figure 6.1e from the interpolated input Figure 6.1b has clearly the tendency towards the mean face. Contrarily, Figure 6.1f shares more personal characteristics with the HR ground truth in Figure 6.1d.

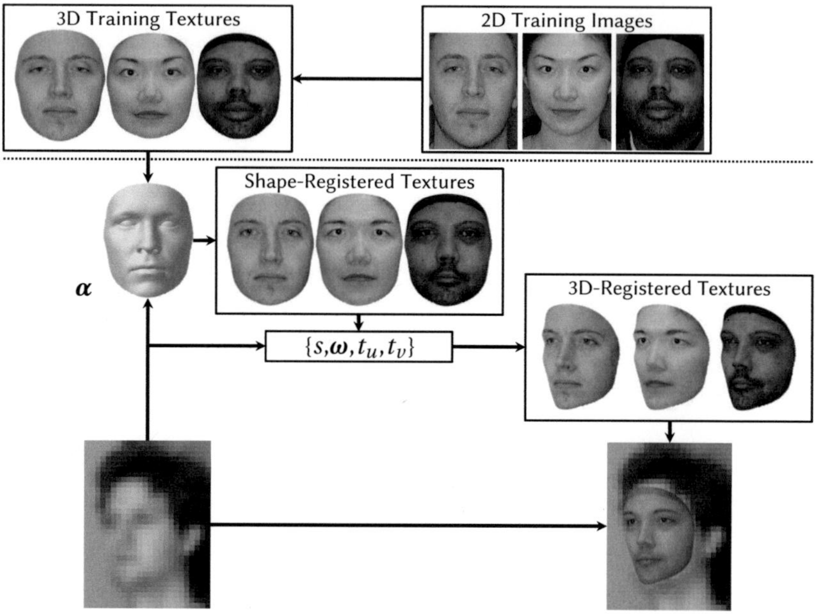

Figure 6.2: Overview of the proposed resolution-aware alignment for FSR.

Inspired by Dedeoğlu *et al.* [Ded06], who reverse the AAM fitting process for LR images to avoid warping the LR data, a resolution-aware approach is presented in Figure 6.2, which inversely warps all training HR textures and directly registers them with the target-specific 3D shape. In particular, the 3D shape of each training face is first recovered in the offline stage for preparation of the 3D training set (above the dotted line in Figure 6.2). Only the textures on the vertices of the 3DMM extracted from the 2D images based on the 3D correspondence is stored, while the 3D shape information is discarded. In contrast, given a test LR face, its 3DMM shape coefficients

$\boldsymbol{\alpha}$ and pose parameters $\{s, \boldsymbol{\omega}, t_u, t_v\}$ are simultaneously estimated, while the LR texture is *not* extracted.

The alignment procedure in which the training 3D textures are projected onto the 3D shape of the test image yields identical face shape to the reference with different HR training textures. If the newly generated *shape-registered textures* are compared with the original data, it is obvious that the shape of the eyes and eyebrows as well as the thickness of the lips in the samples are already adapted to the input image respectively, while the actual textures stay unaffected. Subsequently, the estimated pose parameters for rotation, scaling and translation are imposed on the *shape-registered textures*, revealing the fully *3D-registered textures.* As a result, it ensures that independently from the identity and pose, roughly the same part of the face is located at the same position in the image, which fulfills the prerequisite for FSR. Note that for learning-based FSR, the HR–LR training set is built from the HR textures, whereas the original LR image remains untouched.

6.3 3D Facial Texture Super-Resolution

After the offline data preparation for the 3D training textures, this section details the main 3D framework for super-resolving LR images with an initial fitting of the faces. To start with, a straightforward 2.5D FSR method leveraging the alignment scheme is introduced as the prelude of the 3D algorithm, which is made possible by revisiting the LR image formation model on the mesh surface. With this formulation, the 2D Lucas–Kanade image registration is generalized to the non-rigid 3D domain. Finally, a patch-based 3D approach is presented and the benefit of 3D FSR is demonstrated.

6.3.1 3D-Aided 2D Face Super-Resolution

3D-aided 2D FSR, a.k.a. 2.5D FSR, differs from the conventional 2D family in that a 3DMM is fitted to create correspondence in lieu of 2D registration such as geometric transformation or flow methods. In accordance with the notation in Equations (2.9) and (2.10) of Section 2.2.1 for the PCA subspaces, the coefficients $\boldsymbol{\alpha} \in \mathbb{R}^{Q_s}$ and $\boldsymbol{\beta} \in \mathbb{R}^{Q_t}$ suffice to describe any valid face within the linear subspaces.

When the *3D-registered textures* are available after Section 6.2, a person-specific 2D training set w.r.t. the LR face can be set up by first rendering the

3D textures on the HR lattice of dimension $mN_1 \times mN_2$ determined by the original LR size and the SR upsampling ratio m as the HR training images. In the sequel, the LR counterpart is built by blurring and shrinking the HR images. In this spirit, 3D alignment serves as a preprocessing instrument for 2D FSR. In [Qu15b], the two basic 2D FSR methods eigentransformation [Wan05] and PP [Ma10] are incorporated. In spite of their simplicity, evaluation results superior to more complicated state of the art are achieved, validating the capability of the resolution-aware 3D registration.

Although impressive competence of the 2.5D framework [Qu15b] is shown in both FSR and FR on synthetically generated LR data, several areas of possible improvements are spotted:

- 3D shape reconstruction is performed solely based on a few automatically detected facial landmarks, of which the accuracy is susceptible to image resolution, especially for unconstrained settings [Her15].
- A redundant interpolation step is required to obtain the 3D facial texture, which may again be encountered with quality loss in the course of texture extraction.
- While rendering novel views of the super-resolved face, the real texture in the self-occluded region remains intractable.

Fortunately, these unfavorable aspects can be addressed elegantly with the proposed 3D system.

6.3.2 Image Formation Model

The widely used 2D LR observation process [Par03, Yan10a] depicted in Figure 6.3 models the LR image $\mathbf{z}$ of $N_1 \times N_2$ pixels as a downsampled version of the HR image $\mathbf{x}$ of $mN_1 \times mN_2$ pixels with

$$\mathbf{z} = (\mathbf{B_k} \circ \mathbf{W}(\mathbf{x}; \boldsymbol{\theta})) \downarrow_m + \mathbf{n}, \tag{6.1}$$

where $\mathbf{W}$ first warps the original signal via parametrized motion $\boldsymbol{\theta}$. Then $\mathbf{B}$ imposes the blurring effect with kernel $\mathbf{k}$ and $\downarrow$ denotes decimation with magnification factor m. The imaging noise, often assumed to be white, is reflected in the additive term $\mathbf{n}$.

Learning-based SR brings in extra knowledge from internal or external sources to counteract the ill-posed problem of recovering $\mathbf{x}$ in Equation (6.1). In conventional 2D or 2.5D methods, the motion $\boldsymbol{\theta}$ is compensated for by

2D or 3D alignment techniques and the training data can be warped or rendered to super-resolve the input **z**.

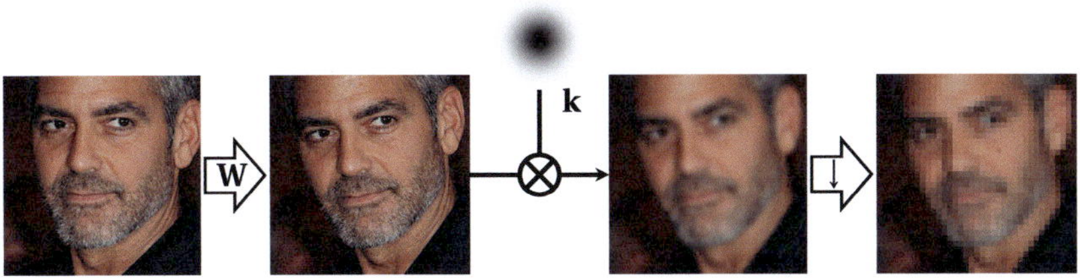

Figure 6.3: The 2D LR image formation process.

Elevating the setup to the 3D level requires establishing a direct connection between the 3D shape **s**, exemplarily illustrated in Figure 6.4, and the LR image **z**, where the key challenge is to take into account the blurring kernel **k**. For the 2D case, a simple convolution operation suffices to serve the purpose, whereas the irregularly distributed vertices on the 3D face make the problem appear intractable. For instance, Dessein *et al.* [Des15] just ignore it and back-project the LR pixel values to the corresponding LR vertices. This oversimplified NN-like approach violates the image formation model [Efr13] and is supposed to struggle with blurred LR faces in real-world imagery.

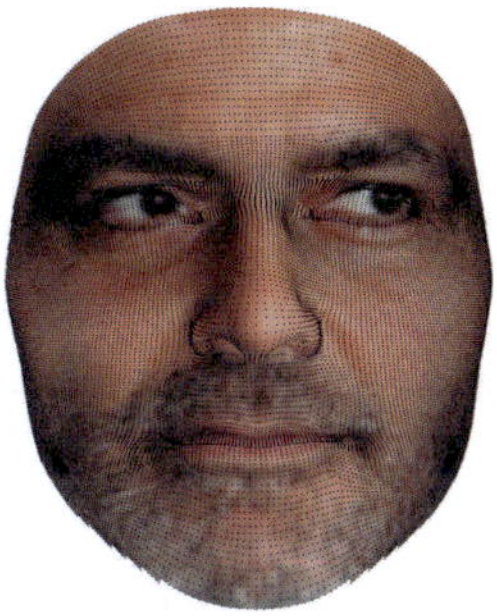

Figure 6.4: Illustration of a 3D face.

Vertex Subsampling

Considering that integrating the blurring kernel **k** directly into the 3D model is not trivial, the idea is to add an intermediate stage to interpolate the 3D surface as an ordinary image before convolving it with kernel **k**. The initial LR 3D shape is first upscaled by factor m onto the HR image coordinates w.r.t. Equation (6.1). Since a 3DMM usually has tens of thousands of vertices and involving all of them causes extra computational overhead (*e.g.*, for triangulation) with hardly any qualitative improvement for rendering, just a small fraction of them is actually necessary and taken into consideration. Only one of those that fall into each HR pixel grid is selected by

$$\mathbf{s}_i^- = \underset{\mathbf{v} \in \mathcal{V}_i}{\arg\min} \|\mathbf{v} - \mathbf{p}_i\|_2 \quad (6.2)$$

after the visible vertices are determined, where $\mathcal{V}_i$ denotes all vertices inside the unit square centered at pixel $\mathbf{p}_i$, revealing a reduced set $\mathbf{s}^-$ of roughly the same cardinality as the number of pixels in the HR face. This nearly one-to-one mapping between vertices and pixels targets to ensure fidelity when downscaled.

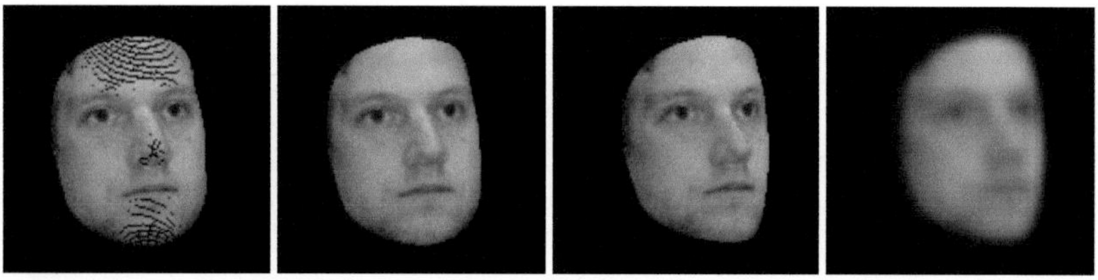

(a) $\{\mathbf{s}^-, \mathbf{t}^-\}$ **(b)** $\mathbf{I}(\mathbf{s}^-)\mathbf{t}$ **(c)** $\mathbf{I}(\mathbf{W}(\mathbf{s}^-;\boldsymbol{\theta}))\mathbf{t}$ **(d)** $\mathbf{H}(\mathbf{W}(\mathbf{s}^-;\boldsymbol{\theta}))\mathbf{t}$

Figure 6.5: From 3D shape to LR image: (a) the subsampled vertices $\mathbf{s}^-$, (b) interpolated result of (a), (c) image output with extra rotation applied using the *same* vertex subsampling $\mathbf{s}^-$, (d) final LR output $\mathbf{z}$ of (c).

Figure 6.5a depicts an image with the pixels from the associated subsampled vertices $\mathbf{s}^-$ of an example 3D face found with Equation (6.2). Note that holes emerge at regions like forehead or jaw where no vertices are present owing to the non-uniform distribution of the mesh. However, these less structured places on $\mathbf{s}^-$ are ignored as they can be completely eliminated by the subsequent interpolation step (see Figure 6.5b). Even after rotating the face by 15°, the *original* subsampling $\mathbf{s}^-$ can still generate natural image output with enough details in Figure 6.5c. This is critical for the 3D extension of the Lucas–Kanade algorithm for post-processing the initial 3D fitting, which alters the face geometry and motion in each iteration.

LR Interpolation for 3D Vertices

After sampling the scattered point cloud $\mathbf{s}^-$, it is interpolated on the HR lattice to obtain a 2D image. Specifically, Delaunay triangulation is carried out on the projected 2D coordinates of $\mathbf{s}^-$ and indices of the triangles in which each pixel is located can be found. At the same time, the barycentric coordinates for the HR pixels w.r.t. the triangulated vertices can also be computed efficiently. Importantly, the whole procedure of linear interpolation is representable as a sparse matrix $\mathbf{I}(\mathbf{s}^-) \in \mathbb{R}^{m^2 N_1 N_2 \times P}$ depending on the current subsampled shape $\mathbf{s}^-$, which has as many rows as the number of HR pixels, and as many columns as the number of 3D vertices. In each row of this matrix for calculating a pixel value $\mathbf{p}_i$, there are exactly three entries storing the barycentric coordinates $\{b_1, b_2, 1 - b_1 - b_2\}$ of the relevant vertices $\{v_1, v_2, v_3\}$. In this way, one can interpolate $\mathbf{p}_i$ with

$$\mathbf{p}_i = b_1\mathbf{t}_1 + b_2\mathbf{t}_2 + (1 - b_1 - b_2)\mathbf{t}_3. \tag{6.3}$$

Accordingly, the vectorized representation for the entire HR image $\mathbf{x}$ is

$$\text{vec}(\mathbf{x}) = \mathbf{I}(\mathbf{s}^-)\mathbf{t}, \tag{6.4}$$

which is a simple matrix multiplication with the grayscale texture $\mathbf{t} \in \mathbb{R}^P$.

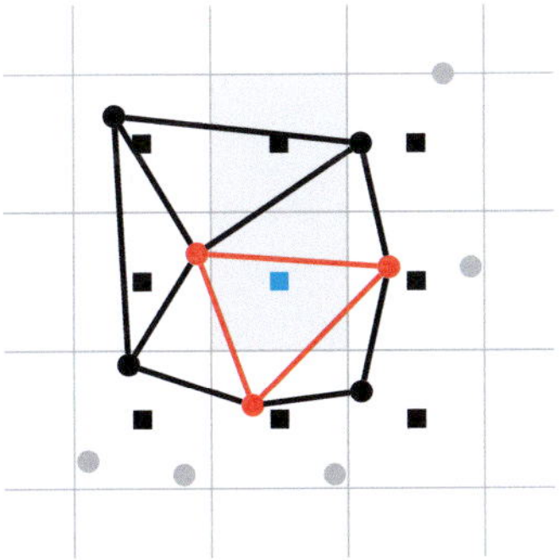

Figure 6.6: Interpolating image pixel values from the scattered 3D vertices.

This operations so far are depicted in Figure 6.6. The grid placed over regular image coordinates (in squares) indicates the neighborhood of the pixels. When subsampling of 3D vertices (in circles) is finished, some are discarded w.r.t. Equation (6.2), which are grayed out in the figure. For the shaded pixels that have no vertex associated to them, interpolation is still possible. As an example, the value of the blue pixel in the middle can be inferred with the three surrounding red vertices by Equation (6.3).

Subsequently, the convolution and decimation operators in Equation (6.1) are converted into sparse matrices $\mathbf{T_k}$ and $\mathbf{S}_m$ respectively, where $\mathbf{T_k}$ denotes a Toeplitz matrix [Lev11] for filter $\mathbf{k}$ and $\mathbf{S}_m \in \mathbb{Z}^{N_1 N_2 \times m^2 N_1 N_2}$ is a shrinkage matrix, *i.e.*, for each LR pixel represented by row i, only column j corresponding to the selected HR pixel is set to one.

Therefore, the complete LR image observation process from the 3D surface can be formulated as a matrix multiplication

$$\mathrm{vec}\,(\mathbf{z}) = \mathbf{H}\,(\mathbf{W}(\mathbf{s}^{-};\boldsymbol{\theta}))\,\mathbf{t} + \mathbf{n}, \tag{6.5}$$

where $\mathbf{H} = \mathbf{S}_m \mathbf{T_k} \mathbf{I}$ is a composition matrix of dimension $N_1 N_2 \times P$ integrating all related operations. Both $\mathbf{H}$ and $\mathbf{I}$ are dependent on the (warped) 3D shape. An example LR image generated by this model is illustrated in Figure 6.5d.

6.3.3 Fitting Enhancement

LR faces pose a huge challenge on 3D fitting because of a significant amount of information loss and diverse nuisance factors such as blur and noise from various sources. Whereas the accuracy of fitting propels the quality of FSR, it can also introduce adverse impact when the precision degrades. Motivated by the classic Lucas–Kanade image registration framework [Bak04a, Luc81], a new algorithm that iteratively optimizes both global motion and 3DMM deformation tailored for LR images is developed.

The original goal of the Lucas–Kanade algorithm is to minimize the Sum of Squared Error (SSE) between a template and an image warped onto the coordinate frame of the template using a predefined parametrized representation. When applied to 3D FSR, the formulation yields

$$\frac{1}{|\boldsymbol{\Omega}|}\left\|\mathbf{H}\,(\mathbf{W}(\mathbf{s}^{-};\boldsymbol{\theta}))\,\mathbf{t}' - \mathrm{vec}\,(\mathbf{z})\right\|_2^2, \tag{6.6}$$

normalized by the pixel count of the facial region $\mathbf{\Omega}$ in the LR template $\mathbf{z}$. Subject to the parametrized warping vector

$$\boldsymbol{\theta} = \left[s, \boldsymbol{\omega}^\top, t_u, t_v, \boldsymbol{\alpha}^\top\right]^\top \in \mathbb{R}^{6+Q_s}, \tag{6.7}$$

which consists of scaling s, 3D rotation vector $\boldsymbol{\omega} = [\omega_1, \omega_2, \omega_3]^\top$ [Sze11b] and 2D translation $\mathbf{t}_{2D} = [t_u, t_v]^\top$ on the image grid for rigid motion, as well as the 3DMM shape coefficients $\boldsymbol{\alpha}$ for local deformation. The warping operation $\mathbf{W}(\mathbf{s}; \boldsymbol{\theta})$ transforms the 3D face shape via

$$\mathbf{W}(\mathbf{s}; \boldsymbol{\theta}) = s\mathbf{R}_{[1:2,:]}\, \Psi_{3\times P}\, (\bar{\mathbf{s}} + \mathbf{S}\boldsymbol{\alpha}) \oplus \mathbf{t}_{2D} \tag{6.8}$$

onto the image coordinate system, where $\oplus$ stands for element-wise addition for the respective matrix rows, and $\mathbf{R}_{[1:2,:]}$ for 2D projection of the 3D rotation matrix

$$\mathbf{R} = \mathbf{R}_{\omega_3} \mathbf{R}_{\omega_2} \mathbf{R}_{\omega_1}. \tag{6.9}$$

It is worth noting that minimizing the expression in Equation (6.6) is a nonlinear optimization task, even if $\mathbf{W}(\mathbf{s}; \boldsymbol{\theta})$ were linear in $\boldsymbol{\theta}$, because the rendered pixel values are nonlinear in the 3D shape $\mathbf{s}$ [Bak04a]. Instead of minimizing Equation (6.6) for the warping parameter $\boldsymbol{\theta}$ at one go, the Lucas–Kanade algorithm solves for the incremental update $\boldsymbol{\Delta\theta}$, such that

$$\frac{1}{|\mathbf{\Omega}|} \left\| \mathbf{H}\left(\mathbf{W}(\mathbf{s}^-; \boldsymbol{\theta} + \boldsymbol{\Delta\theta})\right) \mathbf{t}' - \mathrm{vec}\left(\mathbf{z}\right) \right\|_2^2 \tag{6.10}$$

is minimized subject to $\boldsymbol{\Delta\theta}$, which suits the problem setup of this thesis perfectly, as an initial estimate of the 3D geometry is available with the previous 3D reconstruction module.

Before proceeding to the actual optimization of Equation (6.10), though, the crux regarding $\mathbf{t}'$ in this expression must be addressed. The 3D Lucas–Kanade algorithm requires HR facial texture to guide the warping parameter update towards the "template" $\mathbf{z}$, while up to this stage of the processing chain, the facial texture SR has not taken place yet. On the other hand, applying the nonparametric patch-based SR as in Section 6.3.4 here is suboptimal, since it attempts to hallucinate the HR texture by reconstructing the patches in $\mathbf{z}$ with the training data, even åt incorrectly fitted location.

Thus, to fully account for the semantic connection between the 3D shape and texture model, the holistic PCA texture prior is exploited.

In particular, given an approximate fitting, an intermediate estimate of the HR texture $\mathbf{t}'$ for the Lucas–Kanade algorithm can be computed using the FS–MAP approach [Cap01] with the presented 3D image observation model. In theory, the PCA-based 3DMM texture model $\{\bar{\mathbf{t}}, \mathbf{T}\}$ would be the proper choice as the low-dimensional prior. However, the texture model in the 3DMM is pure albedo with the illumination normalized out. In order to cover a wide range of changes, a new PCA model is constructed on the basis of (in-the-wild) faces with richer variation, which can be shared with the downstream FSR task. Concretely, performing PCA on the extracted textures gives the mean texture $\boldsymbol{\mu}$, a matrix $\mathbf{D}$ composed of eigenvectors and a diagonal matrix $\mathbf{P}$ of eigenvalues resembling Equation (2.10). The texture coefficient $\boldsymbol{\beta}'$ on the PCA space and the resulting holistic HR FS–MAP face

$$\mathbf{t}' = \boldsymbol{\mu} + \mathbf{D}\boldsymbol{\beta}' \tag{6.11}$$

are solved for in closed form via

$$\hat{\boldsymbol{\beta}}' = \underset{\boldsymbol{\beta}'}{\arg\min} \left\| \mathbf{H}(\mathbf{s}^-)\left(\boldsymbol{\mu} + \mathbf{D}\boldsymbol{\beta}'\right) - \mathrm{vec}(\mathbf{z}) \right\|_2^2 + \gamma \left\| \boldsymbol{\beta}' \right\|_{\mathbf{P}^{-1}}^2 \tag{6.12}$$

$$= \mathbf{P}\mathbf{D}^\top \mathbf{H}^\top \left(\mathbf{H}\mathbf{D}\mathbf{P}\mathbf{D}^\top \mathbf{H}^\top + \gamma \mathbf{I}_{\mathrm{id}}\right)^{-1} \left(\mathrm{vec}\left(\mathbf{z} - \mathbf{H}\boldsymbol{\mu}\right)\right) \tag{6.13}$$

based on the initial fitting, where a penalty proportional to the Mahalanobis distance of the features in $\boldsymbol{\beta}'$ to the mean in $\boldsymbol{\mu}$. Capel and Zisserman [Cap01] refer to this as FS–MAP, *i.e.*, a prior over the face space, since the solution is constrained to lie on the subspace spanned by the PCA model, which is later proved to be identical to the soft constraints in [Liu07] by Jin and Bouganis in [Jin13].

Finally, the nonlinear optimization task in Equation (6.10) is linearized by first-order Taylor expansion evaluated at $(\mathbf{s}^-; \boldsymbol{\theta})$ [Bak04a], which yields

$$\frac{1}{|\boldsymbol{\Omega}|} \left\| \mathbf{H}\left(\mathbf{W}(\mathbf{s}^-; \boldsymbol{\theta})\right) \mathbf{t}' + \nabla_{\mathbf{H}\mathbf{t}'} \frac{\partial \mathbf{W}}{\partial \boldsymbol{\theta}} \Delta\boldsymbol{\theta} - \mathrm{vec}(\mathbf{z}) \right\|_2^2 . \tag{6.14}$$

In this expression, $\nabla_{\mathbf{H}\mathbf{t}'}$ is the *gradient* of the rendered image at $(\mathbf{s}^{-};\boldsymbol{\theta})$, and $\frac{\partial \mathbf{W}}{\partial \boldsymbol{\theta}}$ is the *Jacobian* of the warp defined in Equation (6.8), which can be derived as

$$\frac{\partial \mathbf{W}}{\partial \boldsymbol{\theta}} = \begin{bmatrix} \frac{\partial \mathbf{W}_u}{\partial s} & \frac{\partial \mathbf{W}_u}{\partial \omega_1} & \frac{\partial \mathbf{W}_u}{\partial \omega_2} & \frac{\partial \mathbf{W}_u}{\partial \omega_3} & \frac{\partial \mathbf{W}_u}{\partial t_u} & \frac{\partial \mathbf{W}_u}{\partial t_v} & \frac{\partial \mathbf{W}_u}{\partial \boldsymbol{\alpha}} \\ \frac{\partial \mathbf{W}_v}{\partial s} & \frac{\partial \mathbf{W}_v}{\partial \omega_1} & \frac{\partial \mathbf{W}_v}{\partial \omega_2} & \frac{\partial \mathbf{W}_v}{\partial \omega_3} & \frac{\partial \mathbf{W}_v}{\partial t_u} & \frac{\partial \mathbf{W}_v}{\partial t_v} & \frac{\partial \mathbf{W}_v}{\partial \boldsymbol{\alpha}} \end{bmatrix} \tag{6.15}$$

$$= \begin{bmatrix} \mathbf{R}_u\,[u,v,z]^\top & 0 & s\cos(\omega_2)z & -s\cos(\omega_3)y & 1 & 0 & s\mathbf{R}_u\mathbf{H}\mathbf{S} \\ \mathbf{R}_v\,[u,v,z]^\top & -s\cos(\omega_1)z & 0 & s\cos(\omega_3)x & 0 & 1 & s\mathbf{R}_v\mathbf{H}\mathbf{S} \end{bmatrix} \tag{6.16}$$

using the chain rule, where the subscripts u and v denote the respective rows in the matrix w.r.t. the image grid and the last column stands for the shape dictionary in Equation (2.9) projected onto the LR coordinates. Note that to obtain the partial derivative of the rotation vector $\frac{\partial \mathbf{W}}{\partial \boldsymbol{\omega}}$, the approximation

$$\mathbf{R} = \mathbf{R}_{\omega_3}\mathbf{R}_{\omega_2}\mathbf{R}_{\omega_1} \approx \begin{bmatrix} 1 & -\sin\omega_3 & \sin\omega_2 \\ \sin\omega_3 & 1 & -\sin\omega_1 \\ -\sin\omega_2 & \sin\omega_1 & 1 \end{bmatrix} \tag{6.17}$$

is used by setting the cosines to one, if the rotation increment is small [Bla04], which is satisfied with the iterative fashion. The extended Lucas–Kanade algorithm for improving LR fitting is summarized in Algorithm 4. Regarding the nonlinear optimization technique in practice, the LM algorithm is preferred by virtue of its robustness against the more complex problem setup [Bak04a] to Gauss–Newton, *e.g.*, for homography in [Jin15].

An instance of the complete fitting process is visualized in Figure 6.7. At first sight, the 3D FS–MAP texture hallucinated on the initial fit in Figure 6.7b seems plausible. But comparison with Figure 6.7d demonstrates how much the 3D fitting can be improved in all respects. Not only the head pose and the facial contour, but also the local deformation (*e.g.*, the shape of the mouth) better conforms to the HR ground truth in Figure 6.7f. It can be observed that in the first few iterations, mainly the global rotation and translation are corrected to rapidly decrease the error, while in the later stage, local adjustment is made to fine-tune the details.

Algorithm 4: 3D Lucas–Kanade fitting enhancement for LR faces.

Input: Rough 3D fitting initialization and intermediate HR texture $\mathbf{t}'$

Output: Improved 3D fitting

```
while ‖Δθ‖ ≥ ε do
    Alter the 3D face by θ via W(s⁻; θ)
    Obtain the LR projection matrix H(W(s⁻; θ))
    Compute error image vec(z) − Ht'
    Compute the image gradient ∇_Ht' of Ht'
    Evaluate the Jacobian of warping ∂W/∂θ at (s⁻; θ) via Equation (6.16)
    Obtain the steepest descent image ∇_Ht' ∂W/∂θ
    Perform nonlinear optimization for Δθ
    Update the warping parameter θ ← θ + Δθ
end
```

Discussion

According to [Bak04a], the proposed Lucas–Kanade extension falls under the Forwards Additive variant (*c.f.* [Bak04b]). In general, the quadratic expression in Equation (6.10) is non-convex and hence not guaranteed to converge globally. However, unlike the 3DMM fitting [Bla03] initialized with the mean appearance, it starts from relatively good shape and texture estimates so that as few as ten iterations are found sufficient for convergence in practice. Furthermore, not taking into account the illumination parameters gives rise to a considerable benefit in runtime with only a fraction of a second for each iteration. Finally, the well-defined LR observation process ensures excellent versatility w.r.t. different image degradation models in real world compared to, *e.g.*, a fixed number of trained LR 3DMMs [Hu12].

Employing the Lucas–Kanade algorithm to register images for FSR is not new. Liu *et al.* [Liu07] first adopt affine transformation based on solely the mean image, which is revised by Jia and Gong [Jia08] to take into consideration the PCA face space prior and solve the optimization problem in an alternating manner. Jin and Bouganis [Jin13, Jin15] incorporate the more advanced homographic transformation into their unified MAP framework. Nevertheless, the presented work is the first 3D extension for LR fitting of deformable face models, which can also be regarded as a simplified version of the analysis-by-synthesis 3DMM algorithm specially designed for fine-tuning on LR faces.

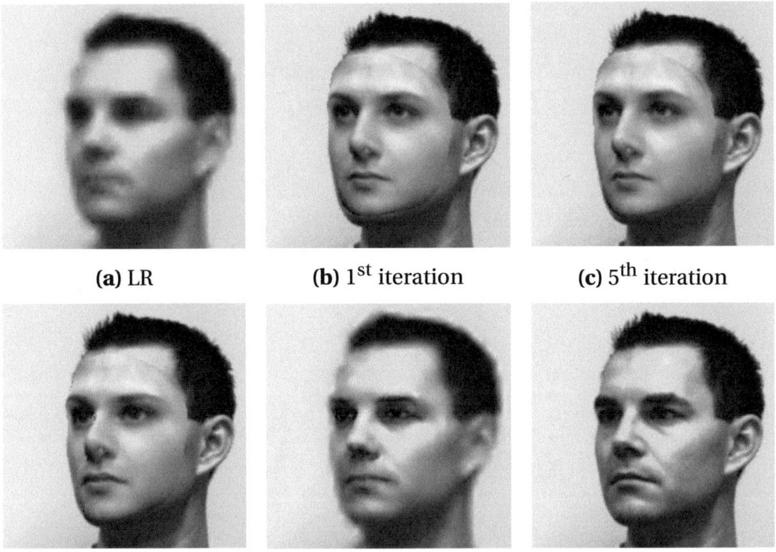

(a) LR **(b)** 1st iteration **(c)** 5th iteration

(d) 10th iteration **(e)** FSR **(f)** HR

Figure 6.7: Improving 3D fitting: From a LR input image in (a), the initial fitting, the results after 5 and 10 iterations with 3D FS–MAP, as well as the final 3D FSR image are shown in (b) to (e), respectively. (f) is the HR ground truth of (a).

6.3.4 Patch-Based Facial Texture Super-Resolution

A key difference of 3D FSR to 2.5D systems as in Section 6.3.1 lies in that the HR 3D texture is directly obtained rather than being extracted separately from the HR image after it is super-resolved by 2D FSR.

The "interface" developed to facilitate 3D FSR, *i.e.*, the image formation model from 3D faces to LR images in Section 6.3.2, is naturally compatible to most 2D FSR methods, if properly redesigned for the 3D case. Similar to Section 6.3.1 (*c.f.* [Qu15b]), the simple idea of the 2D patch-based FSR [Ma10] to divide the LR image into overlapping patches and enforce local subspaces is followed to demonstrate the power of accurate 3D alignment.

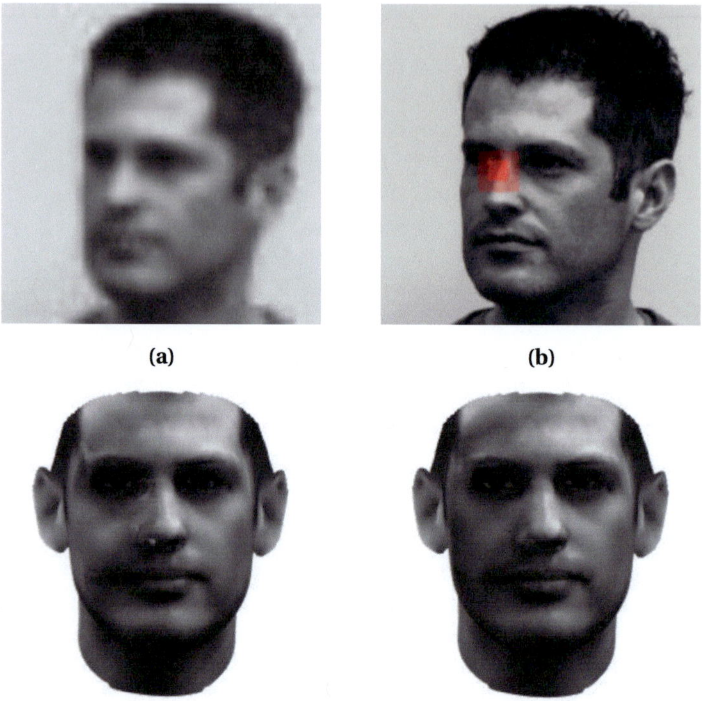

(a) (b)

(c) (d)

Figure 6.8: 3D patch-based FSR: (a) LR input image, (b) a 3D patch superimposed on the HR image, (c) texture extracted from 2.5D FSR, (d) directly super-resolved texture by 3D FSR.

After the segmentation of LR patches, the FSR procedure is conducted on the face mesh. First, the subset of $\mathbf{s}^{-}$ belonging to each patch is determined straightforwardly with the sparse imaging matrix $\mathbf{H}$ in Equation (6.5), *i.e.*, for the respective rows representing the LR pixels, the column indices for vertices with non-empty entries in $\mathbf{H}$ are selected. Figure 6.8b illustrates the corresponding vertices of a patch in solid red. On account of convolution with the blurring kernel, the actual vertices in light red involved for LR patch reconstruction normally have a larger vicinity. For each of the local patch j, the optimal weights $\mathbf{w}_j \in \mathbb{R}^L$ are then obtained by minimizing the reconstruction error with constraint

$$\min_{\mathbf{w}_j} \left\| \sum_{l=1}^{L} w_j^l \mathbf{H}\left(\mathbf{W}\left(\mathbf{s}_j^-;\boldsymbol{\theta}\right)\right) \mathbf{t}_j^l - \text{vec}\left(\mathbf{z}_j\right) \right\|_2^2, \text{ s.t. } \sum_{l=1}^{L} w_j^l = 1 \tag{6.18}$$

by virtue of the 3D observation model, where the superscript l denotes the index of the totally L 3D textures in the training data. To solve Equation (6.18), assume that $\mathbf{Y}_j \in \mathbb{R}^{N_1 N_2 \times L}$ is the matrix of all training samples $\mathbf{H}\left(\mathbf{W}\left(\mathbf{s}_j^-;\boldsymbol{\theta}\right)\right) \mathbf{t}_j^l$ stacked in columns. The local Gram matrix is defined as

$$\mathbf{G}_j = \left(\text{vec}\left(\mathbf{z}_j\right) \mathbf{1}^\top - \mathbf{Y}_j\right)^\top \left(\text{vec}\left(\mathbf{z}_j\right) \mathbf{1}^\top - \mathbf{Y}_j\right), \tag{6.19}$$

where $\mathbf{1} \in \mathbb{Z}^L$ is a column vector of ones. In this manner, the constrained least squares problem for $\mathbf{w}_j$ has the closed-form solution [Cha04]

$$\mathbf{w}_j = \frac{\mathbf{G}_j^{-1}\mathbf{1}}{\mathbf{1}^\top \mathbf{G}_j^{-1}\mathbf{1}}. \tag{6.20}$$

Alternatively, one can solve the linear system of equations

$$\mathbf{G}_j \mathbf{w}_j = \mathbf{1} \tag{6.21}$$

and subsequently normalize the sum of the weight vector $\mathbf{w}_j$ to one. In the end, the complete set $\mathbf{s}$ is recovered using the same weights as for $\mathbf{s}^-$, where the values of the overlapping vertices are averaged.

Note that because there exists no texture outside of the head model in the training data, the border effect must be handled for patch SR. In the implementation, it is discovered that a pragmatic way is to copy the outer area of the LR test image to the training samples, weighted by a reversed face mask, which is interpolated from the hard HR face mask imposed on the background.

A favorable byproduct while directly conducting 3D FSR is the intrinsic filling of the self-occluded texture. In Figure 6.8d, the hidden side of the nose consistent with the illumination condition is learned from the training data and blended seamlessly to the rest of the facial texture, whereas in Figure 6.8c, despite utilizing a dedicate hole-filling technique for faces regarding illumination fidelity and realistic rendering [Qu15a], artifacts cannot be overcome entirely. Even for large poses as in the last one of Figure 7.20, nearly the whole face half under occlusion is still hallucinated realistically.

Moreover, often visible gains w.r.t. sharpness and details are observed (*c.f.* the eyes in Figures 6.8c and 6.8d).

Discussion

It is worth noting that the recent 3D MRF [Des15] is a patch-based FSR approach as well, which uses irregular 3D patches segmented straight on the 3D face model (see Figure 2.7). The advantage of this segmentation scheme is that the patches are divided into approximately the same size, independently from the identity, pose and resolution of the test subject. As such, the compatibility cost of the MRF over the full training set can be precomputed offline. Nevertheless, since the MRF inference with BP is carried out completely on the 3D mesh after the LR pixel values are mapped by the NN principle onto the vertices, the connection to the image space is lost and it is then cumbersome to further incorporate convolution with different blurring kernels as in this work.

6.4 Summary

This chapter concludes the algorithmic part of the proposed 3D facial texture SR system in this thesis. The importance of image alignment for FSR is studied and a resolution-aware approach for 3D FSR under arbitrary poses is presented, which inversely maps the HR textures to the LR input face to generate person-specific training samples, avoiding loss of details through warping the LR image.

In order to allow for a robust 3D texture hallucination framework, the fundamental aspects of LR 3D face fitting and SR are revisited. A novel formulation of the LR image formation process on the 3D mesh is devised, which opens up the possibilities to improve fitting accuracy for the LR scenario and to directly super-resolve the 3D facial texture with natural handling of self-occluded parts of the face.

Algorithm 5 summarizes the work in this chapter. Previous concerns about inaccurate 3D fitting with only automatically detected landmarks on LR faces are successfully addressed. Thanks to precise definition of the actual problems and compact solution proposals, the merit of an efficient and effective workflow is preserved.

Algorithm 5: Robust 3D patch-based facial texture SR.

Input: Rough 3D fitting on the LR face
Output: HR 2D and 3D face with refined fitting

Determine the sparse LR vertex set $\mathbf{s}^-$
Compute the 3D image formation matrix $\mathbf{H}$
while *3D motion* $\boldsymbol{\theta}$ *not converged* **do**
    Compute intermediate texture $\mathbf{t}'$ with 3D FS–MAP
    Update $\boldsymbol{\theta}$ with the 3D Lucas–Kanade extension
    Update $\mathbf{H}$
end
Divide the LR image into overlapping patches
Compute SR weights for the patches on $\mathbf{s}^-$
Reconstruct $\mathbf{t}$ using the same weights

7 Experiments

This chapter extensively evaluates the approaches introduced previously within the context of the entire processing chain. Representative existing work in the literature is compared to the proposed methods in a qualitative and quantitative manner. In Section 7.1, a major flaw of the widespread SR evaluation protocol is addressed with a new FSR dataset collected using a novel dual-camera imaging system. Other public datasets and the evaluation metrics employed in this thesis are described in Section 7.2, before the performance is benchmarked module by module in Section 7.3. Finally, the outcome is summarized in Section 7.4. Table 7.1 lists widely used notation in Chapter 7.

7.1 Capturing Ground Truth Super-Resolution Data

SR offers an effective approach to boost quality and details of LR images to obtain HR images. Despite the theoretical and technical advances in the past decades, it still lacks plausible methodology to evaluate and compare SR algorithms. The main cause to this problem lies in the missing ground truth data for SR. Unlike in many other computer vision tasks, where existing image datasets can be utilized directly, or with extra annotation work, evaluating SR requires that the dataset contain both LR and the corresponding HR ground truth images of the same scene captured at the same time.

Table 7.1: Notation used in Chapter 7.

Symbol	Description
f	Focal length of the lens
F	Number of facial landmarks
k	Severity index for image quality degradation
K	IRLS scaling factor
m	Upscaling factor for SR
P	Number of vertices in the 3DMM
s	Base for image quality degradation
T	Number of triangles in the 3DMM
w	Width of the face image
β	Factor for image quality degradation with blurring
γ	Regularization weight in IRLS for 2D landmark detection
ζ	Factor for image quality degradation with noise
η	Regularization weight for landmark-based 3D shape reconstruction
σ	Standard deviation of the Gaussian blurring kernel
$\mathbf{I}_{\mathrm{id}}$	Identity matrix
$\mathbf{k}$	Blurring kernel of dimension $K \times K$
$\mathbf{n}_i$	Reconstructed normal of the ith vertex
$\mathbf{n}_i^\star$	Ground truth normal of the ith vertex
$\mathbf{s}_i$	Reconstructed 3D coordinates of the ith vertex
$\mathbf{s}_i^\star$	Ground truth 3D coordinates of the ith vertex
$\mathbf{S}_m$	Matrix representation for downsampling of factor m
$\mathbf{T}_\mathbf{x}$	Rearranged image $\mathbf{x}$ by expanding blocks into columns
$\mathbf{W}(\boldsymbol{\xi};\boldsymbol{\theta})$	Warping of the pixels $\boldsymbol{\xi}$ parametrized by $\boldsymbol{\xi}$
$\mathbf{x}$	HR image of dimension $mN_1 \times mN_2$
$\mathbf{x}_i$	Detected location of the ith facial landmark
$\mathbf{x}_i^\star$	Ground truth location of the ith facial landmark
$\mathbf{z}$	Input LR image of dimension $N_1 \times N_2$
$\boldsymbol{\theta}$	Warping vector for translational motion
$\boldsymbol{\xi}$	Pixel coordinates

This section, which is based on the author's publication [Qu16], presents a novel prototype system to address the aforementioned difficulties of acquiring ground truth SR data. Two identical image sensors equipped with a wide-angle lens and a telephoto lens respectively, share the same optical axis by placing a beam splitter into the optical path. The back-end program can then trigger their shutters simultaneously and precisely register the ROIs of the LR and HR image pairs in an automated manner free of subpixel interpolation. Experimental results demonstrate the unique characteristics of the captured HR–LR face images compared to the simulated ones.

The remainder of this section is organized as follows. Section 7.1.1 gives an brief introduction to the motivation and approach. The hardware setup of the proposed prototype is then demonstrated in Section 7.1.2. After acquiring the raw image pairs with the camera system, the algorithmic details for registration and analysis of the images with quantitative and qualitative results are discussed in Section 7.1.3 and Section 7.1.4 respectively. Finally, the section is concluded in Section 7.1.5.

7.1.1 Introduction

In general, many existing computer vision algorithms can only be applied to image data of standard size and quality. When the resolution of the test images falls under a certain limit, the performance is expected to drop dramatically. Instead of employing HR camera systems or specific algorithms for LR data, SR provides the possibility of reusing the existing data and tools. As opposed to interpolation-based methods, SR is able to recover the missing high-frequency information in the original LR image by combining multiple images with subpixel shifts among them [Far04], or through inference of local HR structure from similar HR–LR pairs from external training data [Bak02] or from the internal pyramid of the LR image itself [Gla09].

Considering the surge of interest in SR research, datasets for evaluation purposes have received significantly less attention. Despite the fact that a huge number of datasets have been built in the computer vision society and many of them can be leveraged in various tasks [Gro10, Rus15], unfortunately, evaluation of SR requires a pair of HR–LR images of the same scene, one as input for the algorithms, and the other as ground truth for quantitative assessment of the output. Therefore, to the best of the knowledge of the author, all of the previous work has made a compromise by synthetically generating the LR images using the available HR images in existing datasets, pretty much like the recently published benchmark paper [Yan14]. Nonetheless, if and how much the simulated LR image can model the complicated optical properties of the real image is yet to be justified. Even for the synthesis, strategies regarding blurring, resizing and noise still remain controversial [Efr13].

On the other hand, strict conditions must be met when a new SR dataset is collected, of which the biggest challenges include temporal and spatial consistency. Thus the possibility of taking two images consecutively or the adoption of a parallel multi-camera system similar to stereo vision is eliminated, as different capturing time is not suitable for most scenes which are not completely static, and parallax of the latter setup is also not preferred for the evaluation.

To circumvent these challenging requirements, a prototype of a novel dual-camera setup is proposed. The key idea is to utilize a beam splitter, often found in many optical interferometer systems like the autofocus sensor in CD/DVD/BluRay players [Bey16], which converts the original optical path into two identical ones and redirects them towards the sensors of two cameras respectively. In this way, as long as the images are taken simultaneously, both the temporal and spatial prerequisites are fulfilled. Capturing of LR and HR images is realized with a wide-angle lens and a telephoto lens mounted on the cameras respectively. Automatic image registration based on the Lucas–Kanade algorithm [Bak04a, Luc81] aligns the same ROIs for the pairs of images without subpixel shifts. For the purpose of this thesis, a face SR dataset is collected with the proposed device, which is analyzed in diverse aspects to show its distinct image properties.

7.1.2 Hardware Setup

Capturing ground truth image data for evaluating SR algorithms is not a trivial task. The LR image is given as input to compute the SR result with higher resolution, which should be compared with the original HR image for quantitative or qualitative assessment. Since the SR image is directly computed from the LR input, in order to conduct valid evaluation, the HR image is required to be captured exactly for the same scene at the same instant of time as that of the LR image. Some existing schemes, *e.g.*, taking the HR–LR image pairs in sequence, or on the basis of a stereo camera setup, can only partly meet the prerequisites. Violation of temporal consistency due to unsynchronized recording in the first case, and spatial consistency due to parallax in the second case, forces the method to be applicable to completely static scenes or those with a very large distance, respectively. In comparison, the novel dual-camera setup presented here successfully bypasses these limitations.

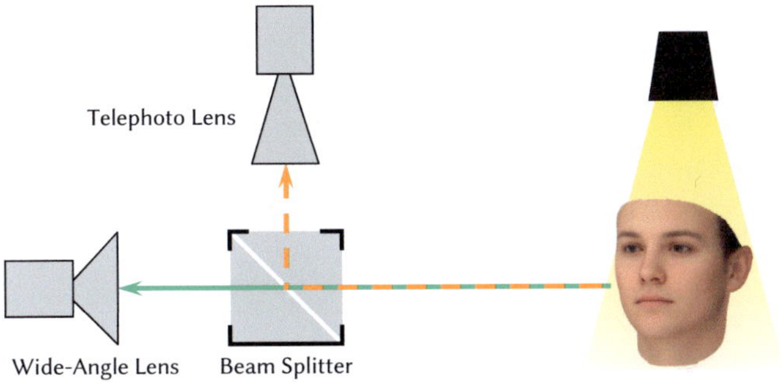

Figure 7.1: Scheme of the proposed dual-camera imaging system.

The scheme of the system is depicted in Figure 7.1. The core idea is the introduction of a beam splitter into the optical path, which splits the incident light from the scene into two identical parts. This can be realized with a beam splitter of 50:50 split ratio. When the light enters through the entrance face of the cube and hits the dielectric coating applied to the hypotenuse surface, which serves as an interference filter, half of the light is reflected and the rest is transmitted. Two identical cameras are directed at the exit faces of the beam splitter, on which a wide-angle lens and a telephoto lens are mounted respectively, such that the first camera with larger field of view (FOV) captures a wider scene with lower resolution, and the other one with smaller FOV captures zoomed HR details.

The upcoming problem is the choice of lenses and the positions of the cameras to achieve the desired magnification factor for the HR–LR image pairs in SR. According to the thin lens formula [Hec01] illustrated in Figure 7.2, the magnification factor m_{Object}, *i.e.*, the size of the image in proportion to the size of the original object is

$$m_{\text{Object}} = -\frac{S_2}{S_1} = \frac{f}{f - S_1} = \frac{f - S_2}{f}, \tag{7.1}$$

where f denotes the focal length of the lens, and S_1 and S_2 are the distances from the lens center to the object and the image respectively. For the magnification factor m which is of more interest, the approximation applies

$$m = \frac{f_{\mathrm{HR}}}{f_{\mathrm{HR}} - S_1} \Big/ \frac{f_{\mathrm{LR}}}{f_{\mathrm{LR}} - S_1} \approx \frac{f_{\mathrm{HR}}}{f_{\mathrm{LR}}}, \tag{7.2}$$

where the object distance is similar for both cameras and much larger than the focal length, *i.e.*, $S_1 \gg f$. On the other side, since m_{Object} for non-macro lenses is very small, one has $S_2 \approx f$, then from Figure 7.2, the camera positions can be determined by

$$S_{2,\mathrm{HR}} - S_{2,\mathrm{LR}} \approx f_{\mathrm{HR}} - f_{\mathrm{LR}}, \tag{7.3}$$

when the focal lengths for HR and LR cameras are approximately computed by Equation (7.2) for the given magnification factor m.

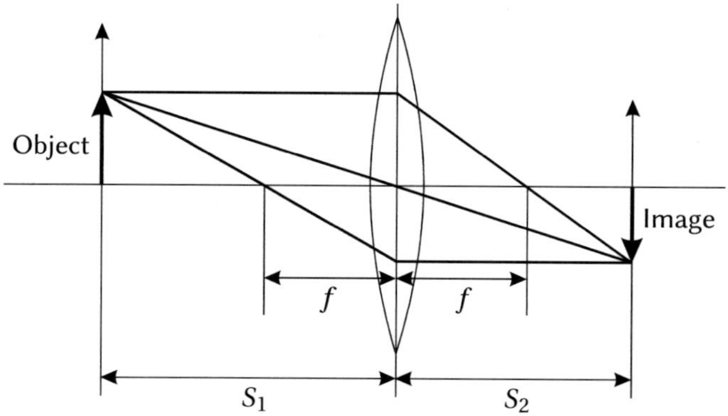

Figure 7.2: Image formation with a thin lens.

However, by virtue of the complex optical elements in real objectives, the thin lens approximation does not always apply. As a consequence, Equations (7.2) and (7.3) do not necessarily hold. Instead of employing prime lenses with the exact focal lengths, zoom lenses are utilized as a workaround, so that the focal lengths can be fine-tuned in the proximity of the theoretical values. An interactive adjustment process is presented in Section 7.1.3.

The built prototype system for the scheme in Figure 7.1 is depicted in Figure 7.3. A 50:50 beam splitter for visible light in the range of 400–700 nm is located at the intersection of the two camera axes. The C-mount cameras possess a large 1/1.2″ CMOS sensor with merely two megapixels (1920 × 1200), which allows for higher Signal-to-Noise Ratio (SNR) thanks to larger pixel size. A wide-angle 4.8 mm f/1.8 prime lens, which serves as the LR lens, and a 12.5–75 mm f/1.2 zoom lens for the HR images are mounted on each camera. The 6× zoom ratio is ideal to experiment with different magnification factors m. The large aperture of both lenses is also fast enough for low-light indoor scenarios, as only half of the light can reach each sensor. In order to mitigate in-plane rotational discrepancy between the pair of images, one camera is installed on a kinetic mounting surface for pitch and roll adjustment.

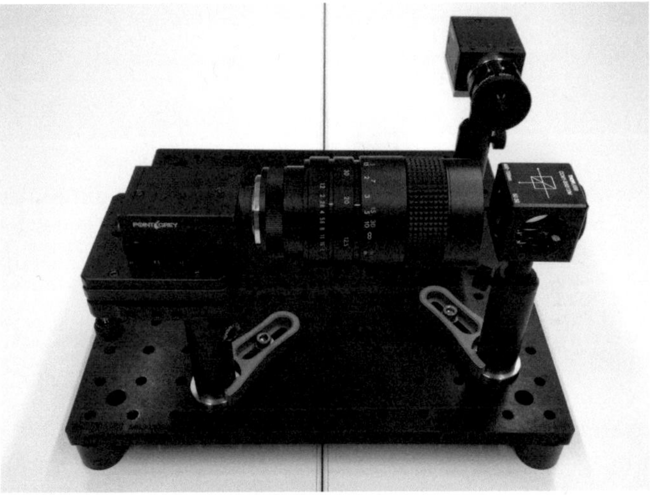

Figure 7.3: Prototype of the proposed camera system.

In summary, the final prototype is able to account for scaling and rotation in the registration process, leaving just the translational offset to be determined algorithmically. As such, concerns that a posterior compensation in scaling and rotation with interpolation could deteriorate the original image quality are addressed.

7.1.3 Image Registration

The hardware prototype in Section 7.1.2 performs a rough presetting of the desired SR ground truth capturing workflow. Raw HR–LR image pairs with approximately the desired magnification factor can be acquired. However, further processing must be done, before the images are ready for evaluation. Since the HR image covers only a small region in the center of the corresponding LR image, the surrounding irrelevant part should be filtered out. In the meantime, fine-tuning of the magnification factor m obtained in Equation (7.2) can also be done in the course of the registration procedure.

Given a coarse alignment in scaling and rotation from the hardware system, only translational motion needs to be estimated, which greatly reduces the degree of freedom (DOF) and computational complexity to exploit the classical but yet powerful Lucas–Kanade algorithm [Bak04a, Luc81, Sze11a], as is already adopted in Section 6.3.3. The objective here is to obtain the update $\boldsymbol{\Delta\theta}$ of the parametrized motion $\boldsymbol{\theta}$ by minimizing the SSE between the fixed template $\mathbf{T}$ and moving image $\mathbf{I}$

$$\sum_{\boldsymbol{\xi}} \|\mathbf{I}(\mathbf{W}(\boldsymbol{\xi};\boldsymbol{\theta}+\boldsymbol{\Delta\theta})) - \mathbf{T}(\boldsymbol{\xi})\|_2^2 \tag{7.4}$$

subject to warping $\mathbf{W}(\boldsymbol{\xi};\boldsymbol{\theta})$ of the pixels $\boldsymbol{\xi}$ [Luc81]. Leveraging Taylor series expansion and the partial derivatives with respect to $\boldsymbol{\theta}$, a closed-form solution can be obtained. Later, it is proved that performing inverse update on the template $\mathbf{T}$ instead of $\mathbf{I}$

$$\sum_{\boldsymbol{\xi}} \|\mathbf{I}(\mathbf{W}(\boldsymbol{\xi};\boldsymbol{\theta})) - \mathbf{T}(\mathbf{W}(\boldsymbol{\xi};\boldsymbol{\Delta\theta}))\|_2^2 \tag{7.5}$$

can substantially boost the efficiency, as the inverse Hessian and steepest descent images can be precomputed at the initial $(\boldsymbol{\xi};\mathbf{0})$ rather than the current iteration $(\boldsymbol{\xi};\boldsymbol{\theta})$ [Bak04a].

Concretely, with a pair of HR–LR images, the template $\mathbf{T}$ is first set as the center of the LR image, or as the ROI detected by some algorithm (*e.g.*, faces by [Vio04]). The moving image $\mathbf{I}$ to be aligned is obtained by downsampling the HR image with the desired magnification factor m. The initial translation $\boldsymbol{\theta}_t^{(0)}$ for $\mathbf{I}$ is set w.r.t. the HR image, or again based on the localized ROI. Subsequently, continuous Lucas–Kanade translational registration is conducted and the result error image is shown to the user. After manual tuning of tip and tilt on the kinetic platform and the focal length f_{HR} for the HR camera, accurate alignment of HR–LR image pairs without subpixel interpolation is computed. The whole image registration procedure is summarized in Algorithm 6.

Algorithm 6: Interactive registration for HR–LR image pairs.

Input: Roughly registered HR–LR image pair
Output: Precisely registered HR–LR image pair

Initialize ROIs for HR and LR images
Crop template **T** from the LR image
Shrink the HR image with factor m as image **I**
Initialize translation $\boldsymbol{\theta}_t^{(0)}$ for **I**
while *not aligned* **do**
    Compute $\boldsymbol{\theta}_t$ using the Lucas–Kanade algorithm
    Crop **I** based on $\boldsymbol{\theta}_t$
    Compare error image of **T** and cropped **I**
    if *in-plane rotation not aligned* **then**
        Adjust tip and tilt of the kinetic platform
    end
    if *magnification not aligned* **then**
        Adjust f_{HR}
    end
end

7.1.4 Image Analysis

As is already studied in Section 6.3.2, the observation model of the conventional image acquisition process for SR turns the HR image $\mathbf{x}$ of dimension $mN_1 \times mN_2$ into the captured LR image $\mathbf{z}$ of dimension $N_1 \times N_2$ with Equation (6.1). The objective of SR is to reversely model the image formation process given the LR image $\mathbf{z}$, which is an ill-posed problem requiring extra knowledge from internal or external sources [Nas14, Wan14a].

In this current task, though, since both the ground truth HR–LR image pairs $\mathbf{x}$ and $\mathbf{z}$ are captured and the motion $\boldsymbol{\theta}$ is compensated for by the image registration process in Section 7.1.3, analysis of the images w.r.t. the unknown blurring kernel $\mathbf{k}$ is a lot easier compared to SR. Akin to Section 6.3.2, manipulation of Equation (6.1) must be performed to convert the intractable convolution and decimation operators into matrix multiplication to allow for further calculation. However, slight modification has to be made w.r.t. the convolution $\mathbf{k} * \mathbf{x}$. Because this time the blurring kernel $\mathbf{k}$ is of interest, it is not transformed into a Toeplitz matrix. Rather for the HR image $\mathbf{x}$, each of its $K \times K$ window is vectorized as a row vector and stacked vertically, which yields a $m^2 N_1 N_2 \times K^2$ matrix $\mathbf{T_x}$. As such, the 2D convolution is replaced again with a matrix multiplication. Thus, Equation (6.1) is equivalent to

$$\mathrm{vec}(\mathbf{z}) = \mathbf{S}_m \mathbf{T_x} \mathrm{vec}(\mathbf{k}_{\mathrm{mirror}}) + \mathbf{n}, \tag{7.6}$$

where the $K \times K$ square blurring kernel $\mathbf{k}$ is mirrored and vectorized into $\mathrm{vec}(\mathbf{k}_{\mathrm{mirror}}) \in \mathbb{R}^{K^2}$.

Assuming independent noise $\mathbf{n}$ with uniform variance facilitates straightforward least squares solution of the blurring kernel $\mathbf{k}$ with MLE by minimizing the SSE

$$\|\mathbf{S}_m \mathbf{T_x} \mathrm{vec}(\mathbf{k}_{\mathrm{mirror}}) - \mathrm{vec}(\mathbf{z})\|_2^2, \tag{7.7}$$

which can also be found in the blind deconvolution literature [Lev11]. A globally optimal solution for the kernel exists by solving for the convex quadratic programming problem [Noc06] in the form of

$$\min_{\mathbf{y}} \left\{ \|\mathbf{A}\mathbf{y} - \mathbf{b}\|_2^2 = \min_{\mathbf{y}} \mathbf{y}^\top \mathbf{A}^\top \mathbf{A}\mathbf{y} - 2\mathbf{b}^\top \mathbf{A}\mathbf{y} \right\}. \tag{7.8}$$

Imposing non-negative and unit ℓ_1 norm constraints ensures a valid estimate of the blurring kernel. Optionally, to resemble Gaussian kernels, an additional symmetry constraint is applicable.

Experimental Analysis

The presented camera system is deployed in an indoor environment to take HR–LR face images for FSR evaluation. A face detector [Vio04] is employed to automatically extract the ROIs from the raw image pairs. The commonly used magnification factor $m = 4$ is chosen as in [Nas14]. The dataset consisting of 31 participants taken at different views, which is made publicly accessible to spur research interest[1].

(a)

(b)

(c)

(d)

Figure 7.4: Center crops of an example pair of (a) HR and (b) LR images captured by the camera system with registered (c) HR and (d) LR ROIs.

An example of the captured and registered images is illustrated in Figure 7.4. By cropping out the background of the LR image, the ROI in Figure 7.4b is roughly equivalent to that of the HR image in Figure 7.4a, with 1/4 of the pixels in both dimensions. The resulting LR face has a width of less than 30 pixels, covering only the central 1.5% of the total 1920 pixels, where optical and chromatic aberration of the 4.8 mm wide-angle lens are negligible, which is critical to the camera system without distortion calibration for being completely free of interpolation.

[1] http://ies.anthropomatik.kit.edu/publ.php?key=ies_2016_qu_capturing

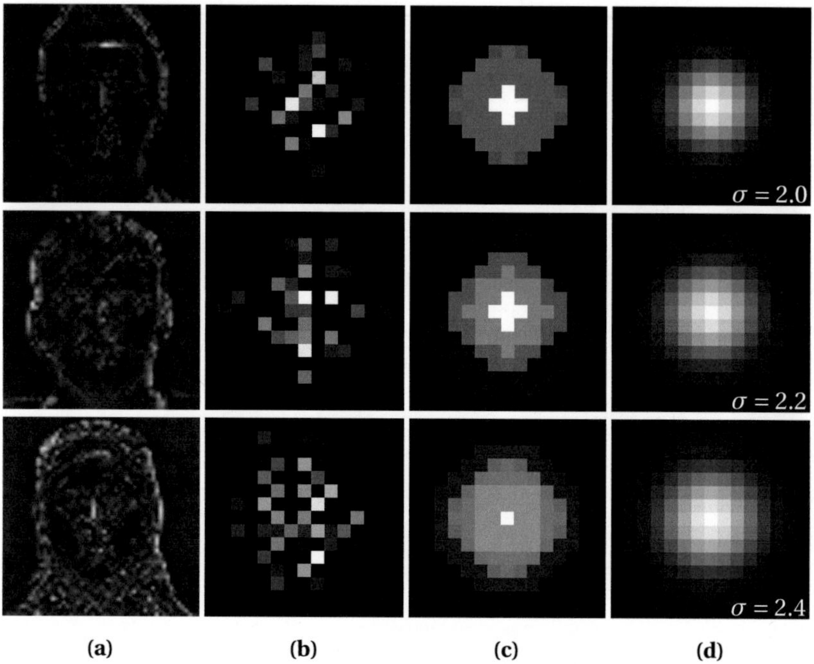

Figure 7.5: Image characteristics analyzed on the sample HR–LR image pairs: (a) the error images between the LR and HR images blurred with the recovered kernels without symmetry constraint in (b) and downsampled, (c) the recovered kernels with symmetry constraint, (d) Gaussian kernels with the lowest HR–LR reconstruction errors.

In Figure 7.5, the blurring kernels for three image pairs are computed and the results are demonstrated. Obviously, the registration process incorporating hardware and algorithmic solutions achieves high precision in both magnification and translational offset. Solely at the silhouette of the faces, where aliasing effects could happen in LR images, more visible error can be spotted in Figure 7.5a. Notably, the true blurring kernels in Figure 7.5b do not resemble the widely accepted Gaussian kernels. By enforcing a symmetry constraint in quadratic programming, the obtained kernels in Figure 7.5c are more akin to the best Gaussian kernels subject to reconstruction error in Figure 7.5d. Moreover, for images with higher error, larger kernel size is seen to smooth out the outliers.

Since noise exists prominently in the data, possibly leading to overfitting the individual kernels to noise, the globally optimal kernels are also recovered by providing $\mathbf{T_x}$ and vec$(\mathbf{z})$ in Equation (7.7) with all HR and LR images respectively, which reveals a more Gaussian-shaped result with vertically a wider span than in horizontal direction (see Figure 7.6a). In terms of Normalized Root Mean Square Error (NRMSE) w.r.t. the dynamic range, the Gaussian kernel in Figure 7.6c is deemed a good approximation. However, note that a slightly wider Gaussian kernel in Figure 7.6d can yield a much higher error. Hereby the unique image properties of ground truth SR data and the importance of accurate blurring kernel estimation for SR algorithms are shown.

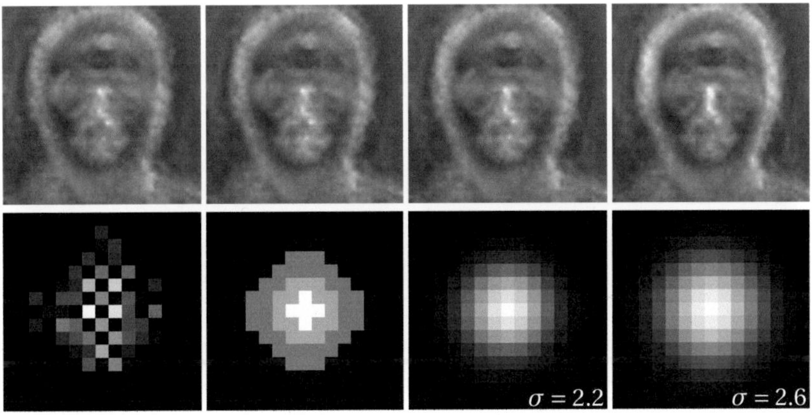

(a) NRMSE: 2.14% **(b)** NRMSE: 2.16% **(c)** NRMSE: 2.18% **(d)** NRMSE: 2.34%

Figure 7.6: Image characteristics analyzed over all HR–LR image pairs. Top row: average error images between all LR and HR images blurred with the kernels in the second row and downsampled. Bottom row: recovered kernels using all HR–LR image pairs (a) without and (b) with symmetry constraint, (c) Gaussian kernel with the lowest HR–LR reconstruction error, (d) an alternative Gaussian kernel.

7.1.5 Summary

The challenges of acquiring a ground truth SR dataset are addressed in this section. A dual-camera imaging system featuring a beam splitter to allow for capturing of HR and LR images with temporal and spatial synchronization is proposed. An interactive process is presented for the nontrivial pixel-accurate registration of the HR–LR image pairs.

The SR community has paid relatively little attention to the impact of the blurring kernels. Those that do often assume Gaussian kernels with the width known beforehand. Hence, the meaning of such ground truth data for SR is justified by the experimental analysis of the unique image characteristics. In the subsequent part of this chapter, the evaluated FSR algorithms are benchmarked on the collected data.

7.2 Experimental Setup

The experimental setup for this chapter regarding evaluation metrics and datasets is elaborated in this section. By reason of the different objectives for the several components of the proposed 3D FSR framework, the respective parts are introduced separately for each submodule.

7.2.1 Evaluation Metrics

Facial Landmark Detection

Since the output of face alignment are the discrete facial landmarks, the overall quality of the methods is commonly evaluated by the distance w.r.t. the ground truth annotations. Among the various metrics found in the literature, the normalized error of the F landmarks is the most widely used one, which has the definition

$$\frac{\sum_{i=1}^{F} \left\| \mathbf{x}_i - \mathbf{x}_i^{\star} \right\|_2}{F \cdot d_{\mathrm{IO}}} \cdot 100\%, \tag{7.9}$$

where $\mathbf{x}_i$ and $\mathbf{x}_i^{\star}$ are the automatically detected location and the ground truth for the facial point i respectively, and d_{IO} is the IOD, *i.e.*, the Euclidean distance between the center of the eyes. This measure can eliminate unreasonable variations caused by different scales of the input faces in comparison with the absolute error [Jin16].

On the basis of the normalized metric for a single image, there are mainly two variants of it for measuring the performance on the entire dataset, *i.e.*, the mean of the normalized errors averaged over all N images, and the Cumulative Error Distribution (CED) curve visualizing the cumulative proportion of the test images with the increase of the normalized error, which is already investigated for the incremental evaluation in Chapter 4. The strength of the CED curve is its robustness against outliers, whereas for the NME, a few samples with extreme errors can have a huge impact on the overall score.

With the dramatic progress of face alignment in the past few years, a normalized error below 5% is conjectured to be close to human level [Yan15b]. On the other hand, some authors consider errors over 10% as failed cases. Thus, the failure rate is a popular measure among the existing work [Bur13, Dan12], too.

3D Face Reconstruction

The 3D face shape reconstruction algorithm in this thesis converts the input set of sparse 2D landmarks into a dense 3D face model. Similar to the 2D case, the recovered shape can be evaluated by the average distance of the P vertices to those of the ground truth 3D shape

$$\epsilon_{\mathbf{s}} = \frac{\sum_{i=1}^{P} \left\| \mathbf{s}_i - \mathbf{s}_i^{\star} \right\|_2}{P} \tag{7.10}$$

in the original size of the 3DMM, which is measured in mm, where $\mathbf{s}_i$ and $\mathbf{s}_i^{\star}$ are the reconstructed and the ground truth 3D coordinates of the ith vertex respectively. In addition to the absolute Euclidean error, the faithfulness of 3D reconstruction is also heavily dependent on the normal of the mesh faces, which measures the resemblance of the two surfaces w.r.t. the orientation of the mesh triangles. Such a metric is defined as

$$\epsilon_{\mathbf{n}} = \frac{1}{T} \sum_{i=1}^{T} \arccos \frac{\mathbf{n}_i \cdot \mathbf{n}_i^{\star}}{\left\| \mathbf{n}_i \right\|_2 \cdot \left\| \mathbf{n}_i^{\star} \right\|_2} \tag{7.11}$$

given the reconstructed and the ground truth normal vectors $\mathbf{n}_i$ and $\mathbf{n}_i^{\star}$ respectively, which can be computed straightforwardly leveraging the cross product of the vectors of the face edges. T denotes the number of triangles of the 3DMM.

In this sense, both the mean shape error $\epsilon_{\mathbf{s}}$ and the mean normal error $\epsilon_{\mathbf{n}}$ are adopted as the benchmark metrics, since they reflect on the reconstruction quality in the vertex and facet perspectives, respectively.

3D Facial Texture Super-Resolution

According to the notation in Table 6.1, SR is able to augment a LR input of $N_1 \times N_2$ pixels by m times in both dimensions into $mN_1 \times mN_2$, which usually has the same size as the HR image. Then, no matter if the LR image is obtained by synthetic downsampling from the HR image or with the dual-camera system in Section 7.1, objective assessment can be made by matching the similarity of the SR output to the HR ground truth. The most frequently used measure for evaluating SR algorithms is probably the Peak Signal-to-Noise Ratio (PSNR), which is closely related to the Mean Square Error (MSE)

$$\epsilon_{\mathrm{MSE}} = \frac{1}{m^2 N_1 N_2} \sum_{i=1}^{mN_1} \sum_{j=1}^{mN_2} \left\| I_{\mathrm{SR}}\left(i,j\right) - I_{\mathrm{HR}}\left(i,j\right) \right\|_2^2, \tag{7.12}$$

where $I\left(i,j\right)$ denotes the value of the pixel $\left(i,j\right)$ in the respective SR or HR images. Correspondingly, the PSNR is in the form of

$$\rho_{\mathrm{PSNR}} = 10 \log_{10} \frac{I_{\max}^2}{\epsilon_{\mathrm{MSE}}} = 20 \log_{10} \frac{I_{\max}}{\epsilon_{\mathrm{RMSE}}}, \tag{7.13}$$

where the Root Mean Square Error (RMSE) is the square root of the MSE in Equation (7.12). $I_{\max}$ stands for the maximum range of image pixels, which, in the case of the common 8-bit color depth, is 255. By virtue of the logarithmic scale, PSNR is reported in dB. Typical values for lossy image compression for wireless transmission, as an example, is between 20 to 30 dB [Tho06]. For an identical image pair, the PSNR is infinite, because the MSE in the denominator of Equation (7.13) is zero.

A vital difference in the SR output of 3D approaches is that only the image part inside the face region is hallucinated (*c.f.* 2D and 3D results in Figures 7.20 and 7.21). Therefore, as is noted in [Jin15] as well, it is more meaningful to consider solely this masked area provided by the fitted 3D model than the entire crop of the face image, which is actually biased concerning the large portion of background pixels (often more than 50%). To this end, another popular Structural Similarity (SSIM) index [Wan04b] measuring image statistics within small windows of the images is not compatible due to the irregular masks. It is noteworthy that the 3D FSR output can be later seamlessly integrated into the interpolated image for better visual appeal.

Like most SR algorithms in the previous work [Wan14b], the 3D FSR algorithm developed in this thesis is applied to the luminance channel only, which is justified by the fact that the human vision system is much more sensitive to variations in intensity than in color [Lee08]. Likewise, evaluation is carried out on the grayscale representation. For color images, the chrominance components are bicubicly upsampled and merged back with the luminance channel processed by SR.

7.2.2 Datasets

Facial Landmark Detection

Apart from the LFPW dataset [Bel11], which is introduced in Chapter 4 for the intermediate evaluation to measure the performance gain w.r.t. each improvement for cascaded shape regression, two more recent and challenging in-the-wild datasets are employed.

- **300-W** is created for the 300 Faces in-the-Wild Challenge [Sag13a], which combines several existing indoor and outdoor datasets, *e.g.*, LFPW [Bel11], AFW [Zhu12] and Helen [Le12], as well as a new collection named IBUG, with annotations of a unified 68-point Multi-PIE markup [Gro10] (see Figure 5.4d). Since the original test dataset is held for future challenges, the whole data are split into a training set of totally 3148 images, consisting of AFW and the training sets of LFPW and Helen, and a test set of 689 images, composed of IBUG and the test sets of LFPW and Helen. Following [Ren14], the 300-W test set is also divided into a common subset of LFPW and Helen, and a challenging subset of IBUG, which contains extremely large variations in pose, expression, occlusion and illumination. An overview of 300-W is given in Table 7.2.
- **COFW** is short for Caltech Occluded Faces in the Wild [Bur13], which complements LFPW [Bel11] with more occluded faces and occlusion annotation for landmarks. All 1,345 training and 507 test images have the same 29-point scheme as LFPW. Note that the occlusion mask is not used to train an occlusion-aware model as in [Bur13]. Instead, standard cascaded regression with exclusively the devised improvements is exploited.

Table 7.2: Overview of the 300-W dataset.

Train		Test		
Dataset	#	Subset	Dataset	#
AFW		Full	LFPW + Helen + IBUG	689
LFPW	3148	Common	LFPW + Helen	554
Helen		Challenging	IBUG	135

3D Face Reconstruction

As opposed to benchmarking 2D landmark detectors, where a plethora of images can be easily crawled from the Internet and annotated by hand or semi-automatically [Sag13b], 3D face datasets are far more difficult to collect, not only requiring expensive and bulky 3D scanners, but involving tedious point cloud registration and a hole filling procedure as well. Therefore, the choice is quite limited. In this work, the high-quality and popular BFM [Pay09] is utilized as the 3DMM.

- **BFM** is built by Paysan *et al.* [Pay09] from the chair of Prof. Thomas Vetter at the University of Basel, who is one of the authors of the pioneering 3DMM paper [Bla99]. The morphable model of BFM is trained with 3D face scans of 100 male and 100 female subjects with an age range from young children to old persons. The registered face model has 53,490 vertices and the resulting 3DMM contains 199 principal modes each for the shape and texture models. Notice that the 200 faces for training PCA are not released. For evaluation purposes, the rendered ten out-of-sample 3D faces included alongside in the dataset are exploited.
- **CMU–PIE** is the abbreviation for the CMU pose, illumination, and expression (PIE) database [Sim02], which is acquired in the 3D room at CMU [Kan98] equipped with multiple cameras and flashes for taking images across pose and illumination simultaneously. CMU–PIE records in total 68 male and female individuals with a wide span of age and ethnicity background. Although there is no 3D information for the faces in CMU–PIE, BFM reconstructs a subset of the faces using the analysis-by-synthesis framework. The recovered 3D shapes with

high precision are regarded as ground truth for benchmarks on real data in addition to the synthetically rendered test subjects in BFM.

3D Facial Texture Super-Resolution

Three publicly available face datasets, ranging from indoor scenarios with controlled pose variation to the outdoor environment with unconstrained conditions, are selected to make qualitative and quantitative assessment of the state-of-the-art FSR systems.

- **Multi-PIE** [Gro10] is the successor of the CMU–PIE database [Sim02]. To further advance researches in facial analysis across pose and illumination, Gross *et al.* address the limitations of CMU–PIE by capturing a larger dataset with more participants across multiple sessions. Since the underlying BFM as the 3DMM for 3D fitting lacks modeling of facial expression and accessories, 120 subjects without glasses appearing in at least two sessions with poses from 0° to 45° (cameras 05_1, 05_0, 04_1 and 19_0) are included in the test subset. The original images are downsized by 50% and cropped according to the face detector [Vio04] as HR data. LR images are blurred with a Gaussian kernel with $\sigma = 2.4$ and subsampled by the scale factor $m = 4$.

  Additionally, a total of 214 Multi-PIE HR shots are employed as the training data for both 2D and 3D methods. Example 3D textures extracted from these images can be seen in Figure 6.2. A fair out-of-sample evaluation in the Multi-PIE experiments is ensured by temporarily excluding the tested subject from the training data.

- **Real-FSR** is the name of the self-collected FSR dataset using the dual-camera setup introduced in Section 7.1, which embodies 31 subjects with yaw and pitch head rotation. Three poses, *i.e.*, frontal, yaw as well as yaw plus pitch, which are abbreviated as F, Y and Y+P respectively in Tables 7.7 to 7.9, are recorded with totally 93 HR–LR image pairs. No preprocessing is needed for Real-FSR as both ground truth LR and HR faces are simultaneously acquired. Upsampling factor is $m = 4$ like in the Multi-PIE experiments.

- **PubFig83** [Pin11] is a refined version of the original PubFig [Kum09], which is made up of a collection of 83 celebrities downloaded from the Internet. The images are cropped by the face bounding boxes and resized to a resolution of 100×100 pixels, which are directly used as the HR ground truth. Altogether 300 images without partial occlusion are chosen to demonstrate 3D FSR primarily in a qualitative point of view. In this sense, the public figures in this dataset are advantageous to verify whether the hallucinated faces are consistent with the actual identities. Following [Jin15], $\sigma = 1.6$ is applied before shrinkage and SR of two to eight times in terms of m.

7.3 Evaluation Results

With the aforementioned metrics and datasets for evaluation, the methods proposed in this thesis are compared against approaches taken from the literature. Evaluation results on 2D alignment, 3D reconstruction and facial texture SR are discussed individually in the respective subsections.

7.3.1 Facial Landmark Detection

Parameters

Before going into details of the face alignment experiments, the technical implementation of the cascaded regression framework is explained. The initial shape for the first cascade stage is generated with the face bounding box either localized by an off-the-shelf face detector [Vio04] for LFPW or included in 300-W and COFW. Rectangular bounding boxes are squared with the mean edge length and their centroids remain unchanged w.r.t. the original ones. Because of the tight bounding boxes provided, the actual face ROIs are expanded by 25% in the directions of the four edges. Afterwards, the mean shape is scaled and centered regarding the normalized square. The feature descriptors are computed initially on 32×32 local support and then projected to the PCA subspace with 98% variance retained to reduce dimensionality. To augment the training data [Xio13], ten perturbed samples per training image, with a standard deviation of 0.05 for translation and scaling, 5° for in-plane rotation, as well as horizontal flipping, are generated. Merely four cascade stages suffice to obtain satisfactory results.

The presented extension of the cascaded regression algorithm has a few parameters that need to be tuned to achieve optimal landmarking accuracy, most notably the regression weight γ and IRLS scaling factor K in Equations (4.9) and (4.14) respectively. γ is responsible for the strength of the regularization, where a higher value penalizes large entries in the regressor.

A sequence of choices for γ in different cascade stages is specified in this test, *i.e.*, constant and monotonically decreasing or increasing values. In IRLS, parameter K controls the weighting matrix $\mathbf{W}^{(s)}$ in Equation (4.14) as well as the convergence speed. In Table 7.3, validation results on LFPW in terms of the NME (with the percentage sign dropped for succinctness) w.r.t. a range of variations for these two parameters are demonstrated, which clearly reveals the outstanding performance with a NME of 3.58% given the parameters $\gamma = [400, 300, 200, 100]$ and $K = 3$. It can be observed that fixing one parameter across identities yields the least average error and highest stability through all test cases against varying values of the other one. It is interesting to see that a decreasing regularization factor γ subject to the cascade stages mostly leads to smaller error in contrast with constant or increasing values, which indicates the necessity of adopting a stronger regularization in early cascades, where significant shape update takes place. The IRLS parameter K, though, tends to have a relatively stable contribution.

Table 7.3: NMEs tested with different IRLS parameters γ and K on LFPW.

γ	K				Mean	Std.
	1	3	5	7		
20	3.74	3.87	3.90	3.94	3.86	0.07
50	3.60	3.72	3.75	3.77	3.71	0.06
100	3.60	3.63	3.65	3.67	3.64	0.03
200	3.68	3.60	3.61	3.62	3.63	0.03
20 ~ 80	3.65	3.73	3.75	3.76	3.72	0.04
50 ~ 200	3.65	3.64	3.66	3.68	3.66	**0.02**
100 ~ 400	3.76	3.64	3.66	3.66	3.68	0.05
200 ~ 800	4.01	3.70	3.69	3.70	3.77	0.13
80 ~ 20	3.62	3.77	3.80	3.83	3.76	0.08
200 ~ 50	**3.57**	3.63	3.66	3.68	3.63	0.04
400 ~ 100	3.65	3.58	3.61	3.62	**3.61**	**0.02**
800 ~ 200	3.90	3.61	3.61	3.62	3.68	0.12
Mean	3.70	**3.68**	3.69	3.71		
Std.	0.13	**0.08**	0.09	0.10		

Regarding the overall performance reported on LFPW, the proposed work (3.58%) is also on par with the best available methods, *e.g.*, Consensus of Exemplars (CE) [Bel11] (3.99%), Explicit Shape Regression (ESR) [Cao12] (3.43%), Supervised Descent Method (SDM) [Xio13] (3.47%), Robust Cascaded Pose Regression (RCPR) [Bur13] (3.5%), Ensemble of Regression Trees (ERT) [Kaz14] (3.8%) and Local Binary Features (LBF) [Ren14] (3.35%). Thus, for the experiments on 300-W and COFW, the parameters above are utilized in favor of those yielding the absolute best result of 3.57%, which might be an exception because $K = 1$ generally gives the worst localization accuracy.

Table 7.4: NMEs and failures on 300-W and COFW.

Method	300-W			COFW	
	Full	Common	Challenging	Error	Failure
ESR [Cao12]	7.58	5.28	17.00	11.2	36%
DRMF [Ast13]	9.22	6.65	19.79	—	—
SDM [Xio13]	7.52	5.60	15.40	—	—
RCPR [Bur13]	8.35	6.18	17.26	8.5	20%
LBF [Ren14]	6.32	4.95	11.98	—	—
CFAN [Zha14a]	—	5.50	—	—	—
HPM [Ghi14]	—	—	—	7.5	13%
RPP [Yan15a]	6.69	5.50	**11.57**	7.5	16%
Baseline	7.40	5.90	13.57	9.9	37%
Proposed	**6.24**	**4.83**	12.02	**6.7**	**10%**
Human	—	—	—	5.6	0%

Comparison

In spite of the state-of-the-art performance on LFPW, it is worth a mention that in consequence of the different size of retrieved data from the URLs released in [Bel11], diverse initialization and restart strategies [Bur13, Cao12], *etc.*, the results are not comparable and conclusive. Particularly, as pointed out in [Wan14a], some deployed face detectors struggle with difficult face images and they are removed from the evaluation, which questionably elevates the average score. Contrarily, 300-W and COFW both provide a fixed number of images and bounding boxes for initializing shapes. Burgos-Artizzu *et al.* [Bur13] note that the performance on standard LFPW is almost saturated, as the lower bound created by human labeling is 3.28%.

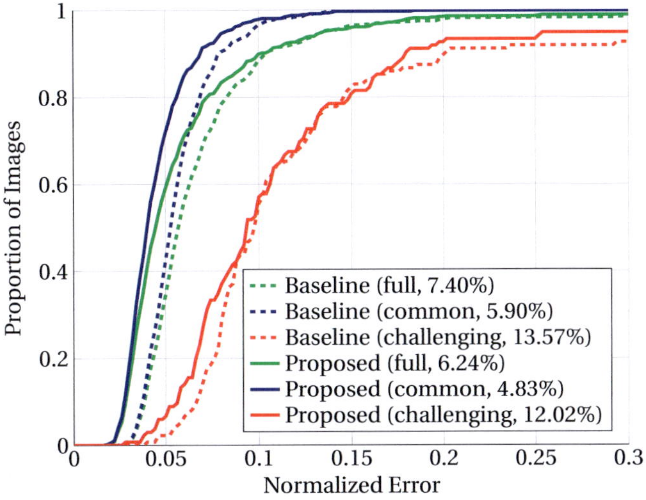

Figure 7.7: CED curves on 300-W. NMEs are reported in parentheses.

The NMEs on 300-W and COFW of existing face alignment approaches, if applicable, are listed in Table 7.4, of which the quantitative results are directly taken from the respective papers. Besides the prior arts evaluated for LFPW, further methods such as Discriminative Response Map Fitting (DRMF) [Ast13] and Coarse-to-Fine Autoencoder Networks (CFAN) [Zha14a] for 300-W, as well as Hierarchical Part Model (HPM) [Ghi14] and Region Predictive Power (RPP) [Yan15a] for COFW are added. Note that the baseline is the own implementation of SDM [Xio13] of this thesis, which performs slightly better than that reported in [Ren14].

Evidently, DRMF within the traditional constrained shape models family (see Section 2.1.2) cannot compete with the rest in the table, which produces the highest error for all test sets on 300-W. RCPR, as an occlusion-aware version of ESR, is of no avail for 300-W, either. Compared to the global binary feature pool in ESR and RCPR learned in the entire face area, the handcrafted SIFT feature of SDM extracted from local patches appears to be more robust for the hard samples. In this spirit, LBF successfully builds on the advantages of the both sides with locally learned binary features, which remarkably improves localization precision for the IBUG subset. By comparison, the developed extension focuses on the essential aspects of the cascaded regression framework, which functions comparably for the challenging subset (12.02% *vs.* 11.98%), and achieves better results for the common images (4.83% *vs.* 4.95%) and the entire set (6.24% *vs.* 6.32%). Moreover, it outperforms DNN-based CFAN on this subset. Interestingly, the power of facial region prediction in RPP is more effective for generic challenging cases in 300-W than for specific occluded faces in COFW.

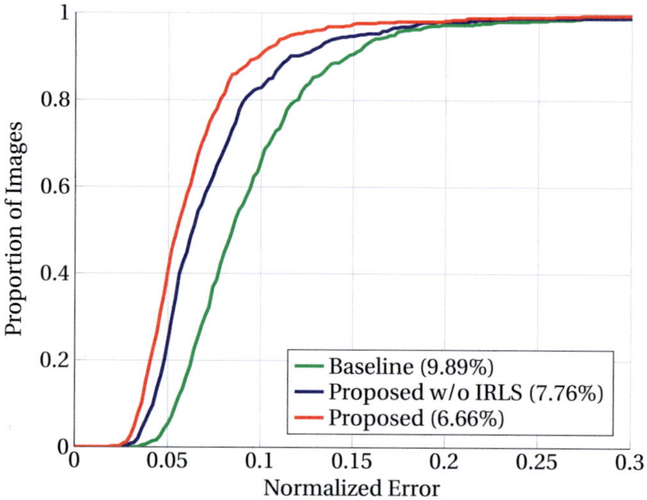

Figure 7.8: CED curves on COFW. NMEs are reported in parentheses.

In contrast to the outcome on 300-W, the occlusion learning in RCPR greatly reduces alignment error and failure w.r.t. its baseline ESR. Two newer algorithms with occlusion handling, *i.e.*, HPM and RPP, make further improvements over RCPR. Surprisingly, even without taking into account the occlusion information in the training, the proposed method outperforms all evaluated systems with explicit occlusion handling, for instance, RCPR by significant error and failure reduction of 20% and 50% respectively.

The CED curves for investigating the performance gain over the baseline are plotted in Figure 7.7 for 300-W and Figure 7.8 for COFW. Obviously, even for the easy subset of 300-W, the blue curve in Figure 7.7 is still worse than Figure 4.7 for the more simple LFPW dataset. The improved cascaded shape regression mainly benefits images of medium difficulty, *i.e.*, with a normalized error of around 5%. It is not until 15% that better convergence emerges for the IBUG subset. That means, it is unable to lower the failure rate for faces with more than 10% fitting error, which consists of over 40% of all IBUG data. On COFW, larger contribution from IRLS is observed than on LFPW in Figure 4.6. The overall localization discrepancy falls 20% from 9.9 to 7.8 for the NME and 50% from 37% to 17% for failure when only ridge regression is applied alongside other presented enhancements. With IRLS, the numbers continue to decrease by approximately 15% to 6.7% and 40% to 10% respectively, which highlights the extra robustness against outliers from partial occlusion brought by IRLS alone.

In Figures 7.9 and 7.10, example detections on the challenging 68-point IBUG subset of 300-W and the 29-point COFW are illustrated. Despite the mixture of diverse unconstrained circumstances including pose, expression, lighting variations and occlusion, good results can still be achieved partly. However, for non-frontal faces, the outline of the face is difficult to localize for lack of distinct features, as discussed in Section 5.3.1. On the other hand, landmarks around the mouth are heavily affected by facial expressions. The extremely large variation considerably impedes their correct localization.

Impact of Image Quality

Facial analysis in the LR domain suffers more seriously than in the HR domain. By studying the prior work in this context, Wang *et al.* [Wan14c] claim that faces smaller than 32 × 24 pixels, or with an IOD under ten pixels, are almost at the limit of the conventional FR systems. Nevertheless, due to various nuisance factors in uncontrolled conditions like image blur, noise and other artifacts, a minimal resolution, or a general definition of LR images is hard to determine, since such a boundary varies among different datasets and methods.

Figure 7.9: Example face alignment results on the challenging IBUG subset of 300-W containing a mixture of unconstrained circumstances including pose, expression, illumination variations and occlusion. Successful fittings and some failure cases are highlighted with green and red frames respectively.

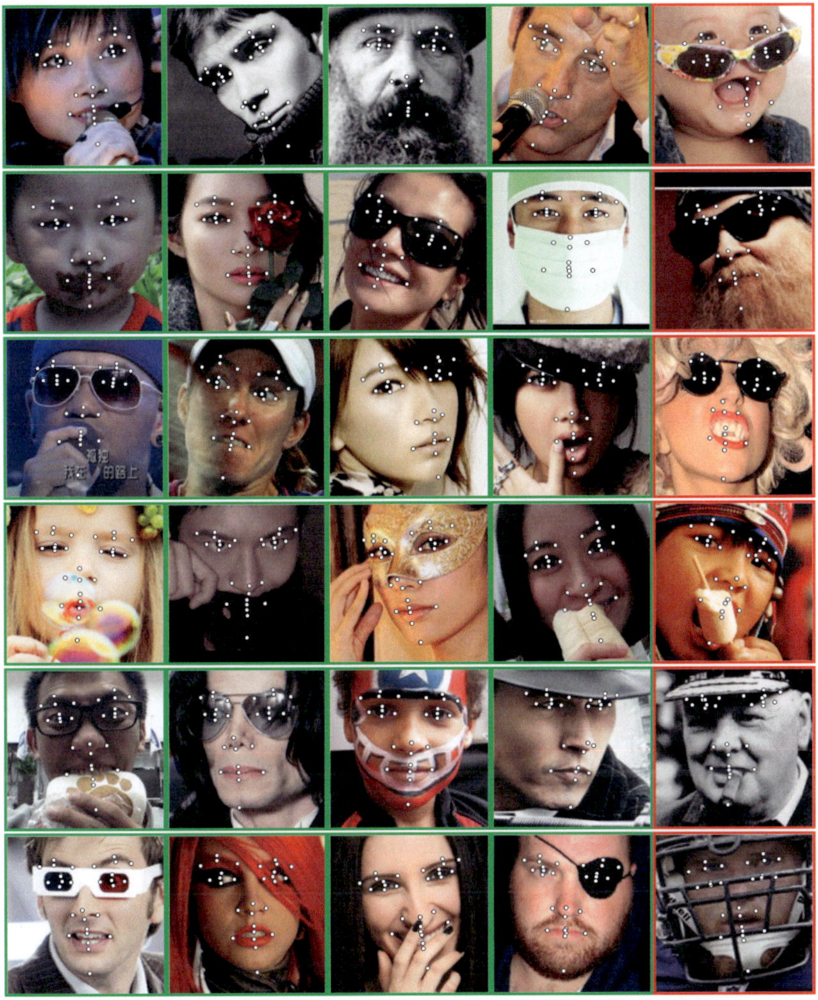

Figure 7.10: Example face alignment results on COFW mainly comprised of occluded faces. Successful fittings and some failure cases are highlighted with green and red frames respectively.

In this part of the evaluation, based on the preliminary research from the author's publication [Her15], a simulation of several crucial degradation aspects on image quality, namely resolution, blurring, noise, and their combination, is conducted and their impact on face alignment as the first module of the entire pipeline is analyzed. The focus here is laid on the effects that are most commonly present in LR scenarios, in particular, spatial resolution, image blur and noise, which also exactly model the LR image acquisition in Equation (6.1). The simulated experiments are carried out in several degradation levels, which are manipulated by the severity index k and a base $s > 1$.

Table 7.5: Control parameters for different effect severities.

k	s^k	w_k (IOD)	σ_k	ζ_k
0	1.0	32 (14.1)	0.64	0.000
1	1.2	27 (11.8)	0.77	0.002
2	1.4	22 (9.9)	0.92	0.004
3	1.7	19 (8.3)	1.11	0.007
4	2.1	15 (6.9)	1.33	0.011
5	2.5	13 (5.8)	1.59	0.015

- **Resolution** is the most critical factor with direct relation to LR imaginary. Starting from a normalized face width of w_0, which is empirically set to 32 pixels following [Wan14c], further downscaled images with a face width of w_k are generated by

$$w_k = s^{-k} \cdot w_0. \tag{7.14}$$

- **Blurring** weakens the high-frequency components and smooths out the gradient transition of structural elements in images. To synthetically blur the base image $\mathbf{I}_0$ with 2D convolution, the widely used Gaussian kernel is adopted, characterized with the standard deviation

$$\sigma_k = \beta s^k \cdot w_0. \tag{7.15}$$

- **Noise** contaminates the source image with random fluctuations of brightness of color values. The typical Gaussian noise is synthesized to deteriorate the original image $\mathbf{I}_0$ in an additive fashion, which can be formulated as

$$\mathbf{I}_k = \mathbf{I}_0 + \zeta\left(s^k - 1\right)\cdot\mathbf{g}, \quad \mathbf{g} \sim \mathcal{N}(\mathbf{0}, \mathbf{I}_{\mathrm{id}}), \tag{7.16}$$

where the random noise $\mathbf{g}$ follows the normal distribution with zero mean and unit variance.

Six levels of degradation are used to evaluate the landmark detection performance. Besides the simulation of the individual effects, a combination of them according to the image formation model defined in Equation (6.1) is exploited, too. The scaling factors β and ζ for image blur and noise are chosen in such a way that realistic deteriorations can be reflected on. With this in mind, $\beta = 0.02$ and $\zeta = 0.01$ are picked, which, together with the base value $s = 1.2$, leads to the parameters in Table 7.5. Sample images from the LFPW dataset are depicted in Figure 7.12.

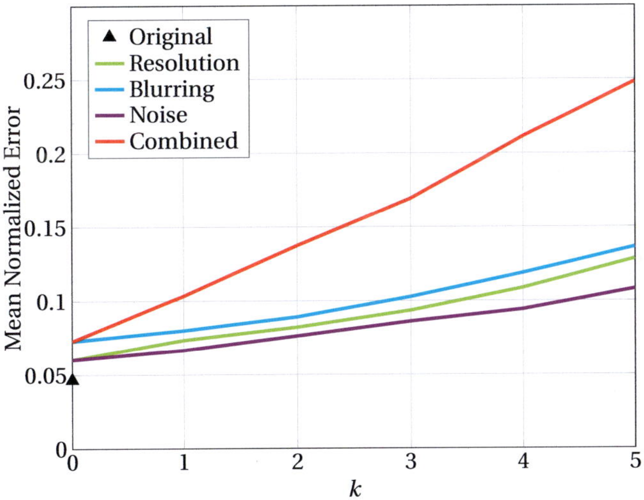

Figure 7.11: Mean alignment errors w.r.t. different kinds and severities of image quality degradation on LFPW.

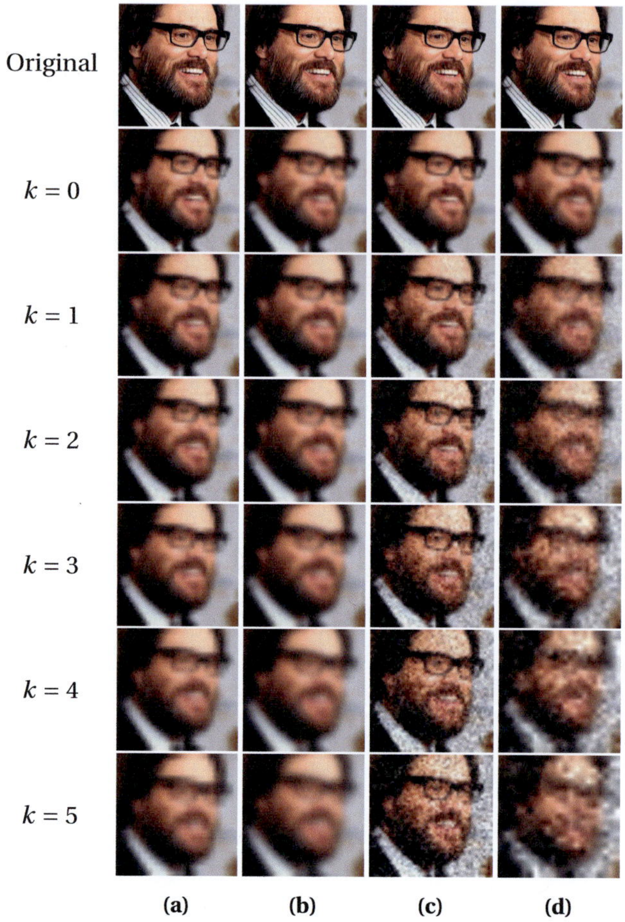

Figure 7.12: Effects of several image quality degradations: (a) resolution, (b) blurring, (c) noise, (d) all combined. The first row shows the original image. Severity level k increases from the second row on.

Figure 7.11 shows how the accuracy of the presented face alignment algorithm trained on 300-W drops with increasing severity on the 68-point LFPW subset of 300-W [Sag13a] (*c.f.* the initial 29-point LFPW in [Bel11]). Because even at the 0th grade, the blurring operation in Equation (7.15) produces a non-zero σ, the starting error at $k = 0$ is slightly higher than the green and the purple curves standing for resolution and noise respectively. Similarly, the NME for the original images marked with a triangle is lower (under 5%) than for the images rescaled to a face width of $w_0 = 32$ (around 6%). As k goes up, the localization precision against single degradation begins to fall gradually with approximately the same rate. From $k = 3$ on, resolution and blurring simultaneously cause more damage with a more steep slope, while the noise curve barely surpasses the 10% mark at the highest level $k = 5$. The reason behind is that in spite of the strong and detrimental visual impact from image noise, there is a relatively good chance to faithfully identify the contour of the eyes under the glasses in the last image of Figure 7.12c compared to Figures 7.12a and 7.12b with fewer details. As expected, combining all three types of degradation almost doubles the error for large k. However, the extreme image quality and up to below six pixels of IOD renders the landmark detection task challenging even for humans.

In summary, the proposed cascade shape regression extension demonstrates stability and robustness against a number of adverse factors w.r.t. the image quality, including resolution. Nonetheless, the post-refinement step developed in Section 6.3.3 is still a complementary and compelling feature for reliable FSR.

7.3.2 3D Face Reconstruction

Parameters

Unlike the cascaded shape regression for localizing fiducial facial feature points, the landmark-based 3D face model reconstruction does not feature a training procedure to learn the regressors for the shape update. Thus, the parameters are only involved in the inference stage, more specifically, during the LM–ICP optimization.

Instead of operating in the continuous 3D shape space for most part of the algorithm, DT works on the discrete image lattice with the contour lines drawn on it (see Figure 5.8b). Hence, the dimension of the DT image is set to 300×300, which is adequate to guarantee reconstruction precision without slowing down the method. The ℓ_2 regularization parameter for the least squares is $\eta = 10^6$ according to [Bla04] in order to balance between person-specific modeling in contrast to the mean shape of the 3DMM and overfitting to noise.

Table 7.6: Influence of the number of LM–ICP iterations on the 3D mean reconstruction errors.

# LM–ICP iterations	1	3	5	10	20	30	40	50
$\epsilon_{\mathbf{s}}$ (mm)	5.49	5.47	5.49	5.48	**5.45**	5.47	5.47	5.47
$\epsilon_{\mathbf{n}}$ (°)	9.32	9.27	9.28	9.28	**9.25**	**9.25**	**9.25**	**9.25**

Another variable directly related to LM–ICP is the number of iterations for the optimization process. The Euclidean distance and the deviation of the normal direction of the mesh faces against the ground truth BFM scans, averaged over all tested subjects and poses, are listed in Table 7.6. Interestingly, even with a single iteration of LM–ICP, the performance is almost on par with that of the best option. With an increasing number of iterations, the least errors in both shape and normal, despite merely marginal difference, are reached after 20 iterations, which costs approximately one second, still orders of magnitude faster than the analysis-by-synthesis 3DMM fitting framework [Bla99, Rom03, Rom05] with over one minute. Therefore, fast convergence and stability of LM–ICP are hereby demonstrated.

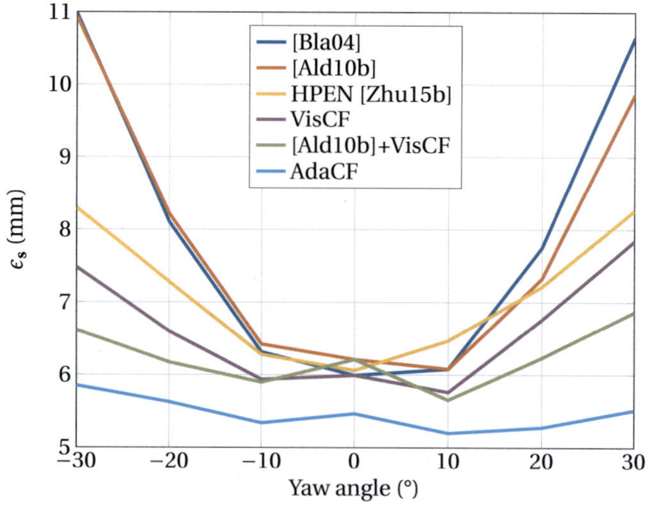

Figure 7.13: Mean 3D shape error in given poses, averaged over ten BFM sample faces.

Comparison

The two algorithms introduced in Chapter 5, coined Visible Contour Fitting (VisCF) (see Section 5.3.1 and [Qu14]) and Adaptive Contour Fitting (AdaCF) (see Section 5.3.3 and [Qu15d]), are evaluated.

Results on BFM The first experiments to measure the efficacy of the devised occlusion-aware shape reconstruction approaches against the prior arts are conducted on BFM. Each of the ten 3D face scans for testing is rendered in seven poses of yaw rotation from −30° to 30° with 10° interval. 68 facial feature points of the rendered images are detected with the cascaded shape regression developed in Chapter 4. The 3D inner and contour vertices conforming to the 2D correspondences are annotated offline, as is illustrated in Figures 5.2 and 5.7a, respectively.

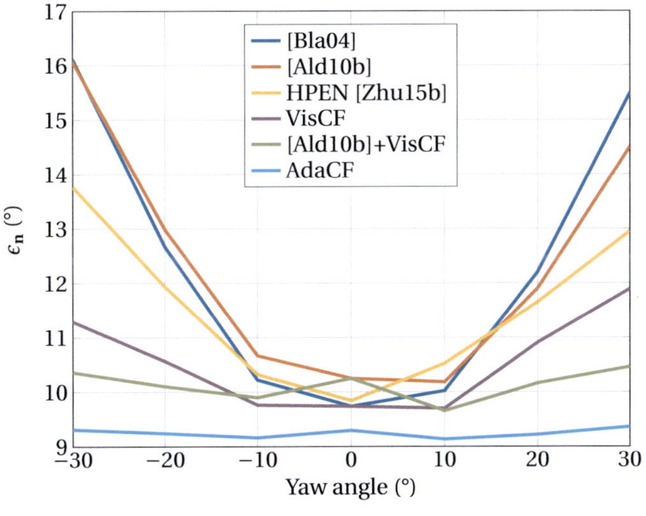

Figure 7.14: Mean normal direction error in given poses, averaged over ten BFM sample faces.

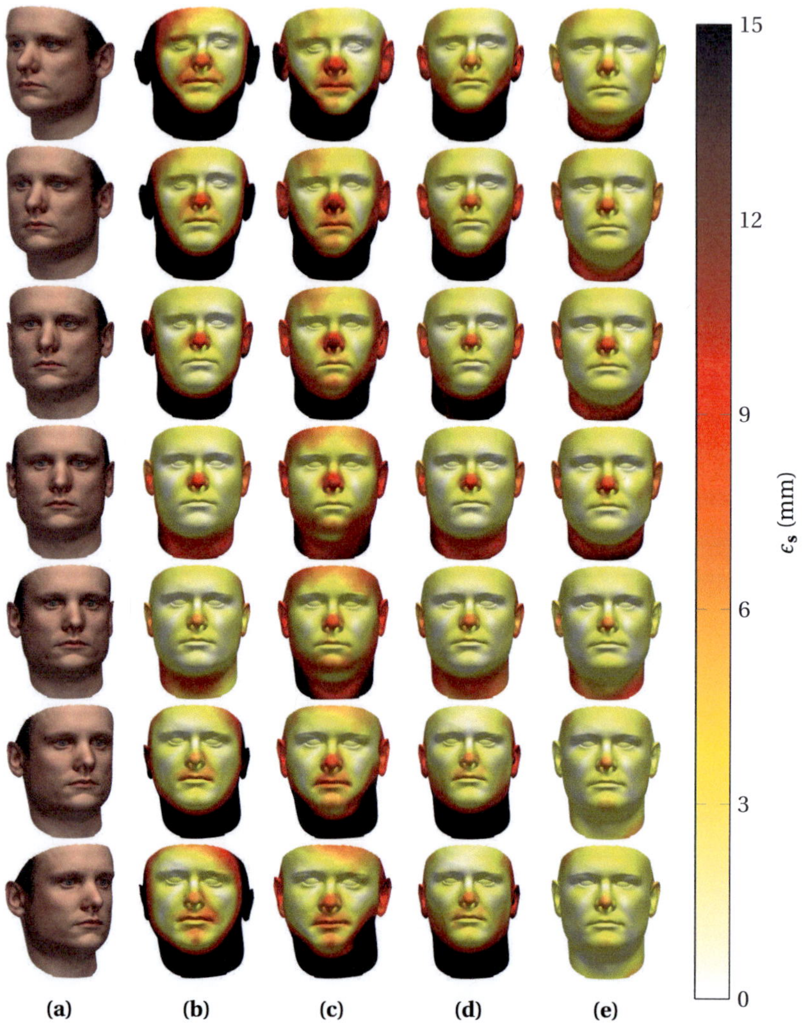

Figure 7.15: BFM sample face No. 4 in (a) and its reconstruction error maps of (b) [Bla04], (c) HPEN [Zhu15b], (d) VisCF and (e) AdaCF.

The basic method [Bla04] takes all 2D landmarks to model the face shape, which is conjectured to be flawed for non-frontal poses. Its variant [Ald10b] relaxes the uniform variance assumption in [Bla04] w.r.t. all landmarks. The uncorrelated Gaussian noise in feature point location in Equations (5.5) and (5.6) is boiled down to generalization error in the model. The individual noise variances are obtained by projecting the out-of-sample face scans onto the PCA shape model to approximate the closest possible face model in a least squares sense, and subsequently computing the mean Euclidean errors of all samples for each of the points. Both [Bla04] and [Ald10b] are implemented in this thesis. Concerning [Ald10b], the noise variances for the 68-point labeling are calculated with the ten BFM test faces. Considering that [Ald10b] and VisCF are mutually non-exclusive, integrating both approaches makes it possible to build a strong baseline, which is denoted [Ald10b]+VisCF. Moreover, the state-of-the-art High-fidelity Pose and Expression Normalization (HPEN) published lately in [Zhu15b] is also taken into consideration. Similar to AdaCF in this work, HPEN exploits the parallel auxiliary points for *horizontal* landmark marching on the occluded half of the face, however, without the DT to facilitate flexible *vertical* movement on the facial contour. The original source code of HPEN released by the authors is adopted[1].

On the basis of the mean 3D shape errors w.r.t. yaw angles plotted in Figure 7.13, clear "U"-shaped curves are seen in the cases of [Bla04] and [Ald10b], which do not take into account the correspondence mismatch of contour vertices at all and thus fail at large angles as anticipated. Employing simple occlusion handling by discarding the invisible contour points in VisCF shows enhanced accuracy for these cases. In contradiction to the theoretical advantage of separate landmark variance modeling in [Ald10b], it is of no avail alone to cope with incorrect correspondence by pose variation. But interestingly, the incorporation of VisCF, namely [Ald10b]+VisCF, turns out to provide remarkable added value to establish itself as the best method among all compared ones, since the assumption in [Ald10b] is only applicable to the visible feature points, which is here validated by VisCF for the automatic landmarking results. Unexpectedly, HPEN struggles with increasing yaw angles, demonstrating merely minor improvement over [Bla04]

[1] http://www.cbsr.ia.ac.cn/users/xiangyuzhu/projects/HPEN/main.htm

and [Ald10b], and is outperformed by both VisCF variants, which implies the necessity of AdaCF to extra model the localization ambiguity *along* the facial contour. By contrast, AdaCF adaptively deals with all contour features and achieves pose-invariant 3D face shape reconstruction with the lowest errors and the most stable error curves across all tested poses. Even for frontal faces, the precision is still higher than the rest, which is attributed to the flexible contour fitting with the continuous feature using DT rather than the discrete point feature easily contaminated by complex landmark discrepancy owing to changing head pose. In Figure 7.14, the mean normal direction errors reveal analogous curves as in Figure 7.13. Note that in both graphs, ±10° sometimes yields better results than the frontal pose. This conforms to the outcome in [Bla03]. An explanation would be that, slight rotation of the head does not impair the face alignment accuracy, but has instant influence on the 3D information, which allows for better inference of the depth, *e.g.*, for the nose.

To help understand the curves in Figures 7.13 and 7.14, fitted face models are depicted in Figure 7.15. The 3D shape error is rendered as skin texture using heat maps on the reconstructed faces respectively. [Bla04] fails to recover the facial form starting from already 10° of yaw angle. VisCF undergoes less performance degradation with increasing head rotation and plausible shapes can be generated at 30°. Nevertheless, reconstruction quality of both the outer area and the inner structure is still heavily limited by not leveraging the valuable self-occluded information and the flawed fixed correspondence on the facial contour. In contrast, superior and constant performance invariant to pose changes is achieved by AdaCF, which matches the quantitative evaluation in Figure 7.13. Although there are no landmarks in the neck and ear region, the error there from AdaCF is massively smaller than from the other approaches. This phenomenon suggests that the possibility of freely moving along the contour prevents skewing these areas, which is unfortunately the case for the fixed 2D–3D mapping scheme.

Results on CMU–PIE The encouraging outcome on the BFM test faces is now verified on CMU–PIE. Unlike the synthetically rendered face images in BFM with just ten samples, CMU–PIE is composed of real capturings in a lab environment with 68 enrolled persons (*c.f.* Figures 7.15a and 7.18a). Given the fact that the cameras deployed in CMU–PIE are positioned approximately 22.5° apart horizontally, five yaw angles from −45° to 45° are adopted for the experiments. However, BFM only releases fitted face models for three poses on CMU–PIE, *i.e.*, 0°, 22.5° and 90°. Hence, the BFM reconstruction of 22.5° is selected for each person as the ground truth by virtue of the aforementioned reason.

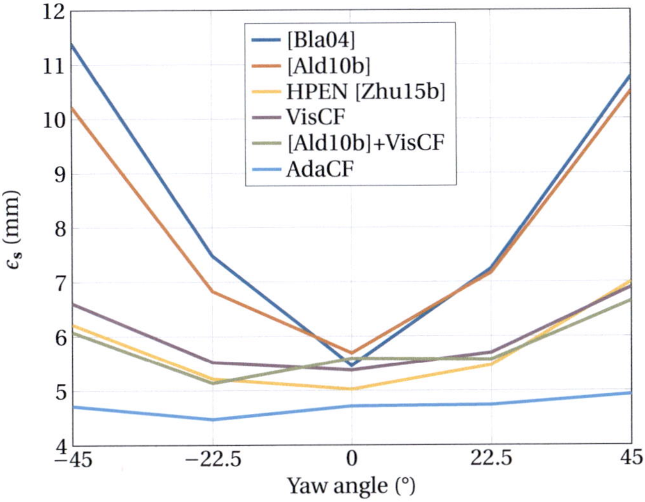

Figure 7.16: Mean 3D shape error in given poses, averaged over 68 faces on CMU–PIE.

The overall shapes of the curves in Figures 7.16 and 7.17 resemble that on BFM in Figures 7.13 and 7.14. [Ald10b] yields marginally lower shape and normal direction errors, both within 1 mm and 1°, in comparison with the basic [Bla04] except for the frontal case. The gap between VisCF and [Ald10b]+VisCF is much smaller on CMU–PIE, which comes down to the fact that the individual generalization errors learned from the *in-sample* BFM test faces are less beneficial to the *out-of-sample* CMU–PIE faces. For the state-of-the-art HPEN method, the huge competitive disadvantage in BFM is finally rectified on the real face images. It has comparable shape error and slightly better fidelity in facet orientation w.r.t. [Ald10b]+VisCF for non-frontal poses. In spite of its lack of continuous feature on the facial contour, the performance on frontal faces is very close to AdaCF, presumably owing to the different parameter and annotation settings in their own implementation. Nonetheless, AdaCF still tops the benchmark with high robustness against head rotation up to 45°. The absolute shape error in Figure 7.16 is even smaller than that in Figure 7.13. But it is worth noting that this is in part caused by the different references in the tests, *i.e.*, the registered 3D scans in BFM *vs.* the 3DMM fittings in CMU–PIE.

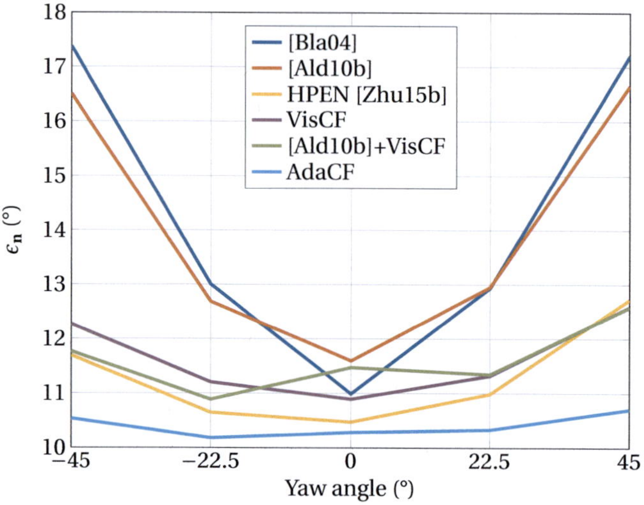

Figure 7.17: Mean normal direction error in given poses, averaged over 68 faces on CMU–PIE.

Qualitative illustrations of the CMU–PIE reconstructions with HPEN, VisCF, [Ald10b]+VisCF and AdaCF on CMU–PIE can be exemplarily found in Figure 7.18. To visualize the recovered face models of pure occlusion-aware algorithms, the weak baseline [Bla04] in Figure 7.15 is replaced with the stronger [Ald10b]+VisCF. HPEN, in contrast to the proposed VisCF and AdaCF, still shows signs of struggling with large yaw rotation of ±45°. The forehead and cheek areas are more twisted. By ignoring the self-occluded feature points, VisCF and [Ald10b]+VisCF leave the shape constraints on the entire face to the underlying 3DMM, which successfully mitigates the skewed effect in Figure 7.18b, at the cost of information loss. For instance, the reddish vertical stripes near the mouth in Figures 7.18c and 7.18d reveal the lowest quality within the face region, which are exactly located on the discarded face silhouette when rotated. On the contrary, AdaCF effectively takes advantage of it to produce highly precise face models. The only visible distinction between VisCF and [Ald10b]+VisCF lies in the nose of the frontal face, which is the consequence of the deficient noise modeling of [Ald10b] for this specific subject in CMU–PIE. Notice that AdaCF also generates the most stable and similar shapes across pose. The nose of HPEN, as an example, leans towards left or right for non-frontal faces.

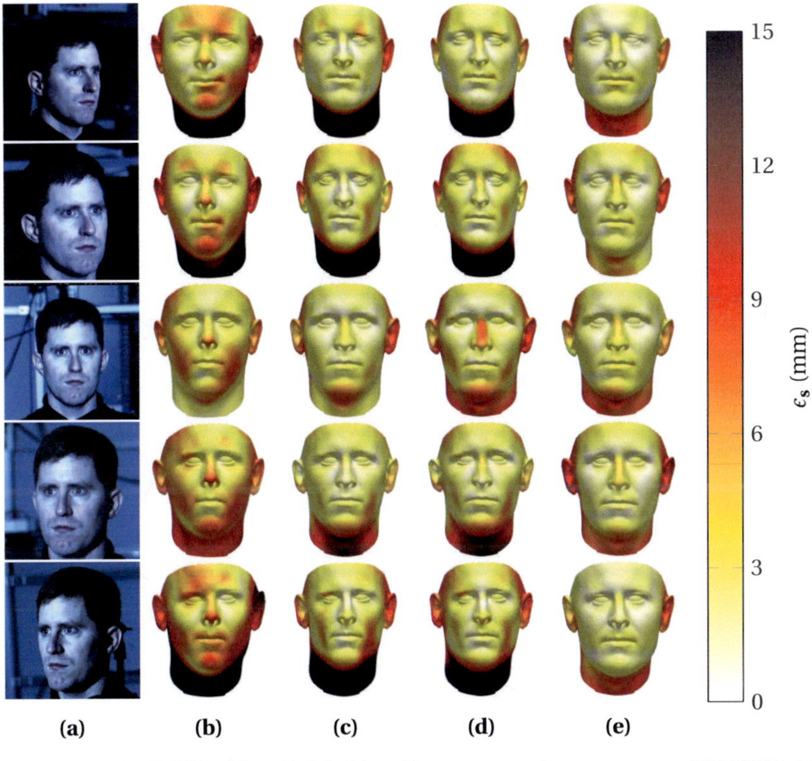

Figure 7.18: CMU–PIE subject 4068 in (a) and its reconstruction error maps of (b) HPEN, (c) VisCF, (d) [Ald10b]+VisCF and (e) AdaCF.

7.3.3 3D Facial Texture Super-Resolution

Comparison

Head-to-Head *vs.* [Mor09] In the first part of the extensive benchmark against the state of the art, the presented 3D FSR work is qualitatively compared with Mortazavian *et al.* [Mor09], which is one of the first ever 3D approaches in the literature.

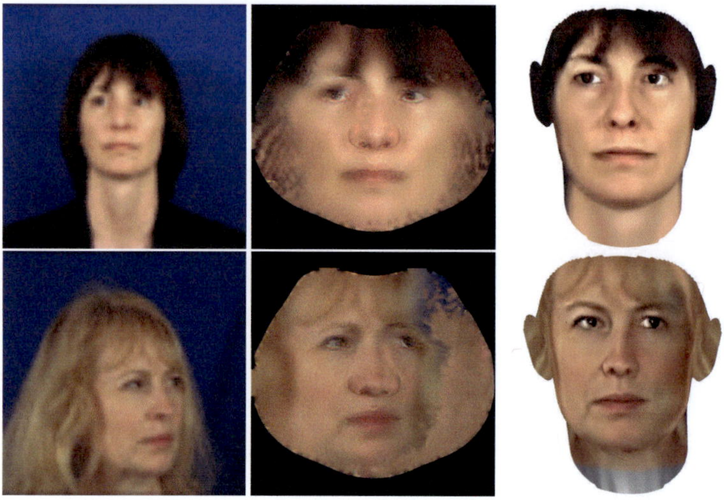

(a) (b) (c)

Figure 7.19: Qualitative comparison against Mortazavian *et al.* [Mor09]: (a) LR input images and 3D FSR outputs from (b) [Mor09] and (c) the proposed work respectively.

Back to Section 6.2, an explanatory experiment showing the potential damage of warping the LR input image as in [Mor09] is done in Figure 6.1 to argue the benefit of the resolution-aware fitting strategy in this thesis. Here in Figure 7.19, a comparison regarding the FSR quality is provided, where the LR images and the FSR results of [Mor09] are directly imported from [Mor13]. With an IOD of around 12 pixels, the XM2VTS [Mes99] images are considered less challenging. Nevertheless, the hallucinated faces in Figure 7.19b from [Mor09] are quite blurred with apparent color artifacts.

The faces in Figure 7.19c, on the contrary, are not only sharper, but also full of details, *e.g.*, in the nasolabial folds of both subjects, which might be already lost during the LR texture extraction stage in [Mor09]. Furthermore, in the bottom example with a head pose of 45°, the fitting error along the silhouette causes gross errors in the facial texture to [Mor09] starting from the left eye horizontally, whereas the devised patch-based 3D FSR fills visually pleasing and homogeneous skin texture in this area. It is noteworthy that the discontinuity close to the left ear is outside the FSR mask, where the super-resolved texture is seamed with that from the mirrored visible half of the face [Qu15a].

Results on Multi-PIE and Real-FSR The performance of the 3D FSR framework in this thesis is first evaluated against prior arts on Multi-PIE and Real-FSR. For 2D methods [Inn13, Ma10, Tap12, Yan13b], the respective authors' original code is employed. Following [Jin15], the convex approach [Inn13] can be regarded as a performance indicator for the Bayesian algorithm [Tap12], as it is shown to be as good as [Tap12]. The texture-normalized version of 3D MRF is further implemented with the same parameters as in [Des15]. For quantitative evaluation, the 3D-aided 2D FSR using the resolution-aware scheme of Section 6.3.1, abbreviated as 2.5D FSR, is also included. An identical 3D fitting engine, namely AdaCF of Section 5.3, is used for all 2.5D and 3D systems, allowing for a fair and convincing comparison. Experimental results are reported in Table 7.7 and Figures 7.20 and 7.21.

Patch-based FSR using positional subspaces is sensitive to deficient fitting caused by the average LR faces with an IOD of merely six to ten pixels on Multi-PIE depending on head rotation. Improved fitting remarkably boosts the final results for all 2D and 3D methods in Table 7.7, where 3D FSR tops all situations except for the frontal pose on Multi-PIE. Qualitative comparison shows that with increasing yaw angle, the visual advantage becomes prominent where 2D registration suffers from large out-of-plane rotation. Notice that for the last subject of Multi-PIE in Figure 7.20, which has 45° yaw rotation, the 3D pose is not perfectly recovered (*c.f.* the nose of the HR and 3D FSR images), which fortunately can still be tolerated by the patch-based facial texture SR approach to generate a realistic hidden half of the face.

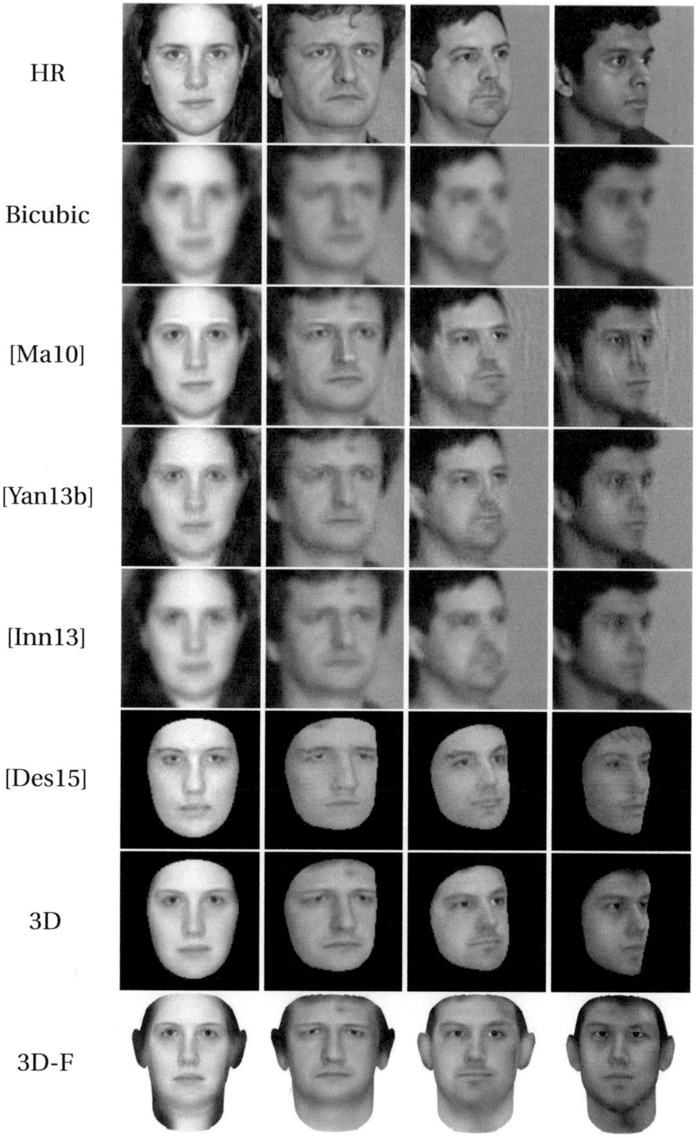

Figure 7.20: Qualitative FSR results on Multi-PIE.

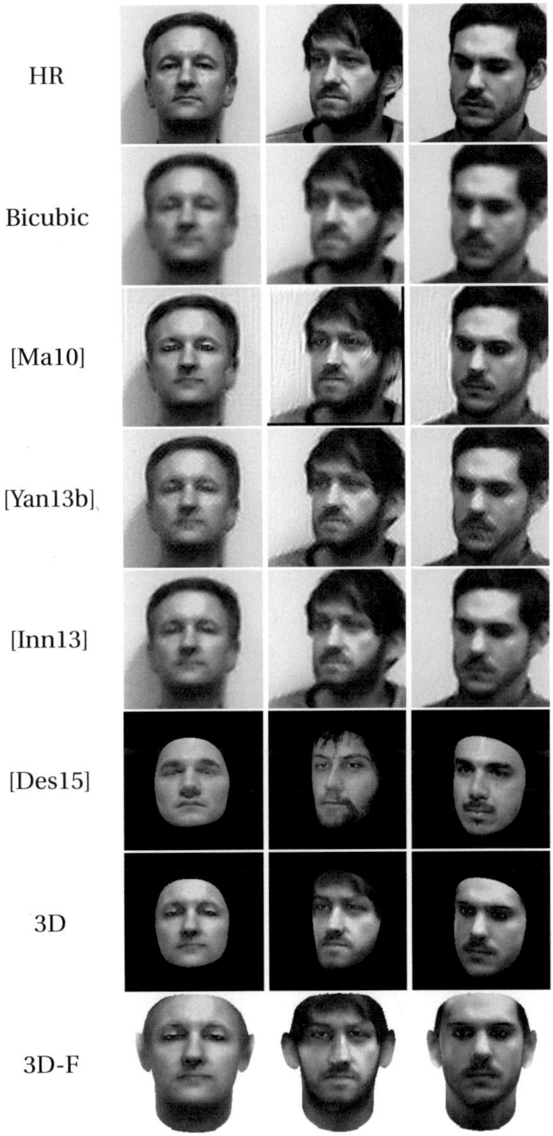

Figure 7.21: Qualitative FSR results on Real-FSR.

Table 7.7: Quantitative FSR results in PSNR (dB) without / with fitting enhancement.

Dataset		Method						
		Bicubic	[Yan13b]	[Inn13]	[Des15]	[Ma10]	2.5D	3D
Multi-PIE	0°	25.60	25.98	26.49	22.10	26.91 / **27.13**	25.92 / 26.25	25.94 / 27.05
	15°	25.49	26.10	26.44	21.52	26.78 / 26.82	26.52 / 26.71	26.56 / **27.15**
	30°	25.27	25.55	26.07	21.38	25.62 / 25.79	25.66 / 26.00	25.69 / **26.35**
	45°	25.27	25.95	26.46	21.34	25.58 / 25.61	26.28 / 26.48	26.31 / **26.62**
Real-FSR	F	26.32	26.02	26.78	18.06	27.11 / 27.04	27.20 / 27.26	27.26 / **27.33**
	Y	25.84	25.71	26.47	16.73	26.16 / 26.35	26.30 / 26.77	26.31 / **26.78**
	Y+P	27.18	26.90	27.82	17.02	27.33 / 27.66	27.50 / 28.03	27.52 / **28.04**

Table 7.8: FR results in identification rate (%) on Multi-PIE and Real-FSR images.

Dataset		Method							
		HR	Bicubic	[Yan13b]	[Inn13]	[Des15]	[Ma10]	3D	3D-F
Multi-PIE	0°	98.3	72.5	87.5	84.2	17.5	**88.3**	85.0	—
	15°	95.0	58.3	75.0	69.2	13.3	70.8	68.3	**80.8**
	30°	62.5	19.2	35.8	27.5	7.5	30.0	30.0	**49.2**
	45°	38.3	12.5	22.5	16.7	7.5	20.0	21.7	**35.0**
Real-FSR	Y	96.8	77.4	80.6	80.6	38.7	83.9	83.9	**100.0**
	Y+P	77.4	67.7	77.4	74.2	29.0	77.4	74.2	**93.5**

On the LR faces of Real-FSR with apparent sensor noise, the frontal case of 3D FSR also outperforms the 2D baseline [Ma10] (*c.f.* the eyes of [Ma10] and 3D FSR in Figure 7.21). By contrast, despite the sophisticated alignment mechanism in [Inn13, Tap12, Yan13b], the output images either are impaired by artifacts and outliers or look blurry. Since the faces in Real-FSR with approximately 12 pixels of IOD are less challenging for most state-of-the-art landmark detectors, such as the one of Chapter 4 here, fitting refinement is less advantageous than for the smaller Multi-PIE faces. Nevertheless, the impact of higher fitting accuracy reiterates the significance for FSR to exploit spatial cues.

As is discussed at the end of Section 6.3.4, the exemplar-based 3D MRF [Des15] generates highly detailed faces, however, with neither realistic appearance nor competitive scores using the simplified image formation model. Apart from the ability of natural frontalization, 2.5D and 3D FSR yield initially almost identical PSNR values by sharing the core fitting and FSR algorithms. The final edge is mainly attributed to the subtle details with improved fitting for 3D FSR, as is revealed in Figures 6.8c and 6.8d.

Results on PubFig83 Figure 7.24 goes beyond controlled environment to testify the robustness on the in-the-wild PubFig83 dataset, where all results except 3D FSR are imported from [Jin15]. Under the challenges of uncontrolled conditions, especially in combination with the faces of as small as approximately six pixels in terms of IOD, the 3D framework in this thesis achieves the most appealing visual quality, surpassing the state-of-the-art [Jin15] in both sharpness and details of facial components with far less training data.

Considering that the picked images in Figure 7.24 from [Jin15] are nearly frontal, well lighted faces, more example results from the 300 subset on PubFig83 are shown in Figures 7.22 and 7.23, which embodies richer variations such as unconstrained poses, expressions and illuminations than in Figure 7.24. Obviously, the entire 3D framework from 2D landmarking to facial texture SR is able to cope with extreme LR scenarios, synthesizing identity-preserving high-quality faces for the celebrity images spanning a variety of age, ethnicity, facial form and style, including beard and makeup.

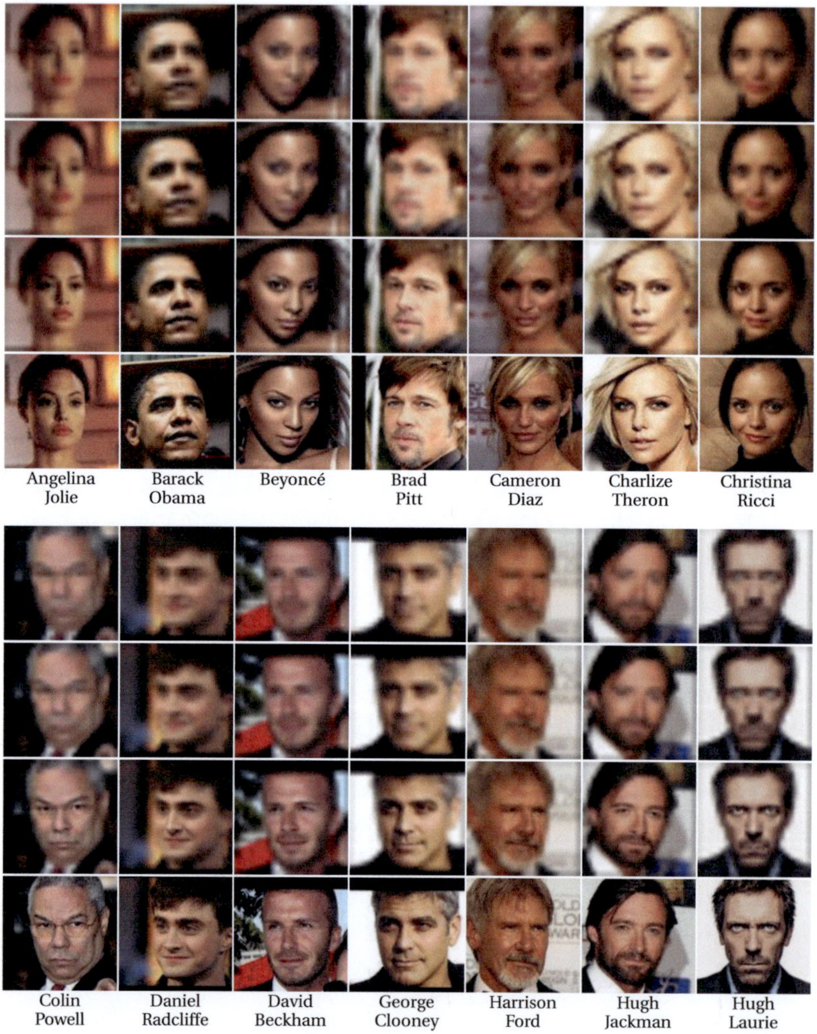

Figure 7.22: Example 3D FSR results on PubFig83. From top to bottom are LR, bicubicly interpolated, 3D FSR and HR images, respectively.

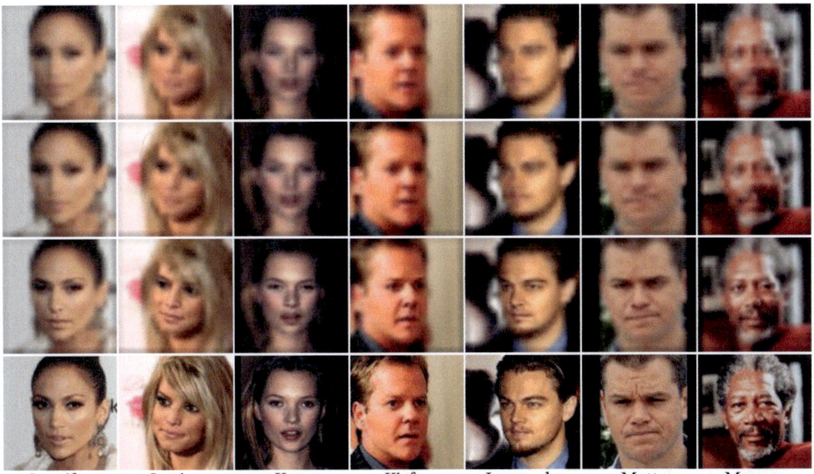

Figure 7.23: Example 3D FSR results on PubFig83 (cont.). From top to bottom are LR, bicubicly interpolated, 3D FSR and HR images, respectively.

In spite of the largely positive results on PubFig83, a couple of flaws can yet be identified. On account of the BFM as the utilized 3DMM with exclusively neutral facial expression, hallucination of novel expressions like in the Will Smith example of Figure 7.24 could lead to artifacts on the mouth. This can be bypassed by adding expression variations, *e.g.*, the FaceWarehouse [Cao14a] as in HPEN [Zhu15b]. Furthermore, missed details such as the glasses of Colin Powell and the aging effect of Morgan Freeman in Figures 7.22 and 7.23 respectively are owed to the extreme resolution in the LR images, where they are completely blurred out from the few remaining pixels. Lastly, the inconsistent gaze directions of Shakira causes poor visual impression as well.

Figure 7.24: Qualitative FSR results on PubFig83 images of Colin Farrell, Ben Affleck, Reese Witherspoon and Will Smith extracted from [Jin15].

Application to Face Recognition

FR is performed with the previous FSR results as probe images to verify the practical application of FSR. Frontal images of the so far unused second subset of the 120 Multi-PIE images serve as gallery. For the Real-FSR data, since only one session is present, the frontal faces are selected instead. Results are reported for each probe set as identification rate, denoting the fraction of probe images which is correctly recognized.

Following [Aho06], faces are first divided into local regions and each region is described by an LBP histogram. All regions are then concatenated to build the final face descriptor. Afterwards, the element-wise square root [Wol08] is computed to enable the matching of $\text{LBP}_{8,1}^{u2}$ patterns with eight sampling points of radius one and uniform patterns with at most two bitwise transitions [Aho06] in the Hellinger space [Ara12].

Evidently, *all* SR images except 3D MRF [Des15] contribute to higher FR scores w.r.t. bicubic interpolation, justifying the importance of FSR for the LR recognition problem. Overall, the identification rate in Table 7.8 is in accordance with the promising FSR outcome. By frontalizing the 3D FSR faces (referred to as 3D-F in Table 7.8), which can be seen in the last rows of Figures 7.20 and 7.21, a significant boost is observed and nearly perfect matching scores are achieved on Real-FSR, even outperforming HR images by a large margin for faces with only moderate yaw and pitch rotation. The synthesized frontal 3D facial texture is hereby verified to be helpful to FR.

Impact of Fitting Enhancement

It is worth noting that as opposed to some 2D and 3D work [Des15, Ma10] where alignment is done manually or on HR images, a more pragmatic setup is adopted in the experiments of this thesis to carry out face alignment and 3D fitting on LR data. To quantitatively evaluate the benefit of 3D fitting enhancement, the NMEs of 2D inner facial landmarks from Equation (7.9) are reported in Table 7.9.

Table 7.9: NMEs for inner facial landmarks without (✗) and with (✓) fitting enhancement on Multi-PIE and Real-FSR.

	Multi-PIE				Real-FSR		
	0°	15°	30°	45°	F	Y	Y+P
✗	**4.23**	**4.53**	6.69	8.49	3.76	5.12	4.72
✓	4.28	4.75	**6.19**	**7.72**	**3.57**	**4.84**	**4.45**

Generally speaking, compared to the initial results, refinement does successfully increase landmarking accuracy. Since the improved landmarks are projected back from the 3D shape, a discrepancy could have negative impact on the error numbers. That means, except for the near-frontal poses on Multi-PIE, this extra stage demonstrates excellent capability to correct the error-prone fitting initialized on LR faces, which is proved to be crucial in the previous FSR experiments.

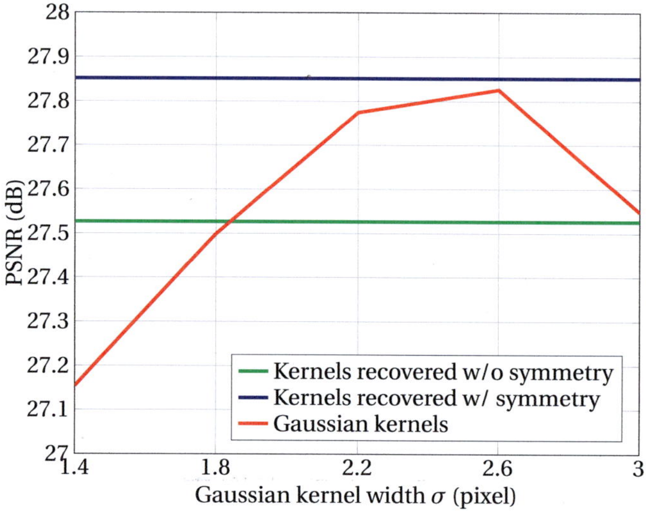

Figure 7.25: Impact of blurring kernels on PSNR values on Real-FSR.

Impact of Blurring Kernels

This study aims to explore the importance of having a correct blurring kernel for SR. The question is extensively analyzed and confirmed in the prior work by Efrat *et al.* [Efr13] using synthetic LR data. The Real-FSR dataset recorded in this thesis with ground truth HR and LR pairs, though, appears to be an ideal instrument to answer if this finding stands for real LR images. Figure 7.25 plots curves of PSNR values with different kernels applied to 3D FSR. The green and blue straight lines are results from individual kernels in Figures 7.5b and 7.5c reconstructed by solving the quadratic programming problem in Equation (7.8) without and with symmetry constraint respectively. The red curve corresponds to standard Gaussian kernels of the given widths, which indicates the optimal standard deviation σ for Real-FSR is around 2.2 to 2.6 pixels. Larger or smaller widths cause detrimental effect to the PSNR values of FSR, which becomes more severe with higher discrepancy w.r.t. the target width. On the other side, the kernels computed with symmetry are at least as good as the optimal Gaussian kernels, which partly validates the correctness of the empirical image formation model in Equation (7.6) employed throughout this thesis and in the SR literature [Par03, Yan10a]. The subpar performance from the asymmetrical kernels probably stems from overfitting due to registration error around the contour of fine structures, *e.g.*, hair (see Figure 7.6), whereas FSR is benchmarked within the facial masks.

(a) (b) (c) (d) (e)

Figure 7.26: Qualitative robustness analysis against motion blur on the PubFig83 image of Kate Winslet. The top row shows the intermediate blurred images with the overlaid (a) Gaussian or (b)–(e) motion blur kernels of 0° to 135°. The bottom row illustrates the HR and the respective 3D FSR results.

Figure 7.26 tries to investigate whether the 3D extension of the LR imaging formulation in Equation (6.5) is capable of dealing with practical cases with non-Gaussian blurring kernels. The top row displays the intermediate images blurred with the respective kernels on the lower right corners before being downscaled by $m = 4$ to the LR inputs for 3D FSR, where the smear effect of the facial components is clearly visible. This tougher condition than the standard PubFig83 setup seems to be well manageable by the proposed 3D framework, as long as the correct blurring kernels are provided, as overall consistent hallucinated faces are observed, especially the gaze, although not in conformity with that in the HR image.

Impact of Input Resolution

The LR input images for the diverse experiments so far have an average IOD of approximately 8 pixels for Multi-PIE, 12 pixels for Real-FSR and 6 pixels for PubFig83, dependent on the original image size of the datasets. However, it is also of paramount interest to delve deeply to see where is the lower bound of the LR faces for 3D FSR. To answer this question, four representative IODs are picked, *i.e.*, 3, 5, 8 and 12 pixels, which correspond to the LR image dimension of 12×12, 20×20, 32×32 and 47×47 respectively on PubFig83 with HR images of 100×100 pixels. Accordingly, these images are super-resolved by two to eight times with 3D FSR (see Table 7.10), and the HR images are slightly downsampled to the target resolutions when necessary to measure the performance. In order to exclude the negative influence of erroneous landmark localization on the FSR quality, the detection is conducted on the HR faces and subsequently rescaled to the LR coordinates.

Table 7.10: Mean PSNR values of 3D FSR from LR inputs with varying IODs on PubFig83.

IOD (pixel)	3	5	8	12
↑	8×	4×	3×	2×
Bicubic	20.47	22.75	24.49	25.11
3D FSR	22.15	24.86	27.11	25.59
Improvement	1.68	2.11	2.62	0.48

The mean PSNR scores of 3D FSR *vs.* bicubic interpolation on the PubFig83 subset are listed in Table 7.10. Increasing the IOD of input images from 3 to 8 pixels gradually opens up the gap between the two counterparts, before it becomes closer for the IOD of 12 pixels, where the SR factor is just two. The qualitative examples in Figure 7.27, on the contrary, acknowledge that the hallucinated details of 3D FSR are still far richer than those from the interpolated ones for this relatively easy case. The quality of 3D FSR remains stable until the IOD reaches 5 pixels. Downwards, it is believed to be too challenging for the algorithm to recover meaningful HR faces, which tends to generate unrecognizable facial texture instead. For instance, the eyes and noses of all samples deviate significantly from the real HR faces.

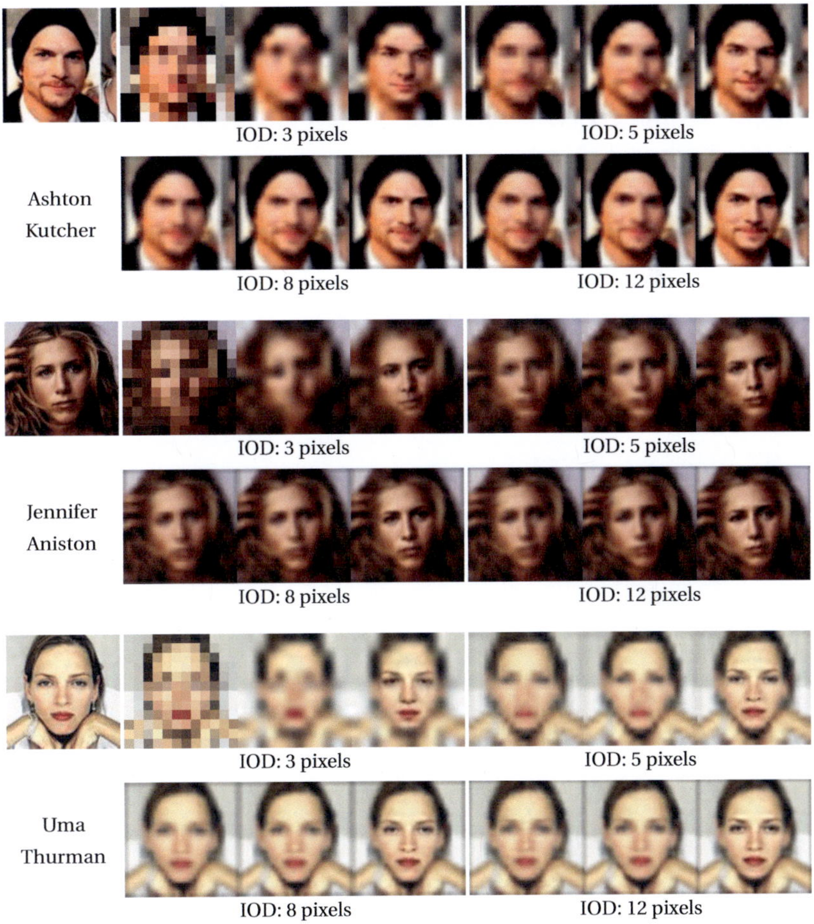

Figure 7.27: Qualitative results of 3D FSR from LR inputs with varying IODs on PubFig83. The leftmost column depicts the HR images. In each triplet for the specified IOD, from left to right are LR, bicubicly interpolated and 3D FSR images.

7.4 Summary

The complete 3D FSR processing chain works fully automatically. The only hyper-parameters to be manually set are the blurring kernel and the upsampling factor. In case of unknown kernels, class-specific face deblurring [Anw15] can be leveraged to obtain an accurate estimate. Regarding the runtime, the unoptimized MATLAB® implementation takes approximately 7 to 25 seconds on a desktop PC with an Intel® Core™ i7 CPU of 3.4 GHz depending on the target HR dimension, markedly below that of the competing algorithms [Des15, Inn13, Tap12, Yan13b] with 2 to 5 minutes and [Jin15] with over 15 minutes.

On a final note, Figure 7.28 reveals a typical failure case of 3D FSR due to incorrect detection of the lips in Figure 7.28c, which produces a phantom mouth at the wrong location. Even the LR fitting refinement in Section 6.3.3 designed for such situation is of no avail. Fortunately, by rectifying a few landmarks, the FSR result in Figure 7.28d is greatly improved in a simple fashion, which shows higher flexibility over all-in-one analysis-by-synthesis approaches [Mor09, Sch15] or DNNs [Tuz16, Yu16, Zhu16a].

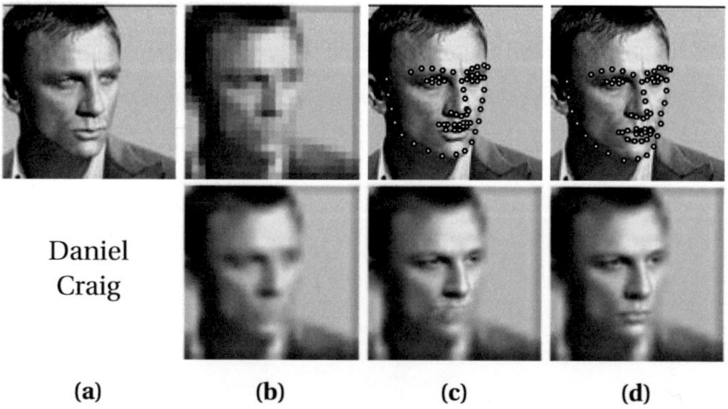

Figure 7.28: A typical failure case of 3D FSR due to incorrect LR landmark detection: (a) HR image, (b) LR and bicubicly interpolated images, (c) 3D FSR given the wrong facial landmarks, (d) revised 3D FSR output with corrected landmarks.

8 Concluding Remarks

In this closing chapter, the improvements made in this thesis, limitations and potential extensions of the proposed 3D FSR framework are outlined with some final remarks.

8.1 Conclusions

Towards effective FSR in real-world applications, where the acquired LR face images cover a range of variations such as blurring, noise, unconstrained pose and illumination, a complete processing chain leveraging 3D face models is presented. 3D representation has long been proved to be a powerful tool for a plethora of computer vision tasks. However, it is extremely challenging to incorporate 3D modeling for FSR. The main reason behind this is the difficulty of directly fitting 3DMMs to uncontrolled images, especially in combination with the ill-posed LR condition. To deal with this problem, a workflow coupling automatic localization of 2D facial feature points and 3D shape reconstruction is developed to obtain a pragmatic solution to the LR scenario, leading to a novel "2D landmarks → 3D dense shape → LR fitting refinement" pipeline. A number of contributions are made thereof to propel robustness and quality of 3D FSR.

The foremost 2D face alignment is built upon the popular cascaded shape regression. The fundamental aspects of this framework including the core regression algorithm, feature descriptors and fitting strategies are revisited. The respective improvements, namely the IRLS, RootSIFT and coarse-to-fine two-pass alignment are evaluated in a progressive manner to demonstrate the benefit of each individual component. State-of-the-art landmarking precision measured on several unconstrained datasets and resistance against image quality degradation sum up to the capability of the approach.

The discrepancy of correspondences between detected 2D points and annotated 3D vertices on the face model is addressed in the second dense shape reconstruction module. Along with an intuitive method excluding the self-occluded ones on the silhouette, an adaptive fitting scheme employing DT and nonlinear LM–ICP is devised to maximize the utility of such landmarks, which at the same time relaxes the unfavorable fixed mapping assumption on the facial contour and achieves superior and stable shape recovery across pose.

In order to exploit the obtained 3D shape and pose for FSR, a resolution-aware approach for registering the training 3D faces with the LR input is designed to avoid warping the LR face, which is confirmed to inevitably result in a loss of discriminative facial details. To facilitate hallucination of the 3D facial texture, the widespread LR image formation procedure from HR images is first reformulated for the 3D face mesh using a straightforward interpolation process. On the basis of this interpretation, the classic Lucas–Kanade algorithm is extended to the case of 3D deformable models to rectify the imperfect landmark-based face modeling on LR images in a posterior fashion. In this way, the final patch-wise SR stage is able to produce a realistic facial texture robust to intrinsic and extrinsic sources of variation, and to synthesize the self-occluded half of the face for non-frontal poses.

Moreover, a novel Real-FSR dataset, which contains both LR and HR pairs acquired with a special dual-camera system, is collected to study the genuine image characteristics related to SR. Extensive analysis and evaluation on Real-FSR validates the correctness of the underlying imaging model within the 3D FSR framework. Further experiments on other benchmark datasets reveal its exceptional ability regarding faithful SR for in-the-wild faces with an IOD of as few as five pixels. Finally yet importantly, the frontalized HR texture is also verified to help boost the performance of FR.

8.2 Outlook

Although the proposed framework reports impressive and consistent SR results for LR input faces of broad scope, it still has its limitations. During the course of this thesis, room for further advancements is also identified. Thanks to the modular design, the individual submodules can be exchanged without influencing the rest of the system.

- A major restriction of the applied landmark-based fitting engine is the maximum permissible head pose of around $\pm 45°$ in yaw rotation. Beyond this angle, the landmarks on the hidden half of the face will become completely occluded by the nose and mouth. The vanished feature on the 2D image causes problems not only to face alignment algorithms, but also to the reliability w.r.t. the manually labeled ground truth. As a consequence, one needs to resort to external sources, *e.g.*, 3DMMs [Jou15], to cope with the large-pose training issue. Since the invisible silhouette can no longer be utilized, additional transformation between the 2D and 3D correspondences [Bul17] is required to introduce further constraints for 3D shape reconstruction. Otherwise, direct 3D dense shape regression with DNNs [Jou16, Zhu16b] offers an alternative option. Their adaptation and applicability to LR images would be an interesting avenue for future work.
- As mentioned earlier, one shortcoming of the present workflow with BFM as the 3DMM is the lack of shape representation for non-neutral expressions, which can be circumvented relatively easily by means of a bilinear 3DMM with separate PCA subspaces for identity and expression [Chu14, Zhu15b]. For the downstream FSR, though, the extra texture of the teeth and tongue for expressions like smile, surprise or scream has to be handled. In practice, the 3D training textures can be noted with an additional flag for whether the mouth is open. After determining the status of the LR input face by the location of the feature points, facial texture SR can be carried out on the respective subset of the training data.
- Furthermore, there are some visionary ideas in terms of the essential SR algorithm. Considering the challenge of accurate LR fitting and the adverse impact of incorrect alignment, it would be preferable to allow the local training patches to deform subject to the LR correspondence [Hua15]. Relatively simple 2D transformation should suffice by virtue of the 3D normalization for the face geometry.

- Another point worth to investigate is the runtime of SR, as the current implementation is still far from real-time capable despite the advantage over prior arts. When more faces are added to the training data, the efficiency is expected to drop further. To alleviate this problem, locally linear regression [Tim13, Yan13c] is able to partition the patch space with clustering and thus greatly reduces computational load. Alternatively, discriminatively learned DNNs provide a feed-forward approach to resolve this issue elegantly.
- Instead of the conventional per-pixel MSE which prefers blurred SR output and produces high error even for two identical images with one pixel offset, advanced loss functions that favor perceptually pleasing results can be adopted by DNNs [Joh16]. The possibilities of incorporating GANs [Goo14] for realistic SR [Led17] and pose-invariant FR [Yin17] are among the most promising topics as well.
- Finally, unconstrained FSR is a long-standing challenge. The 3D FSR pipeline presented in this thesis with the ability to process a single LR input is believed to be a step in this direction. However, although images of reasonably good quality are mostly scarce in surveillance footage, different perspectives of the query face in video data embody supplementary information of the facial texture. Hence, despite the probabilistic solution for similar LR images [Jin15], how to exploit multiple video frames with large pose variation to enhance learning-based FSR robust to illumination and expression changes remains an open question.

Bibliography

[Aho06] T. Ahonen, A. Hadid, and M. Pietikäinen, "Face description with Local Binary Patterns: application to face recognition", *IEEE Transactions on Pattern Analysis and Machine Intelligence,* vol. 28, no. 12, pp. 2037–2041, 2006.

[Ald10a] O. Aldrian and W. A. P. Smith, "A linear approach of 3D face shape and texture recovery using a 3D morphable model", in *Proc. British Machine Vision Conference (BMVC),* 2010, pp. 75.1–75.10.

[Ald10b] O. Aldrian and W. A. P. Smith, "Learning the nature of generalisation errors in a 3D morphable model", in *Proc. IEEE International Conference on Image Processing (ICIP),* 2010, pp. 4557–4560.

[Ald13] O. Aldrian and W. A. P. Smith, "Inverse rendering of faces with a 3D morphable model", *IEEE Transactions on Pattern Analysis and Machine Intelligence,* vol. 35, no. 5, pp. 1080–1093, 2013.

[Amb07] B. Amberg, S. Romdhani, and T. Vetter, "Optimal step nonrigid ICP algorithms for surface registration", in *Proc. IEEE Conference on Computer Vision and Pattern Recognition (CVPR),* 2007, pp. 1–8.

[Amb02] L. Ambrosio, "Optimal transport maps in Monge–Kantorovich problem", in *Proc. International Congress of Mathematicians (ICM),* vol. 3, 2002, pp. 131–140.

[Ant15] E. Antonakos, J. Alabort-i-Medina, and S. Zafeiriou, "Active pictorial structures", in *Proc. IEEE Conference on Computer Vision and Pattern Recognition (CVPR)*, 2015, pp. 5435–5444.

[Anw15] S. Anwar, C. P. Huynh, and F. Porikli, "Class-specific image deblurring", in *Proc. IEEE International Conference on Computer Vision (ICCV)*, 2015, pp. 495–503.

[Ara12] R. Arandjelović and A. Zisserman, "Three things everyone should know to improve object retrieval", in *Proc. IEEE Conference on Computer Vision and Pattern Recognition (CVPR)*, 2012, pp. 2911–2918.

[Ast11] A. Asthana, T. K. Marks, M. J. Jones, K. H. Tieu, and M. V. Rohith, "Fully automatic pose-invariant face recognition via 3D pose normalization", in *Proc. IEEE International Conference on Computer Vision (ICCV)*, 2011, pp. 937–944.

[Ast13] A. Asthana, S. Zafeiriou, S. Cheng, and M. Pantic, "Robust discriminative response map fitting with constrained local models", in *Proc. IEEE Conference on Computer Vision and Pattern Recognition (CVPR)*, 2013, pp. 3444–3451.

[Ast14] A. Asthana, S. Zafeiriou, S. Cheng, and M. Pantic, "Incremental face alignment in the wild", in *Proc. IEEE Conference on Computer Vision and Pattern Recognition (CVPR)*, 2014, pp. 1859–1866.

[Bak03] S. Baker, R. Gross, and I. Matthews, "Lucas–Kanade 20 years on: a unifying framework: part 3", Robotics Institute, Carnegie Mellon University, Tech. Rep. CMU-RI-TR-03-35, 2003.

[Bak00a] S. Baker and T. Kanade, "Hallucinating faces", in *Proc. IEEE International Conference on Automatic Face and Gesture Recognition (FG)*, 2000, pp. 83–88.

[Bak00b] S. Baker and T. Kanade, "Limits on super-resolution and how to break them", in *Proc. IEEE Conference on Computer Vision and Pattern Recognition (CVPR)*, vol. 2, 2000, pp. 372–379.

[Bak02] S. Baker and T. Kanade, "Limits on super-resolution and how to break them", *IEEE Transactions on Pattern Analysis and Machine Intelligence*, vol. 24, no. 9, pp. 1167–1183, 2002.

[Bak04a] S. Baker and I. Matthews, "Lucas–Kanade 20 years on: a unifying framework", *International Journal of Computer Vision*, vol. 56, no. 3, pp. 221–255, 2004.

[Bak04b] S. Baker, R. Patil, K. M. Cheung, and I. Matthews, "Lucas–Kanade 20 years on: part 5", Robotics Institute, Carnegie Mellon University, Tech. Rep. CMU-RI-TR-04-64, 2004.

[Bar09] C. Barnes, E. Shechtman, A. Finkelstein, and D. B. Goldman, "PatchMatch: a randomized correspondence algorithm for structural image editing", *ACM Transactions on Graphics*, vol. 28, no. 3, 24:1–24:11, 2009.

[Bas16] A. Bas, W. A. P. Smith, T. Bolkart, and S. Wuhrer, "Fitting a 3D morphable model to edges: a comparison between hard and soft correspondences", in *Proc. Asian Conference on Computer Vision Workshops (ACCVW)*, 2016, pp. 377–391.

[Bäu13] M. Bäuml, M. Tapaswi, and R. Stiefelhagen, "Semi-supervised learning with constraints for person identification in multimedia data", in *Proc. IEEE Conference on Computer Vision and Pattern Recognition (CVPR)*, 2013, pp. 3602–3609.

[Bel11] P. N. Belhumeur, D. W. Jacobs, D. J. Kriegman, and N. Kumar, "Localizing parts of faces using a consensus of exemplars", in *Proc. IEEE Conference on Computer Vision and Pattern Recognition (CVPR)*, 2011, pp. 545–552.

[Ber12] S. Berretti, A. Del Bimbo, and P. Pala, "Superfaces: a super-resolution model for 3D faces", in *Proc. European Conference on Computer Vision (ECCV)*, 2012, pp. 73–82.

[Bey16] J. Beyerer, F. P. León, and C. Frese, "Methods of image acquisition", in *Machine Vision*, Springer Berlin Heidelberg, 2016, ch. 7, pp. 223–365.

[Bla04] V. Blanz, A. Mehl, T. Vetter, and H.-P. Seidel, "A statistical method for robust 3D surface reconstruction from sparse data", in *Proc. International Symposium on 3D Data Processing, Visualization and Transmission (3DPVT)*, 2004, pp. 293–300.

[Bla99] V. Blanz and T. Vetter, "A morphable model for the synthesis of 3D faces", in *Proc. International Conference on Computer Graphics and Interactive Techniques (SIGGRAPH)*, 1999, pp. 187–194.

[Bla03] V. Blanz and T. Vetter, "Face recognition based on fitting a 3D morphable model", *IEEE Transactions on Pattern Analysis and Machine Intelligence*, vol. 25, no. 9, pp. 1063–1074, 2003.

[Boo89] F. L. Bookstein, "Principal warps: thin-plate splines and the decomposition of deformations", *IEEE Transactions on Pattern Analysis and Machine Intelligence*, vol. 11, no. 6, pp. 567–585, 1989.

[Bre01] L. Breiman, "Random forests", *Machine Learning*, vol. 45, no. 1, pp. 5–32, 2001.

[Bre65] J. E. Bresenham, "Algorithm for computer control of a digital plotter", *IBM Systems Journal*, vol. 4, no. 1, pp. 25–30, 1965.

[Bro04] T. Brox, A. Bruhn, N. Papenberg, and J. Weickert, "High accuracy optical flow estimation based on a theory for warping", in *Proc. European Conference on Computer Vision (ECCV)*, 2004, pp. 25–36.

[Bru14] A. Brunton, A. Salazar, T. Bolkart, and S. Wuhrer, "Review of statistical shape spaces for 3D data with comparative analysis for human faces", *Computer Vision and Image Understanding*, vol. 128, pp. 1–17, 2014.

[Bul17] A. Bulat and G. Tzimiropoulos. (2017). How far are we from solving the 2D & 3D face alignment problem? (and a dataset of 230,000 3D facial landmarks). arXiv: `1703.07332 [cs.CV]`.

[Bur13] X. P. Burgos-Artizzu, P. Perona, and P. Dollár, "Robust face landmark estimation under occlusion", in *Proc. IEEE International Conference on Computer Vision (ICCV)*, 2013, pp. 1513–1520.

[Cal10] M. Calonder, V. Lepetit, C. Strecha, and P. Fua, "BRIEF: binary robust independent elementary features", in *Proc. European Conference on Computer Vision (ECCV)*, 2010, pp. 778–792.

[Cao14a] C. Cao, Q. Hou, and K. Zhou, "Displaced dynamic expression regression for real-time facial tracking and animation", *ACM Transactions on Graphics*, vol. 33, no. 4, 43:1–43:10, 2014.

[Cao13] C. Cao, Y. Weng, S. Lin, and K. Zhou, "3D shape regression for real-time facial animation", *ACM Transactions on Graphics*, vol. 32, no. 4, 41:1–41:10, 2013.

[Cao14b] C. Cao, Y. Weng, S. Zhou, Y. Tong, and K. Zhou, "FaceWarehouse: a 3D facial expression database for visual computing", *IEEE Transactions on Visualization and Computer Graphics*, vol. 20, no. 3, pp. 413–425, 2014.

[Cao12] X. Cao, Y. Wei, F. Wen, and J. Sun, "Face alignment by explicit shape regression", in *Proc. IEEE Conference on Computer Vision and Pattern Recognition (CVPR)*, 2012, pp. 2887–2894.

[Cap01] D. Capel and A. Zisserman, "Super-resolution from multiple views using learnt image models", in *Proc. IEEE Conference on Computer Vision and Pattern Recognition (CVPR)*, vol. 2, 2001, pp. 627–634.

[Cas09] C. D. Castillo and D. W. Jacobs, "Face variation", in *Encyclopedia of Biometrics*, S. Z. Li and A. Jain, Eds. Springer US, 2009, pp. 388–394.

[Cha04] H. Chang, D.-Y. Yeung, and Y. Xiong, "Super-resolution through neighbor embedding", in *Proc. IEEE Conference on Computer Vision and Pattern Recognition (CVPR)*, vol. 1, 2004, pp. 275–282.

[Chr17] G. G. Chrysos, E. Antonakos, P. Snape, A. Asthana, and S. Zafeiriou, "A comprehensive performance evaluation of deformable face tracking "in-the-wild"", *International Journal of Computer Vision*, pp. 1–35, 2017.

[Chu14] B. Chu, S. Romdhani, and L. Chen, "3D-aided face recognition robust to expression and pose variations", in *Proc. IEEE Conference on Computer Vision and Pattern Recognition (CVPR)*, 2014, pp. 1907–1914.

[Coo98] T. F. Cootes, G. J. Edwards, and C. J. Taylor, "Active appearance models", in *Proc. European Conference on Computer Vision (ECCV)*, 1998, pp. 484–498.

[Coo01] T. F. Cootes, G. J. Edwards, and C. J. Taylor, "Active appearance models", *IEEE Transactions on Pattern Analysis and Machine Intelligence*, vol. 23, no. 6, pp. 681–685, 2001.

[Coo92] T. F. Cootes and C. J. Taylor, "Active shape models — 'smart snakes'", in *Proc. British Machine Vision Conference (BMVC)*, 1992, pp. 266–275.

[Coo12] T. F. Cootes, M. C. Ionita, C. Lindner, and P. Sauer, "Robust and accurate shape model fitting using random forest regression voting", in *Proc. European Conference on Computer Vision (ECCV)*, 2012, pp. 278–291.

[Dal05] N. Dalal and B. Triggs, "Histograms of oriented gradients for human detection", in *Proc. IEEE Conference on Computer Vision and Pattern Recognition (CVPR)*, vol. 1, 2005, pp. 886–893.

[Dan12] M. Dantone, J. Gall, G. Fanelli, and L. V. Gool, "Real-time facial feature detection using conditional regression forests", in *Proc. IEEE Conference on Computer Vision and Pattern Recognition (CVPR)*, 2012, pp. 2578–2585.

[Ded06] G. Dedeoğlu, S. Baker, and T. Kanade, "Resolution-aware fitting of active appearance models to low-resolution images", in *Proc. European Conference on Computer Vision (ECCV)*, vol. 2, 2006, pp. 83–97.

[Des15] A. Dessein, W. A. P. Smith, R. C. Wilson, and E. R. Hancock, "Example-based modeling of facial texture from deficient data", in *Proc. IEEE International Conference on Computer Vision (ICCV)*, 2015, pp. 3898–3906.

[Din08] L. Ding and A. M. Martinez, "Precise detailed detection of faces and facial features", in *Proc. IEEE Conference on Computer Vision and Pattern Recognition (CVPR)*, 2008, pp. 1–7.

[Dol10] P. Dollár, P. Welinder, and P. Perona, "Cascaded pose regression", in *Proc. IEEE Conference on Computer Vision and Pattern Recognition (CVPR)*, 2010, pp. 1078–1085.

[Don14] C. Dong, C. C. Loy, K. He, and X. Tang, "Learning a deep convolutional network for image super-resolution", in *Proc. European Conference on Computer Vision (ECCV)*, 2014, pp. 184–199.

[Don16a] C. Dong, C. C. Loy, K. He, and X. Tang, "Image super-resolution using deep convolutional networks", *IEEE Transactions on Pattern Analysis and Machine Intelligence*, vol. 38, no. 2, pp. 295–307, 2016.

[Don16b] C. Dong, C. C. Loy, and X. Tang, "Accelerating the super-resolution convolutional neural network", in *Proc. European Conference on Computer Vision (ECCV)*, 2016, pp. 391–407.

[Don06] D. L. Donoho, "Compressed sensing", *IEEE Transactions on Information Theory*, vol. 52, no. 4, pp. 1289–1306, 2006.

[Dou14] P. Dou, Y. Wu, S. Shah, and I. A. Kakadiaris, "Robust 3D face shape reconstruction from single images via two-fold coupled structure learning", in *Proc. British Machine Vision Conference (BMVC)*, 2014.

[Dov04] R. Dovgard and R. Basri, "Statistical symmetric shape from shading for 3D structure recovery of faces", in *Proc. European Conference on Computer Vision (ECCV)*, 2004, pp. 99–113.

[Dri13] H. Drira, B. B. Amor, A. Srivastava, M. Daoudi, and R. Slama, "3D face recognition under expressions, occlusions, and pose variations", *IEEE Transactions on Pattern Analysis and Machine Intelligence*, vol. 35, no. 9, pp. 2270–2283, 2013.

[Efr13] N. Efrat, D. Glasner, A. Apartsin, B. Nadler, and A. Levin, "Accurate blur models vs. image priors in single image super-resolution", in *Proc. IEEE International Conference on Computer Vision (ICCV)*, 2013, pp. 2832–2839.

[Egg16] B. Egger, A. Schneider, C. Blumer, A. Forster, S. Schönborn, and T. Vetter, "Occlusion-aware 3D morphable face models", in *Proc. British Machine Vision Conference (BMVC)*, 2016, pp. 64.1–64.11.

[Ela97] M. Elad and A. Feuer, "Restoration of a single superresolution image from several blurred, noisy, and undersampled measured images", *IEEE Transactions on Image Processing*, vol. 6, no. 12, pp. 1646–1658, 1997.

[Ela01] M. Elad and Y. Hel-Or, "A fast super-resolution reconstruction algorithm for pure translational motion and common space-invariant blur", *IEEE Transactions on Image Processing*, vol. 10, no. 8, pp. 1187–1193, 2001.

[Fag06] N. Faggian, A. P. Paplinski, and J. Sherrah, "Active appearance models for automatic fitting of 3D morphable models", in *Proc. IEEE International Conference on Advanced Video and Signal Based Surveillance (AVSS)*, 2006, p. 90.

[Fag08] N. Faggian, A. P. Paplinski, and J. Sherrah, "3D morphable model fitting from multiple views", in *Proc. IEEE International Conference on Automatic Face and Gesture Recognition (FG)*, 2008, pp. 1–6.

[Fan16] H. Fan and E. Zhou, "Approaching human level facial landmark localization by deep learning", *Image and Vision Computing*, vol. 47, pp. 27–35, 2016.

[Far04] S. Farsiu, M. D. Robinson, M. Elad, and P. Milanfar, "Fast and robust multiframe super resolution", *IEEE Transactions on Image Processing*, vol. 13, no. 10, pp. 1327–1344, 2004.

[Fat07] R. Fattal, "Image upsampling via imposed edge statistics", *ACM Transactions on Graphics*, vol. 26, no. 3, pp. 95-1–95-8, 2007.

[Fis81] M. A. Fischler and R. C. Bolles, "Random sample consensus: a paradigm for model fitting with applications to image analysis and automated cartography", *Communications of the ACM*, vol. 24, no. 6, pp. 381–395, 1981.

[Fit01] A. W. Fitzgibbon, "Robust registration of 2D and 3D point sets", in *Proc. British Machine Vision Conference (BMVC)*, 2001, pp. 411–420.

[Fre02] W. T. Freeman, T. R. Jones, and E. C. Pasztor, "Example-based super-resolution", *IEEE Computer Graphics and Applications*, vol. 22, no. 2, pp. 56–65, 2002.

[Fre00] W. T. Freeman, E. C. Pasztor, and O. T. Carmichael, "Learning low-level vision", *International Journal of Computer Vision*, vol. 40, no. 1, pp. 25–47, 2000.

[Gao13] H. Gao, "Discriminative appearance models for face alignment", PhD thesis, Karlsruhe Institute of Technology, 2013.

[Gao11] H. Gao, H. K. Ekenel, M. Fischer, and R. Stiefelhagen, "Boosting pseudo census transform features for face alignment", in *Proc. British Machine Vision Conference (BMVC)*, 2011, pp. 54.1–54.11.

[Gao09] H. Gao, H. K. Ekenel, and R. Stiefelhagen, "Pose normalization for local appearance-based face recognition", in *Proc. IAPR/IEEE International Conference on Advances in Biometrics (ICB)*, 2009, pp. 32–41.

[Gao12] H. Gao, H. K. Ekenel, and R. Stiefelhagen, "Face alignment using a ranking model based on regression trees", in *Proc. British Machine Vision Conference (BMVC)*, 2012, pp. 118.1–118.11.

[Gar14] P. Garrido, L. Valgaerts, O. Rehmsen, T. Thormählen, P. Pérez, and C. Theobalt, "Automatic face reenactment", in *Proc. IEEE Conference on Computer Vision and Pattern Recognition (CVPR)*, 2014, pp. 4217–4224.

[Ghi14] G. Ghiasi and C. C. Fowlkes, "Occlusion coherence: localizing occluded faces with a hierarchical deformable part model", in *Proc. IEEE Conference on Computer Vision and Pattern Recognition (CVPR)*, 2014, pp. 1899–1906.

[Gla09] D. Glasner, S. Bagon, and M. Irani, "Super-resolution from a single image", in *Proc. IEEE International Conference on Computer Vision (ICCV)*, 2009, pp. 349–356.

[Gon07] R. C. Gonzalez and R. E. Woods, *Digital Image Processing*, 3rd ed. Prentice Hall, 2007.

[Goo14] I. Goodfellow, J. Pouget-Abadie, M. Mirza, B. Xu, D. Warde-Farley, S. Ozair, A. Courville, and Y. Bengio, "Generative adversarial nets", in *Advances in Neural Information Processing Systems (NIPS)*, 2014, pp. 2672–2680.

[Gre84] P. J. Green, "Iteratively reweighted least squares for maximum likelihood estimation, and some robust and resistant alternatives", *Journal of the Royal Statistical Society. Series B (Methodological)*, vol. 46, no. 2, pp. 149–192, 1984.

[Gro05] R. Gross, I. Matthews, and S. Baker, "Generic vs. person specific active appearance models", *Image and Vision Computing*, vol. 23, no. 12, pp. 1080–1093, 2005.

[Gro10] R. Gross, I. Matthews, J. Cohn, T. Kanade, and S. Baker, "Multi-PIE", *Image and Vision Computing*, vol. 28, no. 5, pp. 807–813, 2010.

[Gu08] L. Gu and T. Kanade, "A generative shape regularization model for robust face alignment", in *Proc. European Conference on Computer Vision (ECCV),* 2008, pp. 413–426.

[Har04] R. I. Hartley and A. Zisserman, *Multiple View Geometry in Computer Vision,* 2nd. New York, NY, USA: Cambridge University Press, 2004.

[Has15] T. Hassner, S. Harel, E. Paz, and R. Enbar, "Effective face frontalization in unconstrained images", in *Proc. IEEE Conference on Computer Vision and Pattern Recognition (CVPR),* 2015, pp. 4295–4304.

[Has09] T. Hastie, R. Tibshirani, and J. Friedman, *The elements of statistical learning: data mining, inference, and prediction,* 2nd ed. Springer, 2009.

[He16] K. He, X. Zhang, S. Ren, and J. Sun, "Deep residual learning for image recognition", in *Proc. IEEE Conference on Computer Vision and Pattern Recognition (CVPR),* 2016, pp. 770–778.

[He04] X. He and P. Niyogi, "Locality preserving projections", in *Advances in Neural Information Processing Systems (NIPS),* 2004, pp. 153–160.

[Hec01] E. Hecht, *Optics,* 4th ed. Addison Wesley, 2001.

[Hen08] P. H. Hennings-Yeomans, S. Baker, and B. V. K. Vijaya Kumar, "Simultaneous super-resolution and feature extraction for recognition of low-resolution faces", in *Proc. IEEE Conference on Computer Vision and Pattern Recognition (CVPR),* 2008, pp. 1–8.

[Her15] C. Herrmann, C. Qu, D. Willersinn, and J. Beyerer, "Impact of resolution and image quality on video face analysis", in *Proc. IEEE International Conference on Advanced Video and Signal Based Surveillance (AVSS),* 2015, pp. 1–6.

[Her16] C. Herrmann, D. Willersinn, and J. Beyerer, "Low-resolution convolutional neural networks for video face recognition", in *Proc. IEEE International Conference on Advanced Video and Signal Based Surveillance (AVSS),* 2016, pp. 221–227.

[Hoe70] A. E. Hoerl and R. W. Kennard, "Ridge regression: biased estimation for nonorthogonal problems", *Technometrics*, vol. 12, no. 1, pp. 55–67, 1970.

[Hor70] B. K. P. Horn, "Shape from shading: a method for obtaining the shape of a smooth opaque object from one view", PhD thesis, Massachussetts Institute of Technology, 1970.

[Hu15] G. Hu, "Face analysis using 3D morphable models", PhD thesis, University of Surrey, 2015.

[Hu12] G. Hu, C. H. Chan, J. Kittler, and W. Christmas, "Resolution-aware 3D morphable model", in *Proc. British Machine Vision Conference (BMVC)*, 2012, pp. 109.1–109.10.

[Hu17] P. Hu and D. Ramanan, "Finding tiny faces", in *Proc. IEEE Conference on Computer Vision and Pattern Recognition (CVPR)*, 2017, pp. 951–959.

[Hu11] Y. Hu, K.-M. Lam, G. Qiu, and T. Shen, "From local pixel structure to global image super-resolution: a new face hallucination framework", *IEEE Transactions on Image Processing*, vol. 20, no. 2, pp. 433–445, 2011.

[Hua08] G. B. Huang, M. Mattar, T. Berg, and E. Learned-Miller, "Labeled faces in the wild: a database for studying face recognition in unconstrained environments", in *Proc. European Conference on Computer Vision Workshops (ECCVW)*, 2008.

[Hua15] J.-B. Huang, A. Singh, and N. Ahuja, "Single image super-resolution from transformed self-exemplars", in *Proc. IEEE Conference on Computer Vision and Pattern Recognition (CVPR)*, 2015, pp. 5197–5206.

[Hua06] X. Huang, N. Paragios, and D. N. Metaxas, "Shape registration in implicit spaces using information theory and free form deformations", *IEEE Transactions on Pattern Analysis and Machine Intelligence*, vol. 28, no. 8, pp. 1303–1318, 2006.

[Hug13] J. F. Hughes, A. van Dam, M. McGuire, D. F. Sklar, J. D. Foley, S. K. Feiner, and K. Akeley, *Computer graphics: principles and practice*, 3rd ed. Addison-Wesley Professional, 2013, p. 1264.

[Inn13] P. Innerhofer and T. Pock, "A convex approach for image hallucination", in *Proc. Annual Workshop of the Austrian Association for Pattern Recognition (ÖAGM–AAPR)*, 2013.

[Ira91] M. Irani and S. Peleg, "Improving resolution by image registration", *CVGIP: Graphical Models and Image Processing*, vol. 53, no. 3, pp. 231–239, 1991.

[Jen15] L. A. Jeni, J. F. Cohn, and T. Kanade, "Dense 3D face alignment from 2D videos in real-time", in *Proc. IEEE International Conference on Automatic Face and Gesture Recognition (FG)*, vol. 1, 2015, pp. 1–8.

[Jen16] L. A. Jeni, S. Tulyakov, L. Yin, N. Sebe, and J. F. Cohn, "The first 3D face alignment in the wild (3DFAW) challenge", in *Proc. European Conference on Computer Vision Workshops (ECCVW)*, 2016, pp. 511–520.

[Jes01] O. Jesorsky, K. J. Kirchberg, and R. Frischholz, "Robust face detection using the Hausdorff distance", in *Proc. International Conference on Audio- and Video-Based Biometric Person Authentication (AVBPA)*, 2001, pp. 90–95.

[Jia08] K. Jia and S. Gong, "Generalized face super-resolution", *IEEE Transactions on Image Processing*, vol. 17, no. 6, pp. 873–886, 2008.

[Jia05] D. Jiang, Y. Hu, S. Yan, L. Zhang, H. Zhang, and W. Gao, "Efficient 3D reconstruction for face recognition", *Pattern Recognition*, vol. 38, no. 6, pp. 787–798, 2005.

[Jia12] J. Jiang, R. Hu, Z. Han, T. Lu, and K. Huang, "Position-patch based face hallucination via locality-constrained representation", in *Proc. IEEE International Conference on Multimedia and Expo (ICME)*, 2012, pp. 212–217.

[Jia13] J. Jiang, R. Hu, Z. Han, Z. Wang, T. Lu, and J. Chen, "Locality-constraint iterative neighbor embedding for face hallucination", in *Proc. IEEE International Conference on Multimedia and Expo (ICME)*, 2013, pp. 1–6.

[Jin16] X. Jin and X. Tan. (2016). Face alignment in-the-wild: a survey. arXiv: `1608.04188 [cs.CV]`.

[Jin13] Y. Jin and C. Bouganis, "Face hallucination revisited: a joint framework", in *Proc. IEEE International Conference on Image Processing (ICIP)*, 2013, pp. 981–985.

[Jin15] Y. Jin and C.-S. Bouganis, "Robust multi-image based blind face hallucination", in *Proc. IEEE Conference on Computer Vision and Pattern Recognition (CVPR)*, 2015, pp. 5252–5260.

[Joh16] J. Johnson, A. Alahi, and F.-F. Li, "Perceptual losses for real-time style transfer and super-resolution", in *Proc. European Conference on Computer Vision (ECCV)*, 2016, pp. 694–711.

[Jou15] A. Jourabloo and X. Liu, "Pose-invariant 3D face alignment", in *Proc. IEEE International Conference on Computer Vision (ICCV)*, 2015, pp. 3694–3702.

[Jou16] A. Jourabloo and X. Liu, "Large-pose face alignment via CNN-based dense 3D model fitting", in *Proc. IEEE Conference on Computer Vision and Pattern Recognition (CVPR)*, 2016, pp. 4188–4196.

[Jun11] C. Jung, L. Jiao, B. Liu, and M. Gong, "Position-patch based face hallucination using convex optimization", *IEEE Signal Processing Letters*, vol. 18, no. 6, pp. 367–370, 2011.

[Kan73] T. Kanade, "Picture processing system by computer complex and recognition of human faces", PhD thesis, Kyoto University, 1973.

[Kan98] T. Kanade, H. Saito, and S. Vedula, "The 3D room: digitizing time-varying 3D events by synchronized multiple video streams", Robotics Institute, Carnegie Mellon University, Tech. Rep. CMU-RI-TR-98-34, 1998.

[Kaz14] V. Kazemi and J. Sullivan, "One millisecond face alignment with an ensemble of regression trees", in *Proc. IEEE Conference on Computer Vision and Pattern Recognition (CVPR)*, 2014, pp. 1867–1874.

[Kem11a] I. Kemelmacher-Shlizerman and R. Basri, "3D face reconstruction from a single image using a single reference face shape", *IEEE Transactions on Pattern Analysis and Machine Intelligence*, vol. 33, no. 2, pp. 394–405, 2011.

[Kem11b] I. Kemelmacher-Shlizerman and S. M. Seitz, "Face reconstruction in the wild", in *Proc. IEEE International Conference on Computer Vision (ICCV)*, 2011, pp. 1746–1753.

[Kem16] I. Kemelmacher-Shlizerman, S. M. Seitz, D. Miller, and E. Brossard, "The MegaFace benchmark: 1 million faces for recognition at scale", in *Proc. IEEE Conference on Computer Vision and Pattern Recognition (CVPR)*, 2016, pp. 4873–4882.

[Kha13] R. A. Khan, A. Meyer, H. Konik, and S. Bouakaz, "Framework for reliable, real-time facial expression recognition for low resolution images", *Pattern Recognition Letters*, vol. 34, no. 10, pp. 1159–1168, 2013.

[Kim16a] J. Kim, J. K. Lee, and K. M. Lee, "Accurate image super-resolution using very deep convolutional networks", in *Proc. IEEE Conference on Computer Vision and Pattern Recognition (CVPR)*, 2016, pp. 1646–1654.

[Kim16b] J. Kim, J. K. Lee, and K. M. Lee, "Deeply-recursive convolutional network for image super-resolution", in *Proc. IEEE Conference on Computer Vision and Pattern Recognition (CVPR)*, 2016, pp. 1637–1645.

[Kim10] K. I. Kim and Y. Kwon, "Single-image super-resolution using sparse regression and natural image prior", *IEEE Transactions on Pattern Analysis and Machine Intelligence*, vol. 32, no. 6, pp. 1127–1133, 2010.

[Kol15] S. Kolouri and G. K. Rohde, "Transport-based single frame super resolution of very low resolution face images", in *Proc. IEEE Conference on Computer Vision and Pattern Recognition (CVPR)*, 2015, pp. 4876–4884.

[Kri12] A. Krizhevsky, I. Sutskever, and G. E. Hinton, "ImageNet classification with deep convolutional neural networks", in *Advances in Neural Information Processing Systems (NIPS)*, 2012, pp. 1097–1105.

[Kum09] N. Kumar, A. C. Berg, P. N. Belhumeur, and S. K. Nayar, "Attribute and simile classifiers for face verification", in *Proc. IEEE International Conference on Computer Vision (ICCV)*, 2009, pp. 365–372.

[Le12] V. Le, J. Brandt, Z. Lin, L. Bourdev, and T. S. Huang, "Interactive facial feature localization", in *Proc. European Conference on Computer Vision (ECCV)*, 2012, pp. 679–692.

[Led17] C. Ledig, L. Theis, F. Huszár, J. Caballero, A. Cunningham, A. Acosta, A. Aitken, A. Tejani, J. Totz, Z. Wang, and W. Shi, "Photo-realistic single image super-resolution using a generative adversarial network", in *Proc. IEEE Conference on Computer Vision and Pattern Recognition (CVPR)*, 2017, pp. 4681–4690.

[Lee08] J.-B. Lee and H. Kalva, "Video coding techniques and standards", in *Encyclopedia of Multimedia*, B. Furht, Ed. Springer US, 2008, pp. 899–904.

[Lee11] S. J. Lee, K. R. Park, and J. Kim, "A SfM-based 3D face reconstruction method robust to self-occlusion by using a shape conversion matrix", *Pattern Recognition*, vol. 44, no. 7, pp. 1470–1486, 2011.

[Lee12] Y. J. Lee, S. J. Lee, K. R. Park, J. Jo, and J. Kim, "Single view-based 3D face reconstruction robust to self-occlusion", *EURASIP Journal on Advances in Signal Processing*, vol. 2012, no. 1, p. 176, 2012.

[Ler02] S. Lertrattanapanich and N. K. Bose, "High resolution image formation from low resolution frames using Delaunay triangulation", *IEEE Transactions on Image Processing*, vol. 11, no. 12, pp. 1427–1441, 2002.

[Lev44] K. Levenberg, "A method for the solution of certain problems in least squares", *Quarterly of Applied Mathematics*, vol. 2, no. 2, pp. 164–168, 1944.

[Lev11] A. Levin, Y. Weiss, F. Durand, and W. T. Freeman, "Efficient marginal likelihood optimization in blind deconvolution", in *Proc. IEEE Conference on Computer Vision and Pattern Recognition (CVPR)*, 2011, pp. 2657–2664.

[Li09] B. Li, H. Chang, S. Shan, and X. Chen, "Locality preserving constraints for super-resolution with neighbor embedding", in *Proc. IEEE International Conference on Image Processing (ICIP)*, 2009, pp. 1189–1192.

[Li14] Y. Li, C. Cai, G. Qiu, and K.-M. Lam, "Face hallucination based on sparse local-pixel structure", *Pattern Recognition,* vol. 47, no. 3, pp. 1261–1270, 2014.

[Lin04] Z. Lin and H.-Y. Shum, "Fundamental limits of reconstruction-based superresolution algorithms under local translation", *IEEE Transactions on Pattern Analysis and Machine Intelligence,* vol. 26, no. 1, pp. 83–97, 2004.

[Liu07] C. Liu, H.-Y. Shum, and W. T. Freeman, "Face hallucination: theory and practice", *International Journal of Computer Vision,* vol. 75, no. 1, pp. 115–134, 2007.

[Liu01] C. Liu, H.-Y. Shum, and C.-S. Zhang, "A two-step approach to hallucinating faces: global parametric model and local nonparametric model", in *Proc. IEEE Conference on Computer Vision and Pattern Recognition (CVPR),* vol. 1, 2001, pp. 192–198.

[Liu11] C. Liu, J. Yuen, and A. Torralba, "SIFT flow: dense correspondence across scenes and its applications", *IEEE Transactions on Pattern Analysis and Machine Intelligence,* vol. 33, no. 5, pp. 978–994, 2011.

[Liu09] X. Liu, "Discriminative face alignment", *IEEE Transactions on Pattern Analysis and Machine Intelligence,* vol. 31, no. 11, pp. 1941–1954, 2009.

[Liu06] X. Liu, P. H. Tu, and F. W. Wheeler, "Face model fitting on low resolution images", in *Proc. British Machine Vision Conference (BMVC),* 2006, pp. 1079–1088.

[Low04] D. G. Lowe, "Distinctive image features from scale-invariant keypoints", *International Journal of Computer Vision,* vol. 60, no. 2, pp. 91–110, 2004.

[Luc81] B. D. Lucas and T. Kanade, "An iterative image registration technique with an application to stereo vision", in *Proc. International Joint Conference on Artificial Intelligence (IJCAI),* vol. 2, 1981, pp. 674–679.

[Ma10] X. Ma, J. Zhang, and C. Qi, "Hallucinating face by position-patch", *Pattern Recognition,* vol. 43, no. 6, pp. 2224–2236, 2010.

[Mad04] K. Madsen, H. B. Nielsen, and O. Tingleff, "Methods for non-linear least squares problems", Informatics and Mathematical Modelling, Technical University of Denmark (DTU), Lecture Note, version 2, 2004. [Online]. Available: http://www2.imm.dtu.dk/pubdb/views/publication_details.php?id=3215.

[Mar63] D. W. Marquardt, "An algorithm for least-squares estimation of nonlinear parameters", *Journal of the Society for Industrial and Applied Mathematics*, vol. 11, no. 2, pp. 431–441, 1963.

[Mar16] B. Martinez and M. F. Valstar, "Advances, challenges, and opportunities in automatic facial expression recognition", in *Advances in Face Detection and Facial Image Analysis*, M. Kawulok, M. E. Celebi, and B. Smolka, Eds. Springer International Publishing, 2016, pp. 63–100.

[Mat07] I. Matthews, J. Xiao, and S. Baker, "2D vs. 3D deformable face models: representational power, construction, and real-time fitting", *International Journal of Computer Vision*, vol. 75, no. 1, pp. 93–113, 2007.

[Mat04] I. Matthews and S. Baker, "Active appearance models revisited", *International Journal of Computer Vision*, vol. 60, no. 2, pp. 135–164, 2004.

[Mes99] K. Messer, J. Matas, J. Kittler, J. Luettin, and G. Maître, "XM2VTSDB: the extended M2VTS database", in *Proc. International Conference on Audio- and Video-Based Biometric Person Authentication (AVBPA)*, 1999.

[Mic13] T. Michaeli and M. Irani, "Nonparametric blind super-resolution", in *Proc. IEEE International Conference on Computer Vision (ICCV)*, 2013, pp. 945–952.

[Mor09] P. Mortazavian, J. Kittler, and W. Christmas, "3D-assisted facial texture super-resolution", in *Proc. British Machine Vision Conference (BMVC)*, 2009, pp. 119.1–119.11.

[Mor13] P. Mortazavian, "Face recognition in low resolution using a 3D morphable model", PhD thesis, University of Surrey, 2013.

[Mor12] P. Mortazavian, J. Kittler, and W. Christmas, "3D morphable model fitting for low-resolution facial images", in *Proc. IAPR International Conference on Biometrics (ICB)*, 2012, pp. 132–138.

[Mur09] E. Murphy-Chutorian and M. M. Trivedi, "Head pose estimation in computer vision: a survey", *IEEE Transactions on Pattern Analysis and Machine Intelligence*, vol. 31, no. 4, pp. 607–626, 2009.

[Nas14] K. Nasrollahi and T. B. Moeslund, "Super-resolution: a comprehensive survey", *Machine Vision and Applications*, vol. 25, no. 6, pp. 1423–1468, 2014.

[Ng14] H.-W. Ng and S. Winkler, "A data-driven approach to cleaning large face datasets", in *Proc. IEEE International Conference on Image Processing (ICIP)*, 2014, pp. 343–347.

[Ngu01] N. Nguyen, P. Milanfar, and G. Golub, "A computationally efficient superresolution image reconstruction algorithm", *IEEE Transactions on Image Processing*, vol. 10, no. 4, pp. 573–583, 2001.

[Noc06] J. Nocedal and S. J. Wright, *Numerical Optimization*, 2nd ed. Springer New York, 2006.

[Oja02] T. Ojala, M. Pietikäinen, and T. Mäenpää, "Multiresolution gray-scale and rotation invariant texture classification with local binary patterns", *IEEE Transactions on Pattern Analysis and Machine Intelligence*, vol. 24, no. 7, pp. 971–987, 2002.

[Oli90] M. A. Oliver and R. Webster, "Kriging: a method of interpolation for geographical information systems", *International Journal of Geographical Information Systems*, vol. 4, no. 3, pp. 313–332, 1990.

[Özu10] M. Özuysal, M. Calonder, V. Lepetit, and P. Fua, "Fast keypoint recognition using random ferns", *IEEE Transactions on Pattern Analysis and Machine Intelligence*, vol. 32, no. 3, pp. 448–461, 2010.

[Pan06] G. Pan, S. Han, Z. Wu, and Y. Wang, "Super-resolution of 3D face", in *Proc. European Conference on Computer Vision (ECCV)*, 2006, pp. 389–401.

[Par08] J.-S. Park and S.-W. Lee, "An example-based face hallucination method for single-frame, low-resolution facial images", *IEEE Transactions on Image Processing*, vol. 17, no. 10, pp. 1806–1816, 2008.

[Par03] S. C. Park, M. K. Park, and M. G. Kang, "Super-resolution image reconstruction: a technical overview", *IEEE Signal Processing Magazine*, vol. 20, no. 3, pp. 21–36, 2003.

[Pat12] A. Patel and W. A. P. Smith, "Driving 3D morphable models using shading cues", *Pattern Recognition*, vol. 45, no. 5, pp. 1993–2004, 2012.

[Pay09] P. Paysan, R. Knothe, B. Amberg, S. Romdhani, and T. Vetter, "A 3D face model for pose and illumination invariant face recognition", in *Proc. IEEE International Conference on Advanced Video and Signal Based Surveillance (AVSS)*, 2009, pp. 296–301.

[Pic06] L. C. Pickup, D. P. Capel, S. J. Roberts, and A. Zisserman, "Bayesian image super-resolution, continued", in *Advances in Neural Information Processing Systems (NIPS)*, 2006, pp. 1089–1096.

[Pin11] N. Pinto, Z. Stone, T. Zickler, and D. Cox, "Scaling up biologically-inspired computer vision: a case study in unconstrained face recognition on Facebook", in *Proc. IEEE Conference on Computer Vision and Pattern Recognition Workshops (CVPRW)*, 2011, pp. 35–42.

[Qu14] C. Qu, E. Monari, T. Schuchert, and J. Beyerer, "Fast, robust and automatic 3D face model reconstruction from videos", in *Proc. IEEE International Conference on Advanced Video and Signal Based Surveillance (AVSS)*, 2014, pp. 113–118.

[Qu15a] C. Qu, E. Monari, T. Schuchert, and J. Beyerer, "Realistic texture extraction for 3D face models robust to self-occlusion", in *Proc. SPIE, Image Processing: Machine Vision Applications VIII*, vol. 9405, 2015, 94050P.

[Qu15b] C. Qu, C. Herrmann, E. Monari, T. Schuchert, and J. Beyerer, "3D vs. 2D: on the importance of registration for hallucinating faces under unconstrained poses", in *Proc. Conference on Computer and Robot Vision (CRV)*, 2015, pp. 139–146.

[Qu15c] C. Qu, H. Gao, E. Monari, J. Beyerer, and J.-P. Thiran, "Towards robust cascaded regression for face alignment in the wild", in *Proc. IEEE Conference on Computer Vision and Pattern Recognition Workshops (CVPRW)*, 2015, pp. 1–9.

[Qu15d] C. Qu, E. Monari, T. Schuchert, and J. Beyerer, "Adaptive contour fitting for pose-invariant 3D face shape reconstruction", in *Proc. British Machine Vision Conference (BMVC)*, 2015, pp. 87.1–87.12.

[Qu16] C. Qu, D. Luo, E. Monari, T. Schuchert, and J. Beyerer, "Capturing ground truth super-resolution data", in *Proc. IEEE International Conference on Image Processing (ICIP)*, 2016, pp. 2812–2816.

[Qu17] C. Qu, C. Herrmann, E. Monari, T. Schuchert, and J. Beyerer, "Robust 3D patch-based face hallucination", in *Proc. IEEE Winter Conference on Applications of Computer Vision (WACV)*, 2017, pp. 1105–1114.

[Rar11] H. M. Rara, A. A. Farag, and T. Davis, "Model-based 3D shape recovery from single images of unknown pose and illumination using a small number of feature points", in *Proc. International Joint Conference on Biometrics (IJCB)*, 2011, pp. 1–7.

[Ren14] S. Ren, X. Cao, Y. Wei, and J. Sun, "Face alignment at 3000 FPS via regressing local binary features", in *Proc. IEEE Conference on Computer Vision and Pattern Recognition (CVPR)*, 2014, pp. 1685–1692.

[Ric17] E. Richardson, M. Sela, R. Or-El, and R. Kimmel, "Learning detailed face reconstruction from a single image", in *Proc. IEEE Conference on Computer Vision and Pattern Recognition (CVPR)*, 2017, pp. 1259–1268.

[Ric16] E. Richardson, M. Sela, and R. Kimmel, "3D face reconstruction by learning from synthetic data", in *Proc. International Conference on 3D Vision (3DV)*, 2016, pp. 460–469.

[Rom03] S. Romdhani and T. Vetter, "Efficient, robust and accurate fitting of a 3D morphable model", in *Proc. IEEE Conference on Computer Vision and Pattern Recognition (CVPR)*, vol. 1, 2003, pp. 59–66.

[Rom05] S. Romdhani and T. Vetter, "Estimating 3D shape and texture using pixel intensity, edges, specular highlights, texture constraints and a prior", in *Proc. IEEE Conference on Computer Vision and Pattern Recognition (CVPR),* vol. 2, 2005, pp. 986–993.

[Rom02] S. Romdhani, V. Blanz, and T. Vetter, "Face identification by fitting a 3D morphable model using linear shape and texture error functions", in *Proc. European Conference on Computer Vision (ECCV),* 2002, pp. 3–19.

[Rot15] J. Roth, Y. Tong, and X. Liu, "Unconstrained 3D face reconstruction", in *Proc. IEEE Conference on Computer Vision and Pattern Recognition (CVPR),* 2015, pp. 2606–2615.

[Rot16] J. Roth, Y. Tong, and X. Liu, "Adaptive 3D face reconstruction from unconstrained photo collections", in *Proc. IEEE Conference on Computer Vision and Pattern Recognition (CVPR),* 2016, pp. 4197–4206.

[Roy03] A. K. Roy-Chowdhury and R. Chellappa, "Face reconstruction from monocular video using uncertainty analysis and a generic model", *Computer Vision and Image Understanding,* vol. 91, no. 1–2, pp. 188–213, 2003.

[Rud92] L. I. Rudin, S. Osher, and E. Fatemi, "Nonlinear total variation based noise removal algorithms", *Physica D: Nonlinear Phenomena,* vol. 60, no. 1–4, pp. 259–268, 1992.

[Rus15] O. Russakovsky, J. Deng, H. Su, J. Krause, S. Satheesh, S. Ma, Z. Huang, A. Karpathy, A. Khosla, M. Bernstein, A. C. Berg, and F.-F. Li, "ImageNet large scale visual recognition challenge", *International Journal of Computer Vision,* vol. 115, no. 3, pp. 211–252, 2015.

[Sag16] C. Sagonas, E. Antonakos, G. Tzimiropoulos, S. Zafeiriou, and M. Pantic, "300 faces in-the-wild challenge: database and results", *Image and Vision Computing,* vol. 47, pp. 3–18, 2016.

[Sag13a] C. Sagonas, G. Tzimiropoulos, S. Zafeiriou, and M. Pantic, "300 faces in-the-wild challenge: the first facial landmark localization challenge", in *Proc. IEEE International Conference on Computer Vision Workshops (ICCVW),* 2013, pp. 397–403.

[Sag13b] C. Sagonas, G. Tzimiropoulos, S. Zafeiriou, and M. Pantic, "A semi-automatic methodology for facial landmark annotation", in *Proc. IEEE Conference on Computer Vision and Pattern Recognition Workshops (CVPRW)*, 2013, pp. 896–903.

[Sar07] J. M. Saragih and R. Goecke, "A nonlinear discriminative approach to aam fitting", in *Proc. IEEE International Conference on Computer Vision (ICCV)*, 2007, pp. 1–8.

[Sar11] J. M. Saragih, S. Lucey, and J. F. Cohn, "Deformable model fitting by regularized landmark mean-shift", *International Journal of Computer Vision*, vol. 91, no. 2, pp. 200–215, 2011.

[Sau03] L. K. Saul and S. T. Roweis, "Think globally, fit locally: unsupervised learning of low dimensional manifolds", *Journal of Machine Learning Research*, vol. 4, pp. 119–155, 2003.

[Sch12] T. Schuchert and F. Oser, "Optical flow estimation with confidence measures for super-resolution based on recursive robust total least squares", in *Proc. International Conference on Pattern Recognition Applications and Methods (ICPRAM)*, 2012, pp. 463–469.

[Sch96] R. R. Schultz and R. L. Stevenson, "Extraction of high-resolution frames from video sequences", *IEEE Transactions on Image Processing*, vol. 5, no. 6, pp. 996–1011, 1996.

[Sch15] M. Schumacher, M. Piotraschke, and V. Blanz, "Hallucination of facial details from degraded images using 3D face models", *Image and Vision Computing*, vol. 40, pp. 49–64, 2015.

[She15] J. Shen, S. Zafeiriou, G. G. Chrysos, J. Kossaifi, G. Tzimiropoulos, and M. Pantic, "The first facial landmark tracking in-the-wild challenge: benchmark and results", in *Proc. IEEE International Conference on Computer Vision Workshops (ICCVW)*, 2015, pp. 1003–1011.

[Shi16] W. Shi, J. Caballero, F. Huszár, J. Totz, A. P. Aitken, R. Bishop, D. Rueckert, and Z. Wang, "Real-time single image and video super-resolution using an efficient sub-pixel convolutional neural network", in *Proc. IEEE Conference on Computer Vision and Pattern Recognition (CVPR)*, 2016, pp. 1874–1883.

[Sim02] T. Sim, S. Baker, and M. Bsat, "The CMU pose, illumination, and expression (PIE) database", in *Proc. IEEE International Conference on Automatic Face and Gesture Recognition (FG)*, 2002, pp. 46–51.

[Sri00] S. Srinivasan, "Extracting structure from optical flow using the fast error search technique", *International Journal of Computer Vision*, vol. 37, no. 3, pp. 203–230, 2000.

[Sta89] H. Stark and P. Oskoui, "High-resolution image recovery from image-plane arrays, using convex projections", *Journal of the Optical Society of America A*, vol. 6, no. 11, pp. 1715–1726, 1989.

[Su05] C. Su, Y. Zhuang, L. Huang, and F. Wu, "Steerable pyramid-based face hallucination", *Pattern Recognition*, vol. 38, no. 6, pp. 813–824, 2005.

[Sun08] J. Sun, Z. Xu, and H.-Y. Shum, "Image super-resolution using gradient profile prior", in *Proc. IEEE Conference on Computer Vision and Pattern Recognition (CVPR)*, 2008, pp. 1–8.

[Sun13] Y. Sun, X. Wang, and X. Tang, "Deep convolutional network cascade for facial point detection", in *Proc. IEEE Conference on Computer Vision and Pattern Recognition (CVPR)*, 2013, pp. 3476–3483.

[Sze11a] R. Szeliski, "Dense motion estimation", in *Computer Vision: Algorithms and Applications*, D. Gries and F. B. Schneider, Eds. Springer London, 2011, ch. 8, pp. 335–374.

[Sze11b] R. Szeliski, "Image formation", in *Computer Vision: Algorithms and Applications*, D. Gries and F. B. Schneider, Eds. Springer London, 2011, ch. 2, pp. 27–86.

[Tai14] Y. Taigman, M. Yang, M. Ranzato, and L. Wolf, "DeepFace: closing the gap to human-level performance in face verification", in *Proc. IEEE Conference on Computer Vision and Pattern Recognition (CVPR)*, 2014, pp. 1701–1708.

[Tap12] M. F. Tappen and C. Liu, "A Bayesian approach to alignment-based image hallucination", in *Proc. European Conference on Computer Vision (ECCV)*, 2012, pp. 236–249.

[Ten07] J. R. Tena Rodríguez, "3D face modelling for 2D+3D face recognition", PhD thesis, University of Surrey, 2007.

[Thi16] J. Thies, M. Zollhöfer, M. Stamminger, C. Theobalt, and M. Nießner, "Face2Face: real-time face capture and reenactment of RGB videos", in *Proc. IEEE Conference on Computer Vision and Pattern Recognition (CVPR)*, 2016, pp. 2387–2395.

[Tho06] N. Thomos, N. V. Boulgouris, and M. G. Strintzis, "Optimized transmission of JPEG2000 streams over wireless channels", *IEEE Transactions on Image Processing*, vol. 15, no. 1, pp. 54–67, 2006.

[Tim13] R. Timofte, V. de Smet, and L. van Gool, "Anchored neighborhood regression for fast example-based super-resolution", in *Proc. IEEE International Conference on Computer Vision (ICCV)*, 2013, pp. 1920–1927.

[Tim15] R. Timofte, V. de Smet, and L. van Gool, "A+: adjusted anchored neighborhood regression for fast super-resolution", in *Proc. Asian Conference on Computer Vision (ACCV)*, 2015, pp. 111–126.

[Tim16] R. Timofte, R. Rothe, and L. van Gool, "Seven ways to improve example-based single image super resolution", in *Proc. IEEE Conference on Computer Vision and Pattern Recognition (CVPR)*, 2016, pp. 1865–1873.

[Tip02] M. E. Tipping and C. Bishop, "Bayesian image super-resolution", in *Advances in Neural Information Processing Systems (NIPS)*, vol. 15, 2002, pp. 1303–1310.

[Tom98] C. Tomasi and R. Manduchi, "Bilateral filtering for gray and color images", in *Proc. IEEE International Conference on Computer Vision (ICCV)*, 1998, pp. 839–846.

[Tri16] G. Trigeorgis, P. Snape, M. A. Nicolaou, E. Antonakos, and S. Zafeiriou, "Mnemonic descent method: a recurrent process applied for end-to-end face alignment", in *Proc. IEEE Conference on Computer Vision and Pattern Recognition (CVPR)*, 2016, pp. 4177–4187.

[Tsa84] R. Y. Tsai and T. S. Huang, "Multiframe image restoration and registration", in *Advances in Computer Vision and Image Processing*, vol. 1, 1984, pp. 317–339.

[Tul15] S. Tulyakov and N. Sebe, "Regressing a 3D face shape from a single image", in *Proc. IEEE International Conference on Computer Vision (ICCV)*, 2015, pp. 3748–3755.

[Tur91] M. A. Turk and A. P. Pentland, "Face recognition using eigenfaces", in *Proc. IEEE Conference on Computer Vision and Pattern Recognition (CVPR)*, 1991, pp. 586–591.

[Tuz16] O. Tuzel, Y. Taguchi, and J. R. Hershey. (2016). Global–local face upsampling network. arXiv: `1603.07235 [cs.CV]`.

[Tzi15] G. Tzimiropoulos, "Project-out cascaded regression with an application to face alignment", in *Proc. IEEE Conference on Computer Vision and Pattern Recognition (CVPR)*, 2015, pp. 3659–3667.

[Tzi13] G. Tzimiropoulos and M. Pantic, "Optimization problems for fast AAM fitting in-the-wild", in *Proc. IEEE International Conference on Computer Vision (ICCV)*, 2013, pp. 593–600.

[Tzi14] G. Tzimiropoulos and M. Pantic, "Gauss–Newton deformable part models for face alignment in-the-wild", in *Proc. IEEE Conference on Computer Vision and Pattern Recognition (CVPR)*, 2014, pp. 1851–1858.

[Ur92] H. Ur and D. Gross, "Improved resolution from subpixel shifted pictures", *CVGIP: Graphical Models and Image Processing*, vol. 54, no. 2, pp. 181–186, 1992.

[Val10] M. Valstar, B. Martinez, X. Binefa, and M. Pantic, "Facial point detection using boosted regression and graph models", in *Proc. IEEE Conference on Computer Vision and Pattern Recognition (CVPR)*, 2010, pp. 2729–2736.

[Vet97] T. Vetter and N. F. Troje, "Separation of texture and shape in images of faces for image coding and synthesis", *Journal of the Optical Society of America A*, vol. 14, no. 9, pp. 2152–2161, 1997.

[Vio04] P. Viola and M. J. Jones, "Robust real-time face detection", *International Journal of Computer Vision*, vol. 57, no. 2, pp. 137–154, 2004.

[vAgr08] U. von Agris, J. Zieren, U. Canzler, B. Bauer, and K.-F. Kraiss, "Recent developments in visual sign language recognition", *Universal Access in the Information Society,* vol. 6, no. 4, pp. 323–362, 2008.

[Vuk05] D. Vukadinovic and M. Pantic, "Fully automatic facial feature point detection using gabor feature based boosted classifiers", in *Proc. IEEE International Conference on Systems, Man and Cybernetics (SMC),* 2005, pp. 1692–1698.

[Wan04a] C. Wang, S. Yan, H. Li, H. Zhang, and M. Li, "Automatic, effective, and efficient 3D face reconstruction from arbitrary view image", in *Advances in Multimedia Information Processing (PCM),* 2004, pp. 553–560.

[Wan14a] N. Wang, X. Gao, D. Tao, and X. Li. (2014). Facial feature point detection: a comprehensive survey. arXiv: `1410.1037 [cs.CV]`.

[Wan14b] N. Wang, D. Tao, X. Gao, X. Li, and J. Li, "A comprehensive survey to face hallucination", *International Journal of Computer Vision,* vol. 106, no. 1, pp. 9–30, 2014.

[Wan12] S. Wang, L. Zhang, Y. Liang, and Q. Pan, "Semi-coupled dictionary learning with applications to image super-resolution and photo-sketch synthesis", in *Proc. IEEE Conference on Computer Vision and Pattern Recognition (CVPR),* 2012, pp. 2216–2223.

[Wan05] X. Wang and X. Tang, "Hallucinating face by eigentransformation", *IEEE Transactions on Systems, Man, and Cybernetics, Part C (Applications and Reviews),* vol. 35, no. 3, pp. 425–434, 2005.

[Wan08] Y. Wang, S. Lucey, and J. F. Cohn, "Enforcing convexity for improved alignment with constrained local models", in *Proc. IEEE Conference on Computer Vision and Pattern Recognition (CVPR),* 2008, pp. 1–8.

[Wan16] Z. Wang, S. Chang, Y. Yang, D. Liu, and T. S. Huang, "Studying very low resolution recognition using deep networks", in *Proc. IEEE Conference on Computer Vision and Pattern Recognition (CVPR),* 2016, pp. 4792–4800.

[Wan14c] Z. Wang, Z. Miao, Q. M. Jonathan Wu, Y. Wan, and Z. Tang, "Low-resolution face recognition: a review", *The Visual Computer,* vol. 30, no. 4, pp. 359–386, 2014.

[Wan04b] Z. Wang, A. C. Bovik, H. R. Sheikh, and E. P. Simoncelli, "Image quality assessment: from error visibility to structural similarity", *IEEE Transactions on Image Processing*, vol. 13, no. 4, pp. 600–612, 2004.

[Whe07] F. W. Wheeler, X. Liu, and P. H. Tu, "Multi-frame super-resolution for face recognition", in *Proc. IEEE International Conference on Biometrics: Theory, Applications and Systems (BTAS)*, 2007, pp. 1–6.

[Whe11] F. W. Wheeler, X. Liu, and P. H. Tu, "Face recognition at a distance", in *Handbook of Face Recognition*, S. Z. Li and A. K. Jain, Eds. Springer London, 2011, ch. 14, pp. 353–381.

[Wol11] L. Wolf, T. Hassner, and I. Maoz, "Face recognition in unconstrained videos with matched background similarity", in *Proc. IEEE Conference on Computer Vision and Pattern Recognition (CVPR)*, 2011, pp. 529–534.

[Wol08] L. Wolf, T. Hassner, and Y. Taigman, "Descriptor based methods in the wild", in *Proc. European Conference on Computer Vision Workshops (ECCVW)*, 2008.

[Woo80] R. J. Woodham, "Photometric method for determining surface orientation from multiple images", *Optical Engineering*, vol. 19, no. 1, pp. 139–144, 1980.

[Xio13] X. Xiong and F. De la Torre, "Supervised descent method and its applications to face alignment", in *Proc. IEEE Conference on Computer Vision and Pattern Recognition (CVPR)*, 2013, pp. 532–539.

[Yan13a] J. Yan, Z. Lei, D. Yi, and S. Z. Li, "Learn to combine multiple hypotheses for accurate face alignment", in *Proc. IEEE International Conference on Computer Vision Workshops (ICCVW)*, 2013, pp. 392–396.

[Yan13b] C.-Y. Yang, S. Liu, and M.-H. Yang, "Structured face hallucination", in *Proc. IEEE Conference on Computer Vision and Pattern Recognition (CVPR)*, 2013, pp. 1099–1106.

[Yan14] C.-Y. Yang, C. Ma, and M.-H. Yang, "Single-image super-resolution: a benchmark", in *Proc. European Conference on Computer Vision (ECCV)*, 2014, pp. 372–386.

[Yan13c] C.-Y. Yang and M.-H. Yang, "Fast direct super-resolution by simple functions", in *Proc. IEEE International Conference on Computer Vision (ICCV)*, 2013, pp. 561–568.

[Yan15a] H. Yang, X. He, X. Jia, and I. Patras, "Robust face alignment under occlusion via regional predictive power estimation", *IEEE Transactions on Image Processing*, vol. 24, no. 8, pp. 2393–2403, 2015.

[Yan15b] H. Yang, X. Jia, C. C. Loy, and P. Robinson. (2015). An empirical study of recent face alignment methods. arXiv: `1511.05049 [cs.CV]`.

[Yan13d] H. Yang and I. Patras, "Sieving regression forest votes for facial feature detection in the wild", in *Proc. IEEE International Conference on Computer Vision (ICCV)*, 2013, pp. 1936–1943.

[Yan10a] J. Yang and T. Huang, "Image super-resolution: historical overview and future challenges", in *Super-Resoluton Imaging*, P. Milanfar, Ed. CRC Press, 2010, ch. 1, pp. 1–33.

[Yan13e] J. Yang, Z. Lin, and S. Cohen, "Fast image super-resolution based on in-place example regression", in *Proc. IEEE Conference on Computer Vision and Pattern Recognition (CVPR)*, 2013, pp. 1059–1066.

[Yan10b] J. Yang, J. Wright, T. S. Huang, and Y. Ma, "Image super-resolution via sparse representation", *IEEE Transactions on Image Processing*, vol. 19, no. 11, pp. 2861–2873, 2010.

[Yan08] J. Yang, J. Wright, T. Huang, and Y. Ma, "Image super-resolution as sparse representation of raw image patches", in *Proc. IEEE Conference on Computer Vision and Pattern Recognition (CVPR)*, 2008, pp. 1–8.

[Yin17] X. Yin, X. Yu, K. Sohn, X. Liu, and M. Chandraker. (2017). Towards large-pose face frontalization in the wild. arXiv: `1704.06244 [cs.CV]`.

[You78] D. C. Youla, "Generalized image restoration by the method of alternating orthogonal projections", *IEEE Transactions on Circuits and Systems*, vol. 25, no. 9, pp. 694–702, 1978.

[Yu08] J. Yu and B. Bhanu, "Super-resolution of facial images in video with expression changes", in *Proc. IEEE International Conference on Advanced Video and Signal Based Surveillance (AVSS)*, 2008, pp. 184–191.

[Yu16] X. Yu and F. Porikli, "Ultra-resolving face images by discriminative generative networks", in *Proc. European Conference on Computer Vision (ECCV)*, 2016, pp. 318–333.

[Zei11] M. D. Zeiler, G. W. Taylor, and R. Fergus, "Adaptive deconvolutional networks for mid and high level feature learning", in *Proc. IEEE International Conference on Computer Vision (ICCV)*, 2011, pp. 2018–2025.

[Zha15] J. Zhang, M. Kan, S. Shan, and X. Chen, "Leveraging datasets with varying annotations for face alignment via deep regression network", in *Proc. IEEE International Conference on Computer Vision (ICCV)*, 2015, pp. 3801–3809.

[Zha14a] J. Zhang, S. Shan, M. Kan, and X. Chen, "Coarse-to-fine autoencoder networks (CFAN) for real-time face alignment", in *Proc. European Conference on Computer Vision (ECCV)*, 2014, pp. 1–16.

[Zha06a] L. Zhang and D. Samaras, "Face recognition from a single training image under arbitrary unknown lighting using spherical harmonics", *IEEE Transactions on Pattern Analysis and Machine Intelligence*, vol. 28, no. 3, pp. 351–363, 2006.

[Zha10] S. Zhang, "Recent progresses on real-time 3D shape measurement using digital fringe projection techniques", *Optics and Lasers in Engineering*, vol. 48, no. 2, pp. 149–158, 2010.

[Zha14b] Z. Zhang, P. Luo, C. C. Loy, and X. Tang, "Facial landmark detection by deep multi-task learning", in *Proc. European Conference on Computer Vision (ECCV)*, 2014, pp. 94–108.

[Zha16] Z. Zhang, P. Luo, C. C. Loy, and X. Tang, "Learning deep representation for face alignment with auxiliary attributes", *IEEE Transactions on Pattern Analysis and Machine Intelligence*, vol. 38, no. 5, pp. 918–930, 2016.

[Zha06b] M. Zhao, T.-S. Chua, and T. Sim, "Morphable face reconstruction with multiple images", in *Proc. IEEE International Conference on Automatic Face and Gesture Recognition (FG)*, 2006, pp. 597–602.

[Zha01] W. Y. Zhao and R. Chellappa, "Symmetric shape-from-shading using self-ratio image", *International Journal of Computer Vision*, vol. 45, no. 1, pp. 55–75, 2001.

[Zha02] W. Zhao and H. S. Sawhney, "Is super-resolution with optical flow feasible?", in *Proc. European Conference on Computer Vision (ECCV)*, 2002, pp. 599–613.

[Zho13] E. Zhou, H. Fan, Z. Cao, Y. Jiang, and Q. Yin, "Extensive facial landmark localization with coarse-to-fine convolutional network cascade", in *Proc. IEEE International Conference on Computer Vision Workshops (ICCVW)*, 2013, pp. 386–391.

[Zho15] E. Zhou, H. Fan, Z. Cao, Y. Jiang, and Q. Yin, "Learning face hallucination in the wild", in *Proc. AAAI Conference on Artificial Intelligence (AAAI)*, 2015, pp. 3871–3877.

[Zhu15a] S. Zhu, C. Li, C. C. Loy, and X. Tang, "Face alignment by coarse-to-fine shape searching", in *Proc. IEEE Conference on Computer Vision and Pattern Recognition (CVPR)*, 2015, pp. 4998–5006.

[Zhu16a] S. Zhu, S. Liu, C. C. Loy, and X. Tang, "Deep cascaded bi-network for face hallucination", in *Proc. European Conference on Computer Vision (ECCV)*, 2016, pp. 614–630.

[Zhu15b] X. Zhu, Z. Lei, J. Yan, D. Yi, and S. Z. Li, "High-fidelity pose and expression normalization for face recognition in the wild", in *Proc. IEEE Conference on Computer Vision and Pattern Recognition (CVPR)*, 2015, pp. 787–796.

[Zhu12] X. Zhu and D. Ramanan, "Face detection, pose estimation, and landmark localization in the wild", in *Proc. IEEE Conference on Computer Vision and Pattern Recognition (CVPR)*, 2012, pp. 2879–2886.

[Zhu16b] X. Zhu, Z. Lei, X. Liu, H. Shi, and S. Z. Li, "Face alignment across large poses: a 3D solution", in *Proc. IEEE Conference on Computer Vision and Pattern Recognition (CVPR)*, 2016, pp. 146–155.

[Zhu15c] X. Zhu, J. Yan, D. Yi, Z. Lei, and S. Z. Li, "Discriminative 3D morphable model fitting", in *Proc. IEEE International Conference on Automatic Face and Gesture Recognition (FG)*, vol. 1, 2015, pp. 1–8.

[Zhu07] Y. Zhuang, J. Zhang, and F. Wu, "Hallucinating faces: LPH super-resolution and neighbor reconstruction for residue compensation", *Pattern Recognition*, vol. 40, no. 11, pp. 3178–3194, 2007.

[Zou12] W. W. W. Zou and P. C. Yuen, "Very low resolution face recognition problem", *IEEE Transactions on Image Processing*, vol. 21, no. 1, pp. 327–340, 2012.

Publications

[Qu13] C. Qu, E. Monari, and T. Schuchert, "Resolution-aware constrained local model with mixture of local experts", in *Proc. IEEE International Conference on Advanced Video and Signal Based Surveillance (AVSS)*, 2013, pp. 454–459.

[Qu14] C. Qu, E. Monari, T. Schuchert, and J. Beyerer, "Fast, robust and automatic 3D face model reconstruction from videos", in *Proc. IEEE International Conference on Advanced Video and Signal Based Surveillance (AVSS)*, 2014, pp. 113–118.

[Qu15a] C. Qu, E. Monari, T. Schuchert, and J. Beyerer, "Realistic texture extraction for 3D face models robust to self-occlusion", in *Proc. SPIE, Image Processing: Machine Vision Applications VIII*, vol. 9405, 2015, 94050P.

[Qu15b] C. Qu, C. Herrmann, E. Monari, T. Schuchert, and J. Beyerer, "3D vs. 2D: on the importance of registration for hallucinating faces under unconstrained poses", in *Proc. Conference on Computer and Robot Vision (CRV)*, 2015, pp. 139–146.

[Qu15c] C. Qu, H. Gao, E. Monari, J. Beyerer, and J.-P. Thiran, "Towards robust cascaded regression for face alignment in the wild", in *Proc. IEEE Conference on Computer Vision and Pattern Recognition Workshops (CVPRW)*, 2015, pp. 1–9.

[Qu15d] C. Qu, E. Monari, T. Schuchert, and J. Beyerer, "Adaptive contour fitting for pose-invariant 3D face shape reconstruction", in *Proc. British Machine Vision Conference (BMVC),* 2015, pp. 87.1–87.12.

[Qu15e] C. Qu, H. Gao, and H. K. Ekenel, “Rotation update on manifold in probabilistic NRSFM for robust 3D face modeling”, *EURASIP Journal on Image and Video Processing,* vol. 2015, no. 1, p. 45, 2015.

[Qu16] C. Qu, D. Luo, E. Monari, T. Schuchert, and J. Beyerer, “Capturing ground truth super-resolution data”, in *Proc. IEEE International Conference on Image Processing (ICIP),* 2016, pp. 2812–2816.

[Qu17] C. Qu, C. Herrmann, E. Monari, T. Schuchert, and J. Beyerer, “Robust 3D patch-based face hallucination”, in *Proc. IEEE Winter Conference on Applications of Computer Vision (WACV),* 2017, pp. 1105–1114.

[Her15a] C. Herrmann, C. Qu, D. Willersinn, and J. Beyerer, “Impact of resolution and image quality on video face analysis”, in *Proc. IEEE International Conference on Advanced Video and Signal Based Surveillance (AVSS),* 2015, pp. 1–6.

[Her15b] C. Herrmann, C. Qu, and J. Beyerer, “Low-resolution video face recognition with face normalization and feature adaptation”, in *Proc. IEEE International Conference on Signal and Image Processing Applications (ICSIPA),* 2015, pp. 89–94.

[Jon15a] C. Jonietz, E. Monari, H. Widak, and C. Qu, “Towards mobile and touchless fingerprint verification”, in *Proc. IEEE International Conference on Advanced Video and Signal Based Surveillance (AVSS),* 2015, pp. 1–6.

[Jon15b] C. Jonietz, E. Monari, and C. Qu, “Towards touchless palm and finger detection for fingerprint extraction with mobile devices”, in *Proc. International Conference of the Biometrics Special Interest Group (BIOSIG),* 2015, pp. 1–8.

[Ham16] J. H. Hammer, C. Qu, M. Voit, and J. Beyerer, “2D hand tracking with motion information, skin color classification and aggregated channel features”, in *Proc. International Conference on Image Processing, Computer Vision, and Pattern Recognition (IPCV),* 2016, pp. 365–371.

List of Figures

List of Tables

Acronyms

*k*NN	*k*-Nearest Neighbors
300-W	300 Faces in-the-Wild Challenge
3DMM	3D Morphable Model
AAM	Active Appearance Model
AdaCF	Adaptive Contour Fitting
AFW	Annotated Faces in the Wild
ASM	Active Shape Model
BFM	Basel Face Model
BP	Belief Propagation
BTV	Bilateral Total Variation
CBN	Cascaded Bi-Network
CCTV	Closed-Circuit Television
CE	Consensus of Exemplars
CED	Cumulative Error Distribution
CFAN	Coarse-to-Fine Autoencoder Networks
CLM	Constrained Local Model
CNN	Convolutional Neural Network
COFW	Caltech Occluded Faces in the Wild
DNN	Deep Neural Network
DOF	degree of freedom
DRMF	Discriminative Response Map Fitting
DT	Distance Transform
EM	Expectation–Maximization

ERT	Ensemble of Regression Trees
ESR	Explicit Shape Regression
FFD	Free-Form Deformation
FH	face hallucination
FOV	field of view
FR	face recognition
FS–MAP	Face Space–Maximum a Posteriori
FSR	face super-resolution
GAN	Generative Adversarial Network
GMM	Gaussian Mixture Model
HOG	Histogram of Oriented Gradients
HPEN	High-fidelity Pose and Expression Normalization
HPM	Hierarchical Part Model
HR	high-resolution
IBP	Iterative Back-Projection
ICP	Iterative Closest Point
IOD	interocular distance
IRLS	Iteratively Reweighted Least Squares
IS–MAP	Image Space–Maximum a Posteriori
LBF	Local Binary Features
LBP	Local Binary Patterns
LFPW	Labeled Face Parts in the Wild
LFW	Labeled Faces in the Wild
LLE	Locally Linear Embedding
LM	Levenberg–Marquardt
LM–ICP	Levenberg–Marquardt Iterative Closest Point
LPP	Locality Preserving Projection
LR	low-resolution
MAP	Maximum a Posteriori
MFF	Multi-Features Fitting
MLE	Maximum Likelihood Estimation
MRF	Markov Random Field
MSE	Mean Square Error
NME	Mean Normalized Error
NMF	Nonnegative Matrix Factorization
NN	Nearest Neighbor
NRMSE	Normalized Root Mean Square Error
PCA	Principal Component Analysis

PCR	Principal Component Regression
PDM	Point Distribution Model
PIE	pose, illumination, and expression
PO–CR	Project-Out Cascaded Regression
POCS	Projection onto Convex Sets
PP	Position-Patch
PS	Photometric Stereo
PSF	Point Spread Function
PSNR	Peak Signal-to-Noise Ratio
RANSAC	Random Sample Consensus
RBF	Radial Basis Function
RCPR	Robust Cascaded Pose Regression
RMSE	Root Mean Square Error
ROI	region of interest
RPP	Region Predictive Power
SDM	Supervised Descent Method
SFM	Structure from Motion
SFS	Shape from Shading
SIFT	Scale-Invariant Feature Transform
SNR	Signal-to-Noise Ratio
SR	super-resolution
SSE	Sum of Squared Error
SSIM	Structural Similarity
SVD	Singular Value Decomposition
SVM	Support Vector Machine
SVR	Support Vector Regression
TPS	Thin-Plate Spline
TV	Total Variation
VisCF	Visible Contour Fitting

Karlsruher Schriftenreihe zur Anthropomatik (ISSN 1863-6489)

Herausgeber: Prof. Dr.-Ing. habil. Jürgen Beyerer

Band 1 Jürgen Geisler
Leistung des Menschen am Bildschirmarbeitsplatz. 2006
ISBN 3-86644-070-7

Band 2 Elisabeth Peinsipp-Byma
Leistungserhöhung durch Assistenz in interaktiven Systemen zur Szenenanalyse. 2007
ISBN 978-3-86644-149-1

Band 3 Jürgen Geisler, Jürgen Beyerer (Hrsg.)
Mensch-Maschine-Systeme. 2010
ISBN 978-3-86644-457-7

Band 4 Jürgen Beyerer, Marco Huber (Hrsg.)
Proceedings of the 2009 Joint Workshop of Fraunhofer IOSB and Institute for Anthropomatics, Vision and Fusion Laboratory. 2010
ISBN 978-3-86644-469-0

Band 5 Thomas Usländer
Service-oriented design of environmental information systems. 2010
ISBN 978-3-86644-499-7

Band 6 Giulio Milighetti
Multisensorielle diskret-kontinuierliche Überwachung und Regelung humanoider Roboter. 2010
ISBN 978-3-86644-568-0

Band 7 Jürgen Beyerer, Marco Huber (Hrsg.)
Proceedings of the 2010 Joint Workshop of Fraunhofer IOSB and Institute for Anthropomatics, Vision and Fusion Laboratory. 2011
ISBN 978-3-86644-609-0

Band 8 Eduardo Monari
Dynamische Sensorselektion zur auftragsorientierten Objektverfolgung in Kameranetzwerken. 2011
ISBN 978-3-86644-729-5

Die Bände sind unter www.ksp.kit.edu als PDF frei verfügbar oder als Druckausgabe bestellbar.

Band 9 Thomas Bader
Multimodale Interaktion in Multi-Display-Umgebungen. 2011
ISBN 3-86644-760-8

Band 10 Christian Frese
Planung kooperativer Fahrmanöver für kognitive Automobile. 2012
ISBN 978-3-86644-798-1

Band 11 Jürgen Beyerer, Alexey Pak (Hrsg.)
Proceedings of the 2011 Joint Workshop of Fraunhofer IOSB and Institute for Anthropomatics, Vision and Fusion Laboratory. 2012
ISBN 978-3-86644-855-1

Band 12 Miriam Schleipen
Adaptivität und Interoperabilität von Manufacturing Execution Systemen (MES). 2013
ISBN 978-3-86644-955-8

Band 13 Jürgen Beyerer, Alexey Pak (Hrsg.)
Proceedings of the 2012 Joint Workshop of Fraunhofer IOSB and Institute for Anthropomatics, Vision and Fusion Laboratory. 2013
ISBN 978-3-86644-988-6

Band 14 Hauke-Hendrik Vagts
Privatheit und Datenschutz in der intelligenten Überwachung: Ein datenschutzgewährendes System, entworfen nach dem „Privacy by Design" Prinzip. 2013
ISBN 978-3-7315-0041-4

Band 15 Christian Kühnert
Data-driven Methods for Fault Localization in Process Technology. 2013
ISBN 978-3-7315-0098-8

Band 16 Alexander Bauer
Probabilistische Szenenmodelle für die Luftbildauswertung. 2014
ISBN 978-3-7315-0167-1

Band 17 Jürgen Beyerer, Alexey Pak (Hrsg.)
Proceedings of the 2013 Joint Workshop of Fraunhofer IOSB and Institute for Anthropomatics, Vision and Fusion Laboratory. 2014
ISBN 978-3-7315-0212-8

Band 18 Michael Teutsch
Moving Object Detection and Segmentation for Remote Aerial Video Surveillance. 2015
ISBN 978-3-7315-0320-0

Band 19 Marco Huber
Nonlinear Gaussian Filtering: Theory, Algorithms, and Applications. 2015
ISBN 978-3-7315-0338-5

Band 20 Jürgen Beyerer, Alexey Pak (Hrsg.)
Proceedings of the 2014 Joint Workshop of Fraunhofer IOSB and Institute for Anthropomatics, Vision and Fusion Laboratory. 2014
ISBN 978-3-7315-0401-6

Band 21 Todor Dimitrov
Permanente Optimierung dynamischer Probleme der Fertigungssteuerung unter Einbeziehung von Benutzerinteraktionen. 2015
ISBN 978-3-7315-0426-9

Band 22 Benjamin Kühn
Interessengetriebene audiovisuelle Szenenexploration. 2016
ISBN 978-3-7315-0457-3

Band 23 Yvonne Fischer
Wissensbasierte probabilistische Modellierung für die Situationsanalyse am Beispiel der maritimen Überwachung. 2016
ISBN 978-3-7315-0460-3

Band 24 Jürgen Beyerer, Alexey Pak (Hrsg.)
Proceedings of the 2015 Joint Workshop of Fraunhofer IOSB and Institute for Anthropomatics, Vision and Fusion Laboratory. 2016
ISBN 978-3-7315-0519-8

Band 25 Pascal Birnstill
Privacy-Respecting Smart Video Surveillance Based on Usage Control Enforcement. 2016
ISBN 978-3-7315-0538-9

Band 26 Philipp Woock
Umgebungskartenschätzung aus Sidescan-Sonardaten für ein autonomes Unterwasserfahrzeug. 2016
ISBN 978-3-7315-0541-9

Band 27 Janko Petereit
Adaptive State × Time Lattices: A Contribution to Mobile Robot Motion Planning in Unstructured Dynamic Environments. 2017
ISBN 978-3-7315-0580-8

Band 28 Erik Ludwig Krempel
Steigerung der Akzeptanz von intelligenter Videoüberwachung in öffentlichen Räumen. 2017
ISBN 978-3-7315-0598-3

Band 29 Jürgen Moßgraber
Ein Rahmenwerk für die Architektur von Frühwarnsystemen. 2017
ISBN 978-3-7315-0638-6

Band 30 Andrey Belkin
World Modeling for Intelligent Autonomous Systems. 2017
ISBN 978-3-7315-0641-6

Band 31 Chettapong Janya-Anurak
Framework for Analysis and Identification of Nonlinear Distributed Parameter Systems using Bayesian Uncertainty Quantification based on Generalized Polynomial Chaos. 2017
ISBN 978-3-7315-0642-3

Band 32 David Münch
Begriffliche Situationsanalyse aus Videodaten bei unvollständiger und fehlerhafter Information. 2017
ISBN 978-3-7315-0644-7

Band 33 Jürgen Beyerer, Alexey Pak (Eds.)
Proceedings of the 2016 Joint Workshop of Fraunhofer IOSB and Institute for Anthropomatics, Vision and Fusion Laboratory. 2017
ISBN 978-3-7315-0678-2

Band 34 Jürgen Beyerer, Alexey Pak and Miro Taphanel (Eds.)
Proceedings of the 2017 Joint Workshop of Fraunhofer IOSB and Institute for Anthropomatics, Vision and Fusion Laboratory. 2018
ISBN 978-3-7315-0779-6

Band 35 Michael Grinberg
Feature-Based Probabilistic Data Association for Video-Based Multi-Object Tracking. 2018
ISBN 978-3-7315-0781-9

Die Bände sind unter www.ksp.kit.edu als PDF frei verfügbar oder als Druckausgabe bestellbar.

Band 36 Christian Herrmann
Video-to-Video Face Recognition for Low-Quality Surveillance Data. 2018
ISBN 978-3-7315-0799-4

Band 37 Chengchao Qu
Facial Texture Super-Resolution by Fitting 3D Face Models. 2018
ISBN 978-3-7315-0828-1